MEET THE PRESS

MEET THE PRESS

McGRAW-HILL
New York San Francisco Washington, D.C. Auckland Bogotá
Caracas Lisbon London Madrid Mexico City Milan
Montreal New Delhi San Juan Singapore
Sydney Tokyo Toronto

Fifty Years of History in the Making

BY RICK BALL AND NBC NEWS

McGraw-Hill

A Division of The ***McGraw-Hill*** *Companies*

Library of Congress Catalog Card Number: 97-073866

1 2 3 4 5 6 7 8 9 0 VNH/VNH 9 0 2 1 0 9 8 7

ISBN 0-07-046614-9

McGraw-Hill books are available at special quantity discounts to use as premiums and sales promotions, or for use in corporate training programs. For more information, please write to the Director of Special Sales, McGraw-Hill, 11 West 19th Street, New York, NY 10011. Or contact your local bookstore.

GRATEFUL ACKNOWLEDGMENT to AP/Wide World Photos for the use of the photos on pages: 7, 10, 20, 21, 22, 23, 54, 55, 56, 57, 70, 73, 76, 77, 83, 102, 103, 104, 105, 108, 110, 113, 124, 125, 139, 140, 141, 143, 144, 145, 146, 147, 152, 160, 164, 165, 178, 181, 182, 183, 184, 185, 191, 203, 206, 207, 209, 211, 212, 214, 215, 216, and 217.

All other photos for NBC News: John DiJoseph and Richard Ellis.

This project was produced in conjunction with BTD.

For NBC

CLARE TULLY

BETTY COLE DUKERT

SHANNON STEELE

For BTD

PROJECT MANAGEMENT:

MELISSA PROIOS, BETH TONDREAU

ART DIRECTION, DESIGN, AND PHOTO RESEARCH:

BETH TONDREAU

PRODUCTION:

EMILY BARCLIFFE, CLAIRE BONAHOOM, SUE CARLSON, CECILIE DAHL, ARLENE GOLDBERG, ANN OBRINGER

EDITORIAL ASSISTANCE PROVIDED BY K&N BOOKWORKS INC.

For McGRAW-HILL

CLAUDIA RIEMER BOUTOTE

SUSAN BARRY

Contents

WNBQ
5
2
6

Acknowledgments

Many people have made very real contributions to this book, not least the producers, panelists, moderators, and guests who have kept *Meet the Press* a vital part of the democratic process for fifty years. Certain people have made outstanding direct contributions to this book, and I owe them heartfelt thanks.

Tim Russert has not only kept the spirit of Lawrence E. Spivak alive in his *Meet the Press* interviews, but he also provided the impetus and original ideas that made this book possible.

Clare Tully, director of business development at NBC News in New York, put together the team who produced the book. Her enthusiasm and judgment were crucial and constant factors throughout. I thank her in particular for sacrificing so many evenings and weekends to the project.

Claudia Riemer Boutote of McGraw-Hill demonstrated early faith in the project. Her determination to publish this anniversary book was ably supported throughout by the editorial work of her colleague Susan Barry.

The staff in the Manuscript Division of the Library of Congress, where the Lawrence E. Spivak archive is housed, was impressively professional and invariably helpful beyond the call of duty. The staff's guidance made research productive and pleasurable.

Patti Gandolfini's organizational and editorial skills were invaluable in judging more than two thousand *Meet the Press* transcripts.

I am in awe at the speedy efficiency with which Tory Klose and Joan B. Nagy of K&N Bookworks brought order to the manuscript.

I am indebted to Bill Monroe for his splendid anecdotes and an injection of humor at a critical point in the project. I thank him sincerely for both.

Beth Tondreau organized the entire job from beginning to end, under constant pressure and with endless grace and humor. All those who have worked with her know she is unsurpassably professional and endlessly creative. This project repeatedly justified and enhanced that reputation. The artistry in this book is entirely hers.

Above all, Betty Cole Dukert is the key to this book, just as she is the key to *Meet the Press.* Much of the knowledge in this book is hers, as are most of the memories, many of the ideas, and a large number of the best words. Without her generosity, her journalistic skills, her prodigious memory, her unflappable attention to detail, and her meticulous archiving of *Meet the Press* material, this book most certainly could not have happened. *Meet the Press* is lucky to have met Betty Cole Dukert in 1956. I am lucky to have met her in 1997. Democracy is well served by her.

My wife Liney Li and our son Oliver conspired to give me the time to research and write this book. This is not easy, and I dedicate my work to them with love.

Foreword by Tim Russert

When I was selected as moderator of *Meet the Press* in December 1991, I immediately called the program's legendary founder Lawrence E. Spivak, then ninety-one. His advice was as precise as was his on-air questioning: "Learn everything about your guests' positions on the issues—and take the other side!"

That in fact defines the mission of *Meet the Press* for all its fifty years: a thoughtful exchange of ideas, sometimes tense, even feisty, occasionally humorous, but always fair and always civilized.

High quality demands constancy and breeds consistency. Perhaps that explains why in a television industry that specializes in turnover, there have been only nine moderators of *Meet the Press* over a half century: Spivak, Martha Rountree, Ned Brooks, Bill Monroe, Marvin Kalb, Roger Mudd, Chris Wallace, Garrick Utley, and me. Journalists of different generations and backgrounds and diverse personalities, to be sure, but all singular in their shared dedication to excellence.

Meet the Press was born on NBC television on November 6, 1947. The first guest was James A. Farley, the former chairman of the Democratic National Committee and Franklin Roosevelt's postmaster general. Twenty-five hundred programs later *TV Guide* still describes *Meet the Press* as "*the* preeminent political talk show."

John F. Kennedy once called it the "fifty-first state." Since the Kennedy presidency, every man who has occupied the Oval Office has appeared on *Meet the Press* during his career. In January 1980 President Carter announced on the program the United States would not participate in the Olympic Games in Moscow because of the Soviet occupation of Afghanistan. The story reverberated worldwide. Likewise when President Clinton decreed on *Meet the Press* on Sunday, November 7, 1993, "North Korea cannot be allowed to develop a nuclear bomb. We have to be very firm about it." Clinton went on: "They know that any attack on South Korea is an attack on the United States." A line established in the fifties, redrawn in the nineties.

Foreign policy has always been a staple of *Meet the Press* interviews. World leaders like Castro, Mitterrand, Indira Gandhi, Ben-Gurion, and Marcos have all held forth. Post–World War II, Korea, Vietnam, the Gulf War, and Bosnia have all been chronicled.

Every American secretary of state from John Foster Dulles to Madeleine Albright has been interviewed. Albright, the first woman ever to be secretary of state, gave her first extended television interview on *Meet the Press.* No surprise. Women have always been central to the program. *Meet the Press*'s first moderator was Martha Rountree. Eleanor Roosevelt was interviewed after she was first lady, Nancy Reagan while she was first lady, and Rosalynn Carter on her way to becoming first lady. Newsmakers from Phyllis Schlafly to Gloria Steinem, Madame Chiang Kai-shek to Golda Meir, Bernadette Devlin to Elizabeth Dole have all presented their views with verve.

The other Dole, as in Bob, holds the record for the most appearances on *Meet the Press*—fifty-six—in a career that ranged from congressman, senator, Republican National Committee chairman, vice presidential candidate, and finally presidential nominee. In fact my very first question as a panelist of *Meet the Press* on September 16, 1990 was to Senator Dole: "Senator, let's talk political reality. If you were back in Russell, Kansas, this morning in the coffee shop and someone said, 'You're going to tax my beer, you're going to tax filling up my gas tank, you're going to tax buying an automobile, and now I read you're giving a tax cut to those who make over fifty thousand dollars, Why? . . .'"

It was a question I hoped would satisfy Lawrence Spivak's journalistic standards yet interest my working-class family in Buffalo. It is that test I try to meet each and every Sunday morning. In recent years our viewers have heard Bill Clinton on the underclass, Al Gore on the environment, Newt Gingrich on the welfare state, Jack Kemp on taxes, Colin Powell on volunteerism, Pat Buchanan on immigration, and Jesse Jackson on race. All were asked to explain their views in concise but understandable answers.

Sometimes I haven't been artful in my questions. Ross Perot was so frustrated in 1992 at my demanding the specifics of his budget plan he playfully put me in a headlock and proclaimed, "I hope you think you proved your manhood." By far my most embarrassing exchange was with the decorated Vietnam veteran Sen. Bob Kerrey of Nebraska. I asked Kerrey whether he felt President Clinton would remain loyal to congressional Democrats if they reformed entitlement programs such as Medicare and Social Security, or would the president "put you out on a limb and saw your limb off"? Kerrey, an amputee, exclaimed, ". . . [S]omebody's already sawed one of them off!" I was horrified. Of all the metaphors available, I chose the absolutely most joltingly inappropriate. Senator Kerrey was most gracious and to this day jokes about the exchange. I now assiduously avoid *any* tree analogies.

Tone and temperament are essential to on-air professionalism. The only time I believe I became too emotional in my questioning was with former Ku Klux Klan leader and Nazi sympathizer David Duke. He was running for governor of Louisiana, and I asked him to name the three largest employers in his state. He couldn't name one. The audience clearly saw his inadequacies, but I persisted in behaving like a prosecutor, yelling, "You don't know the biggest employers in your state!" jabbing my finger all the while.

I regretted my behavior but hoped that I had redeemed myself when I dispassionately asked Mr. Duke, "What was it about this country, the United States of America, that made you choose to become a Nazi?" He had no answer. Forty-eight hours later he lost the election.

Not all *Meet the Press* programs are as dramatic, but all are of considerable news value. Sunday's interviews do make Monday's headlines. Sometimes from unexpected sources like Yogi Berra explaining his witticisms or Michael Jordan urging young men to accept responsibility for their behavior. But the mainstay has always been the exchanges with our political leadership. They're all here—Kennedy, Johnson, Nixon, King, Ford, Carter, Reagan, Perot, Dole, Gingrich, and Clinton—making *Meet the Press* the longest-running and most quoted television program in the world.

Meet the Press really is a national treasure. And I am honored to be its custodian in this fiftieth anniversary year.

TIM RUSSERT
Washington, D.C.

David S. Broder

The principle carrying *Meet the Press* through fifty years is a simple one: A prominent guest answers a reporter's questions. The formula works well only if the reporters are well prepared, nimble witted, and capable of posing clear, probing questions. David S. Broder of the *Washington Post* has made more *Meet the Press* appearances than any other non-NBC journalist in the history of the program. Since he put his first question as a panelist in 1963, he has faced the guest on more than three hundred occasions.

I can hardly credit the fact that I have been involved with *Meet the Press* for more than two-thirds of its fifty years of life. I almost wrote "appeared on" *Meet the Press*, but luckily *Meet the Press* has never been about appearance. Otherwise some of us would never have been asked aboard.

The program was an important part of my life long before I came to Washington. May Craig and her hats, Jack Bell and his laconic but penetrating questions, Richard Wilson and his orotund formulations, and of course Larry Spivak and his terrier tenacity were all familiar figures.

The first time I sat down on the simple set where I had watched them, I was scared as hell. It was the summer of 1963, and the guest was Sen. John Tower of Texas, who was heading up the drive to draft Barry Goldwater for the Republican presidential nomination. I had written one of the first stories about the effort. That's why I was invited onto the panel.

There was no rehearsal, no discussion—just right into it. I managed to get my questions out without too much stammering, and so began what has become a wonderfully rewarding set of experiences. The program has taken me to Hawaii (for a conference of mayors) and even to Russell, Kansas. The friendships with moderators and off-camera production people and researchers and makeup artists have been like marrying into a family with more than its share of outsize characters. Best of all has been the delicious sensation that when you sit down at the start of the program, you have no idea what is about to happen. It can be a brawl or a howl or, with luck, something that is enlightening and revealing.

From the start *Meet the Press* has been serious journalism—and nothing else. That is surely why it has built this big and loyal audience. Mr. Spivak used to say something at the start of each program to this effect: "Remember, the questioners are not expressing their point of view. It's their way of getting a story for you." *Meet the Press* has never been about the panelists or even the guests being interviewed. It's always been about the public, the audience, and "getting a story for you."

Long may it remain so!

Robert D. Novak

Columnist Robert D. Novak has made more than two hundred appearances on *Meet the Press*, a record surpassed only by David Broder and the indomitable May Craig.

Imagine my delight in 1964 when, as a thirty-two-year-old syndicated columnist, I was asked for the first time to come to *Meet the Press* to interview Senate Majority Leader Mike Mansfield. As my late mother once told a somewhat discomfited Larry Spivak, "Bob always watched you when you were a little boy."

Indeed I did. And as an aspiring journalist I was enthralled by the questioners more than the guests: the smoothly competent Jack Bell; the unpredictable May Craig; the impervious Richard Wilson (who once told the equally impervious Sen. Robert S. Kerr, "Senator, *we* ask the questions here!"—a formulation I have borrowed more than once).

And of course there was Lawrence Spivak, who had two rules all television interrogators might follow: (1) Prepare as if your life depended on it; (2) always regard the person being interviewed as your adversary. Tim Russert certainly has upheld that tradition, and I always tried to as a *Meet the Press* panelist over four separate decades.

A good example came in 1972, when George McGovern and Hubert Humphrey, during their bitter and decisive California presidential primary campaign, debated on a one-hour *Meet the Press* special. I was considered so anti-McGovern that his aides protested my selection for the panel. But I followed the Spivak rules, preparing carefully to approach each candidate as my adversary. I succeeded so well that Humphrey's people complained after the broadcast that I was tougher on their man than on McGovern.

Another memorable program was aired just before the 1968 election. Richard Nixon, sitting on a big lead, had avoided television interviews. But as Hubert Humphrey's softer stand on Vietnam narrowed the margin, Nixon moved. He finally agreed to go on *Meet the Press* the last Sunday of the campaign. He brilliantly manipulated the questioning to turn the tables on Humphrey and make it appear that Nixon was the prudent peace candidate and Humphrey would lead to war or surrender. I can tell you the panel was frustrated by being outwitted by Nixon, because I was one of the questioners.

But the triumph of the guest is rare. From Spivak to Russert, the great figures in American public life have seldom dominated on *Meet the Press*. Nearly a half century ago Whittaker Chambers in *Witness* wrote that the program "can be summed up as fun for the boys but death for the frogs." That's still true, and I'm pleased to have been a part of this important contribution to our political scene.

Ross Perot

Moderator Tim Russert asked three seasoned *Meet the Press* guests to provide an insight into the program from the guest's point of view.

When Ross Perot first appeared on *Meet the Press* in 1992, guests were no longer questioned by a panel of four reporters. Russert was joined by Lisa Myers (NBC News) and Al Hunt (the *Wall Street Journal*) for a memorable encounter. Stimulated by the battle, Perot has readily accepted the challenge of return matchups with Russert.

***What's the best way to prepare for an appearance on* Meet the Press?**

Do your homework. Get your facts straight. Make sure your numbers are accurate. Get a good night's sleep.

After the interview, are you generally satisfied with the questions? With your answers?

The questions are fair, clear, and professional. I am generally satisfied, but as I review my answers, I can always think of things I should have included.

What reaction do you receive from the viewing public about your appearance?

Anytime I am in public over a period of several days after appearing on *Meet the Press,* large numbers of people come up to me and say almost exactly the same thing: "Ross, I saw you on *Meet the Press* last Sunday."

Daniel Patrick Moynihan

Sen. Daniel Patrick Moynihan first faced the *Meet the Press* panel in 1965. More than thirty years later, as the program entered its fiftieth year, he made his twenty-fourth appearance.

Daniel Patrick Moynihan

United States Senate
Washington, D.C.
March 7, 1997

Dear Tim:

For the forthcoming fiftieth, here are my brief comments:

***What's the best way to prepare for an appearance on* Meet the Press?**
Don't.

After the interview, are you generally satisfied with the questions? With your answers?
In the great Spivak era the program ended at the stroke of noon, whereupon a silver tray ladened with Bloody Marys appeared and anxiety evanesced accordingly. After which he would take you to lunch. Now you get orange juice at ten o'clock in the morning, as if you had just given blood. Next, you wonder whether you really have to be off to eleven o'clock Mass.

What reaction do you receive from the viewing public about your appearance?
My first appearance was the most important. In the spring of 1965, I prepared for the White House—I was assistant secretary of labor for policy planning and research—a position paper entitled *The Negro Family: The Case for National Action.* President Johnson got the idea, and I was asked to draft a speech for him to give at Howard University on June 4, 1965. His speech was an enormous success, but soon rioting broke out in Watts. Bill Moyers as press secretary was besieged by questions. What was going on? We were told everything was going well. And such like. Of a sudden, on August 17, 1965, he passed out to the press my report, saying we have been on to this inner-city problem for some while, that sort of thing. The next

day Evans and Novak's column covered it under the headline THE MOYNIHAN REPORT. In short order I had become hugely disliked and indeed in some quarters anathematized. In the meantime I had left Washington and lost a primary election in New York City. Not the happiest of sequences. Whereupon I received a call from Larry Spivak asking if we could have lunch. Which we did at a steakhouse on Third Avenue in Manhattan, the kind of place men of his generation enjoyed. We talked about the report, and at the end of lunch he asked if I would come on the show. I did, on December 12, 1965, and all of a sudden became a name with a face, as it were. A respectable participant in a legitimate national debate. A debate which goes on to this day, a generation, or is it two generations, later. It could not have happened without *Meet the Press*.

I have been on some twenty-three times since. None nearly so terrifying, but all almost as rewarding. As Tim Russert says, "If it's Sunday, it's *Meet the Press*." Which means on Monday people will have heard you with that little extra attention and willing suspension of disbelief which one associates with pronouncements made Sunday mornings.

Best,

Daniel Patrick Moynihan

Bob Dole

Bob Dole has been a guest on *Meet the Press* more often than anyone else, with twice the number of appearances of the closest contender, Sam Nunn. He is the perfect guest—witty, articulate, independent, well informed, and willing to give clear, unequivocal answers to difficult questions. His statements on *Meet the Press* have made Monday-morning headlines on many occasions.

February 25, 1997

Timothy J. Russert
Moderator
Meet the Press
4001 Nebraska Avenue, NW
Washington, D.C. 20016

Dear Tim,

Thanks for the opportunity to provide comments for the forthcoming book commemorating the fiftieth anniversary of *Meet the Press*. If you asked just three questions on the show, I might come back more often!

***What's the best way to prepare for an appearance on* Meet the Press?**
Read your briefing book, read the Sunday morning papers, watch the weekend news shows, be aware of any issues the panelists may have been writing about during the week, and get a good night's sleep. Also, always try to come with some kind of newsmaking statement or announcement. If all else fails, try to read the questions upside down across the table.

After the interview, are you generally satisfied with the questions? With your answers?
I'm usually more satisfied with my answers than with the questions. If I could ask the questions, maybe it would be different. I also usually get a second chance at any answers I'm not happy with at the sidewalk press conference—the stakeout—which greets all Sunday show guests outside the studio.

What reaction do you receive from the viewing public about your appearance?
Why weren't you in church on Sunday?

Tim, congratulations on your tremendous success with the show, and all the best for *Meet*'s next fifty years. If we can get a recount, I'd still be happy to do that fiftieth anniversary show in the Oval Office. Let's stay in touch.

Sincerely,

Bob Dole

"The pleasantries having been dispensed with, we now go right for the jugular."

ALASTAIR BURNET
THE ECONOMIST
GREAT BRITAIN
MELOR STURUA
IZVESTIA
USSR
MEET
THE
PRESS

WOL

Introduction

Meet the Press is the longest running network television show in the world. For fifty years it has questioned the newsmakers, and for fifty years it has been making news. It has probably produced more news stories than any other television or radio program in history.

One name dominates the first four decades of *Meet the Press:* Lawrence E. Spivak, cofounder of *Meet the Press,* fearless inquisitor of the great and the would-be great. Spivak dared ask the direct question on behalf of the American people. He made *Meet the Press* part of the democratic process.

Spivak was born in Brooklyn on June 11, 1900. In 1921, soon after he graduated cum laude from Harvard, he became business manager of *Antiques* magazine. By 1930 he was circulation director and assistant to the publisher at the *National Sportsman* and *Hunting and Fishing*. He joined H. L. Mencken's *The American Mercury* magazine in 1934 and bought it twice: from the publisher Alfred A. Knopf in 1935 and again in 1939 from the editor Paul Palmer, to whom he had sold a controlling interest in 1936. From 1944 to 1950—when he sold *The American Mercury*—he acted as both editor and publisher.

Lawrence Spivak held a fierce conviction that the conflict between the individual and the state was the great issue of the age, with power-hungry central authority the enemy of the individual's freedom. He made the *Mercury* a crusading anti-Communist magazine. It also fought discrimination against any minority group and had the honor of being one of the first magazines banned by Hitler's Germany.

Spivak was a visionary pioneer in paperback publishing, the first man to apply magazine-selling tactics to the marketing of books. James M. Cain's *The Postman Always Rings Twice* was his first twenty-five-cent title; it sold fifty thousand copies at city newsstands. Among Spivak's other innovations: *Ellery Queen's Mystery Magazine,* the *Magazine of Fantasy and Science Fiction,* and—in 1950—*Detective.*

In an effort to boost the circulation of *The American Mercury,* Spivak ventured into radio.

In 1945 he was sponsoring a WQXR radio program called *The American Mercury.* The show dramatized articles in *The American Mercury* in an attempt to sell subscriptions to the magazine. Spivak told how this undistinguished show gave birth to *Meet the Press:* "Some-

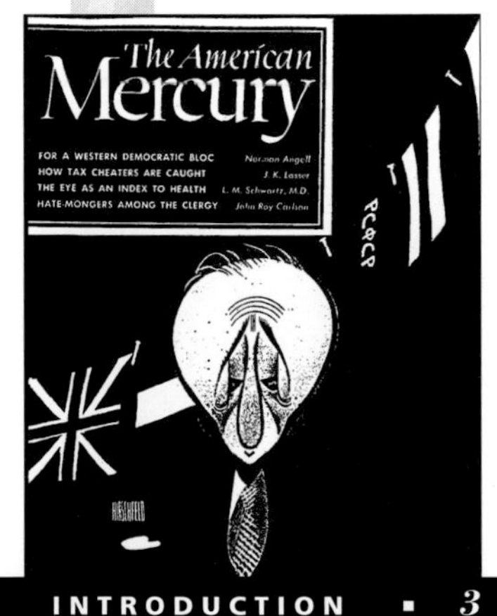

There was little legroom for the panelists in the studio for the early radio broadcasts of Meet the Press, *moderated by the ever-elegant Martha Rountree.*

time in early 1945 Norman Cousins, who was then editing the *Saturday Review of Literature,* sent a young lady by the name of Martha Rountree to see me. She had written an article based on some statistics which indicated that there were now more women than men in the population and that if all the eligible women registered to vote, they might have a profound effect on elections. . . . I learned that she was producing a radio program called *Listen to the Women,* which had a panel of four women and a moderator. The moderator put questions to the women that were received through the mails on a variety of subjects, and the women gave their answers and frequently got into controversy because of differences of opinion. We both agreed after listening to a series of *The American Mercury* that they were not very effective or interesting, and we then began a discussion to see if we could come up with a program that might be more interesting and effective in promoting *The American Mercury.*"

The idea of a radio press conference with four journalists confronting a newsworthy guest emerged, and Rountree thought it was an idea a network might buy. After Spivak had failed to interest the big networks in a show whose aim was "to ferret out news, to report news and to clarify news by having the best reporters we could find put challenging questions to the great and the near great," Rountree suggested the Mutual Broadcasting System, which was by then broadcasting her successful show *Leave It to the Girls,* billed as "a battle of wits between the sexes" and "a roundtable of romance featuring glamorous career girls." She acted as moderator of *Leave It to the Girls,* and Spivak made occasional guest appearances in the "Man Strikes Back" segment, in which, according to *Tide* magazine (August 8, 1945), "the male guest gets a chance to challenge the four experts on love and romance who preside at the roundtable."

In spite of Rountree's credentials, the Mutual executives were solidly hostile to the idea of *Meet the Press.* The breakthrough came at a meeting with Ed Kobak, president of Mutual, when Rountree asked, "How would you like to have a program on Mutual in which people like Stalin and Roosevelt and Churchill and Henry Wallace were asked challenging and unrehearsed questions by a panel of top newsmen?" Kobak was enthusiastic. "Can you get people like that?" "Maybe not all, but some," said Rountree confidently. Spivak was appalled, but Rountree soon soothed him: "I didn't say we could get Roosevelt, Churchill, and Stalin. I said people *like* them—and Henry Wallace. I'm sure you can get *him* to appear." Kobak decided to put the show on the air.

On June 24, 1945, *Meet the Press* made its debut

December 29, 1947: Press Productions, Inc., is incorporated. The first meeting is held on January 14, 1948, when the corporation takes over the contract with Mutual dated December 12, 1947, along with acetate recordings of the *Meet the Press* programs. Martha Rountree and Lawrence Spivak each receive fifty shares.

The first woman reporter to appear on the radio version of *Meet the Press* was Dorothy Thompson of the *New York Post* on December 7, 1945.

on the Mutual network on a one-time experimental basis. The first guest was not Henry Wallace but Edmund Stevens of the *Christian Science Monitor*, who had just returned from Stalin's Soviet Union. Coproducers Spivak and Rountree described their new show as "a forum-type program appealing to an audience interested in the mechanics of a genuine press conference" (*Tide*, November 15, 1945), but this first program was more of a discussion than a press conference. Fortunately it was good enough for Kobak to offer *Meet the Press* a run beginning in October, as long as Spivak and Rountree could attract big-name guests—if not Roosevelt or Stalin, at least Henry Wallace.

Meet the Press began its run on Mutual on October 5, 1945. The guest on the first show was Eric Johnston, president of the U.S. Chamber of Commerce, and on the following week Secretary of Commerce Henry Wallace finally appeared. Wallace, the former vice president of the United States, used the program to advocate a 15 to 20 percent wage increase, the first time a major administration figure had spoken in public on the subject. His comments made news, and *Meet the Press* was heard weekly on Mutual until August 1950.

Response to *Meet the Press* was instant and positive. Only five months after the launch, *Tide* was reporting that "radio has managed to turn the tables on the news services, which for once have found themselves taking their headline news from a radio program." In 1946 *Meet the Press* featured on many reviewers' "Best of the Year" lists. In the *New York World-Telegram* 1946 radio awards,

Anti-Communist crusader Sen. Joseph McCarthy (right) made several dramatic appearances on Meet the Press. *He once sat through the show with a gun in his lap in response to rumors of an assassin in the studio audience.*

"Best balladeers" accolade went to Bing Crosby and Dinah Shore, and the "Most disappointing special event" was judged to be the first atom bomb test at Bikini, but "Best program dealing with current events" was *Meet the Press*, "the only program that backed both [Theodore] Bilbo and [Eugene] Talmadge against the wall and made them give straight answers."

The notorious Bilbo interview made national headlines and led to the Senate's taking action against the rogue senator from Mississippi.

Sen. Theodore Bilbo, Democrat of Mississippi, was a leading segregationist and racist. His August 9, 1946 *Meet the Press* appearance was one of the most dramatic programs in the history of the program. When news of the upcoming interview became public, angry letters and telegrams arrived at Mutual, demanding cancellation of Bilbo's appear-

Meet the Press *cofounder Lawrence E. Spivak (second from right) and the panel meet Earl Warren (left) before a radio broadcast.*

ance. There were threats to the senator's life if he dared go on the air, and demonstrators were waiting for him outside the WOL studio at 1627 K Street, NW, in Washington, D.C. Organized by the Washington Council of the National Negro Congress, the peaceful protesters carried placards reading OUST BILBO and WE VETS KNOW—SENATOR BILBO'S RACE PREJUDICE IS UN-AMERICAN; TO SAVE OUR DEMOCRACY OUST BILBO.

That day Bilbo had taken out a permit to carry a gun. "He came to the studio," Spivak explained, "with four armed guards, and a gun in his hip pocket. . . . He was virtual mayor of Washington, and as such, he had more than forty policemen protecting him in and outside the studio." The program opened on a note of extraordinary tension and excitement.

Bert Andrews of the *New York Herald Tribune* was on the panel that day. As Spivak later recalled, "He took a look at the gunmen with Senator Bilbo, and he said, 'Let's not fool around with this so-and-so too long.' I asked him to start the questioning."

Andrews's question was designed to raise the temperature.

> ANDREWS: I would like to go back to the fact that some of the Washington correspondents of a magazine poll voted you . . . the worst man in the Senate. Do you agree with their opinion, sir?
>
> BILBO: I heard the story published in the press and made an investigation and found that it was absolutely untrue. It was an overheard conversation between two newspaper boys who were merely popping off.
>
> . . .
>
> CECIL B. DICKSON (Gannett Publications): Senator, Senator Taft was quoted as saying in the Senate, and I quote: "I am shocked at the sudden outburst of hate and intolerance against minority groups. There is no excuse for him, and he is a disgrace to the Senate. . . ."
>
> BILBO: Well, I have this to say: Senator Taft, as you know, is a very strong Republican, and he has played every string on the instrument in his effort to line up what we call the pinks and the reds and the off brand of the political life of America, to further his interest as a candidate for the presidency of the United States.
>
> QUESTION: Senator, do you think seriously that Senator Taft is after Communist support?
>
> BILBO: Yes, sir. . . . We know him in the Senate as the blah-blah-blah of the Senate. . . . Well, when I think of him, I think of a young mockingbird, just out of his shell—all mouth and no bird at all.
>
> . . .
>
> SPIVAK: Senator, are you or have you ever been a member of the Ku Klux Klan?
>
> BILBO: I have.
>
> SPIVAK: Do you think . . .
>
> BILBO: I am a member of the Ku Klux Klan number forty, called Bilbo, Bilbo Klan number forty, Mississippi. I attended one meeting and have not attended it since, because I was not in sympathy with some of the things in it.
>
> . . .
>
> SPIVAK: Do you think you would get any Klan support now?
>
> BILBO: I do.
>
> SPIVAK: You never left the Klan, in effect?
>
> BILBO: No man can leave the Klan. He takes an oath not to do that. He is a—once a Ku Klux, always a Ku Klux.

BILBO ADMITS HE'S KU KLUXER boomed the front page of the *New York Post* on August 10, and the paper printed a full transcript of the program.

Astonishingly Bilbo used the show in his reelection campaign. It was his practice to obtain transcripts of all such broadcasts and flood Mississippi with photocopies, with the message "See what the damn Yankees are doing to me."

Equally astonishingly Bilbo was duly reelected.

But his appalled fellow senators began an investigation. On November 20, 1946, *Variety* reported that "when the Republican steering committee first met to discuss the matter, a committee representative phoned from Washington to Martha Rountree, producer of Mutual's 'Meet the Press,' in New York, asking for a recording of the show some weeks ago in which Senator Bilbo appeared and admitted that he was a Klansman.

"It is believed this is the first time radio is being called on for such vital evidence."

Senator Bilbo died of cancer before the investigation was completed.

The transcript of the Bilbo show was, like many other *Meet the Press* radio shows, reprinted in Spivak's *American Mercury* magazine. The only mention of the magazine in the program came in the opening announcement: "Mutual and the editors of *The American Mercury,* America's distinguished magazine of opinion . . ." At the end of the show listeners were invited to write in with their comments, encouraged by the offer of a prize—a set of encyclopedias—to the writer of the week's best letter. Spivak used the names and addresses of these *Meet the Press* fans as a mailing list to sell subscriptions to *The American Mercury.*

Meet the Press was making news, and Martha Rountree thought the show was ready to move to television. In 1947 Rountree and Spivak accepted an invitation from an advertising agency to put *Meet the Press* on television for Maxwell House on the NBC network.

After the program started I began to appear because the questions were not challenging enough.

—Lawrence Spivak

IN THE NEWS

1947

- President Truman asks Congress for aid to Greece and Turkey, to fight the spread of communism.
- Secretary of State George C. Marshall aids Europe under the Marshall Plan.
- Jackie Robinson breaks baseball's color barrier as a Brooklyn Dodger.
- The Dodgers lose to the Yankees in the World Series.
- The Taft-Hartley Act outlawing strikes is vetoed by Truman, but Congress overrides the veto.
- Chuck Yeager breaks the sound barrier.
- *Meet the Press* premieres on NBC-TV.

1948

- India's spiritual leader Mahatma Gandhi is assassinated.
- Alger Hiss is denounced as a Communist.
- The Kinsey report on male sexuality is published.
- The newly proclaimed state of Israel is immediately recognized by President Truman.
- Mao Tse-tung defeats Chiang Kai-shek. Chiang retreats to Formosa (Taiwan).
- The Berlin Airlift begins after the Russians blockade the city.

- Satchel Paige, at age forty-two, becomes the first black pitcher in the American League. He pitches in the World Series for the Cleveland Indians.
- Ceaseless rain dampens the London Olympics.
- The 33⅓ rpm LP appears in record stores.
- DEWEY DEFEATS TRUMAN claims the headline in the *Chicago Daily Tribune*, but Truman is elected president.
- Eleanor Roosevelt chairs the UN Commission on Human Rights, which announces the Universal Declaration of Human Rights.
- There are a million television sets in America.

1949

- American troops are withdrawn from Korea.
- The North Atlantic Treaty Organization (NATO) is born.
- Mao Tse-tung proclaims the People's Republic of China.
- Puerto Rican nationalists attempt to kill President Truman.

The bomb that ends World War II brings a brief peace and changes the world forever. Nazism is smashed, its evil revealed as the Allied armies enter the Third Reich's concentration camps. Now the free world faces a new enemy in communism and its ideological powerhouse—Stalin's Soviet Union. Under the Truman Doctrine, President Truman asks Congress to provide aid to Greece and Turkey, to stop them from turning to communism, and Secretary of State George Marshall's Marshall Plan pours massive aid into a Western Europe shattered by war.

The battle between the rival ideologies is destined to dominate world history for more than forty years. The first confrontation occurs in Berlin, the old German capital occupied by the four Allied powers: the United States, the Soviet Union, Great Britain, and France. When the Russians blockade the city in April 1948, the United States responds with the Berlin Airlift, which ends on September 13, 1949.

In the United States the House Committee on Un-American Activities (HUAC) investigates Communist infiltration and influence in Hollywood. None are found, but lives are ruined by the investigation, and a group of actors and directors—among them John Huston, Lauren Bacall, Humphrey Bogart, and Danny Kaye—come to Washington, D.C., to protest HUAC's methods.

Washington does not escape investigation. The denunciation of Alger Hiss fuels fears of Communists influencing State Department policy making, and implacable Communist hunter Sen. Joseph McCarthy (R-WI) begins his crusade to root out the red menace.

As *Meet the Press* prepares to move from radio to television in 1947, Jackie Robinson ends his first season as a Brooklyn Dodger. He is the first black player in major-league baseball. As the struggle against communism dominates the world stage, the battle to break down racial barriers affects domestic politics throughout *Meet the Press*'s first fifty years.

A third battleground also emerges from World War II. The state of Israel is declared on May 14, 1948. It is instantly recognized by the United States and denounced by its Arab neighbors. Israel's struggle for security remains in the news—and on *Meet the Press*—for the next five decades.

Before the decade's end another major state takes the stage. Following his decisive victory over Chiang Kai-shek at the Battle of Huai-hai in October 1948, Mao Tse-tung declares the People's Republic of China. His enemy retreats to the island of Formosa (Taiwan), which becomes another meeting point in the long face-off between the capitalist and Communist worlds.

In 1949 terrorism shoots its way into public awareness, as Puerto Rican nationalists make an attempt on President Truman's life.

NA ONAL BROADCASTING COMPANY, INC. TELEVISION RD-4 10-46

PROGRAM TITLE GENERAL FOODS "Meet the Press" DAY Thus TIME 8:00-8:30 pm

STATIONS WNBT ONLY STARTING DATE

PROGRAM DESCRIPTION As of 11/20/47 - WNBT & NET CLOSING DATE

Nov 6-Dec 4, 1947 Meet the Press - usual format

Guests:

WNBT ONLY	Nov 6, 1947	James Farley, former Post Master General (in Roosevelt's cabinet)
WNBT ONLY	Nov 13, 1947	no script in master book for this date Eric Johnston Motion Picture Association
WNBT & NET	Nov 20, 1947	Harold Knutson, US Representative of Minnesota (R)
WNBT & NET	Nov 27, 1947	Claude Pepper, US Senator of Florida (D)
WNBT & NET	Dec 4, 1947	Robert A Taft, US Senator of Ohio (R)

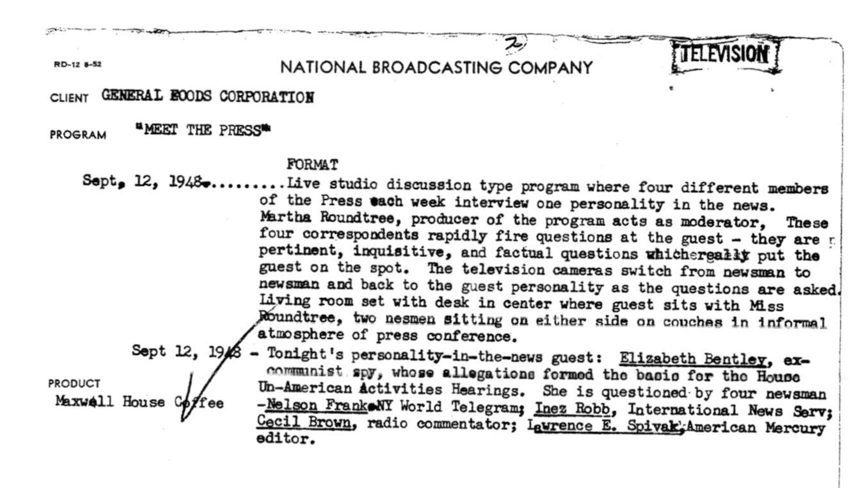

RD-12 8-52 NATIONAL BROADCASTING COMPANY TELEVISION

CLIENT GENERAL FOODS CORPORATION

PROGRAM "MEET THE PRESS"

FORMAT

Sept, 12, 1948.........Live studio discussion type program where four different members of the Press each week interview one personality in the news. Martha Roundtree, producer of the program acts as moderator, These four correspondents rapidly fire questions at the guest - they are pertinent, inquisitive, and factual questions whichgenerally put the guest on the spot. The television cameras switch from newsman to newsman and back to the guest personality as the questions are asked. Living room set with desk in center where guest sits with Miss Roundtree, two nesmen sitting on either side on couches in informal atmosphere of press conference.

Sept 12, 1948 - Tonight's personality-in-the-news guest: Elizabeth Bentley, ex-communist spy, whose allegations formed the basis for the House Un-American Activities Hearings. She is questioned by four newsman -Nelson Frank, NY World Telegram; Inez Robb, International News Serv; Cecil Brown, radio commentator; Lawrence E. Spivak, American Mercury editor.

PRODUCT Maxwell House Coffee

Program cards (above) for the first Meet the Press *programs broadcast by NBC.*
Ronald Reagan (opposite), president of the Screen Actors Guild from 1947 to 1952.

On Thursday, November 6, 1947, at 8:00 P.M. *Meet the Press* makes its NBC television debut. The guest is James A. Farley, former postmaster general under Franklin D. Roosevelt and former chairman of the Democratic National Committee. The show is unrehearsed and live. For the next fifty years it was always unrehearsed and almost invariably broadcast live.

The voice of the announcer opens the early shows, while viewers watch newspapers churning from the presses: "It's the roar of the presses, working day and night in the north, south, east, and west of our nation. These daily presses pour out over forty-eight million newspapers, and behind these millions of headlines are the country's ace reporters, men and women who bring you the inside story. Tonight the makers of Maxwell House Coffee bring you America's Press Conference of the Air: *Meet the Press.*"

The camera then picks up the four aces, whom Spivak usually selected from the Washington press corps, supported by the occasional guest outsider. They are seated on what the *Washington Journalism Review* described later as looking "like borrowed funeral parlor chairs."

The American Mercury drama critic and cofounder George Jean Nathan strongly advised Spivak against a move into television, warning him that "they'll change the way you dress, the way you part your hair, and you'll end up looking at your reflection as you pass store windows." Spivak did indeed begin parting his hair on the left side rather than in the middle. Had he looked at his reflection, he would have seen a slight, pale, bespectacled man standing five feet three inches, quite unlike the eager tiger sniffing out the truth from reluctant guests on *Meet the Press.*

> **The added dimension brought to the radio program by television came from the simple fact that most faces are revealing—and great impact often resulted when facial expressions either matched or failed to match the words spoken. —Lawrence Spivak**

The debut show was seen only on NBC's New York station, WNBT, although it was produced in Washington, D.C., at the WRC-TV studio in the Wardman Park Hotel at Connecticut Avenue and Woodley Road (today site of the Sheraton Washington Hotel). Spivak made his home in the hotel, as did Herbert Hoover, Dwight D. Eisenhower, and Lyndon Johnson. Hotel living suited Spivak. He never had to worry about household problems and had extra time for work—by far his favorite pastime.

Martha Rountree served as moderator of *Meet the Press* for six years, from its debut on NBC until November 1, 1953. Rountree's South Carolina accent was familiar to fans of radio's first panel show, *Leave It to the Girls*, which she created after setting up her New York company, Radio House, in 1940. Rountree and Lawrence Spivak share the credit for creating *Meet the Press*, and the two coproduced the show. Like Spivak, Rountree maintained homes and offices in both New York and Washington, where she was known as one of the capital's most popular—and most influential—hostesses. In 1952 Rountree married advertising agency executive Oliver Presbrey. The birth of two daughters—Martha and Mary—soon followed, and in 1953 Rountree sold her interest in *Meet the Press* to Spivak.

The agreement between the two stated that she would not make a program like *Meet the Press* for at least two years after her departure from *Meet the Press*. On July 4, 1956, she launched *Press Conference* on NBC television, coproduced by her husband, in which sixteen reporters questioned a leading political figure, with Rountree moderating. Guests guaranteed that they would break news on the show. This raised howls of protest from newspapers, and the stipulation was quickly dropped. The show soon moved to ABC, where it was put up against the invincible Ed Sullivan and Steve Allen.

In 1959 Rountree began *Capital Closeups*, a daily news show on WOR, broadcast from her home on R Street in Washington's embassy section. The house was the first Washington home of a young assistant secretary of the navy named Franklin D. Roosevelt.

FIRST FISTICUFFS

The radio guest on February 2, 1947 is Elliott Roosevelt, son of Eleanor and Franklin Roosevelt. The *Boston Herald* reported: "Following his return from Russia . . . Elliott Roosevelt was confronted by Fulton Lewis, Jr., long his most implacable enemy, and Mr. Lewis tore into poor Elliott like a tiger. It was, indeed, the most mercilessly cunning inquisition I've ever heard on the air."

After the show the confrontation develops. The *New York Daily News* reported under the headline FULTON LEWIS SOCKED IN ELLIOTT, FAYE BRAWL: "Elliott Roosevelt, his wife, Faye Emerson, and a friend tangled with Fulton Lewis, Jr., radio commentator, in the studio of the Mutual Broadcasting System, 1440 Broadway last night—and Lewis got socked.

"The punch was thrown by Elliott's pal and literary promoter, Dick Harrity of Duell, Sloan and Pearce, the firm which published Elliott's book, *As I Saw It*. Lewis said it didn't hurt."

Lawrence Spivak so enjoyed the hotel life that he lived in two hotels in two different cities. Friday through Sunday he stayed at the Wardman Park Hotel in Washington, D.C. After the show he traveled by train to New York, where he spent the rest of the week at the Barclay Hotel on East Forty-eighth Street.

The third telecast marked *Meet the Press*'s elevation to network status, as Washington's WRC-TV broadcast the program, but after only five shows *Meet the Press* was canceled. In June and July 1948 four *Meet the Press* interviews were telecast over the DuMont television network from the two major political conventions. The radio broadcasts were continuing, and in August 1948 *Meet the Press* played a key role in one of the most famous spy cases of the century.

August 27, 1948

Whittaker Chambers—for the first time without congressional immunity—accuses Alger Hiss of being a Communist.

Hiss was a distinguished diplomat, Chambers a self-confessed ex-Communist and a former foreign editor at *Time* magazine. Before the House Committee on Un-American Activities, Chambers denounced Hiss as a member of the Communist party, an accusation Hiss hotly denied.

"The congressional investigation of Hiss had more or less reached a stalemate," Spivak recalled. "The public was evenly divided in its conviction as to who had lied, Chambers or Hiss. Chambers had been making his accusations against Hiss under congressional immunity, and Hiss challenged Chambers to call him a Communist without immunity. It was at that point that *Meet the Press* interviewed Chambers."

Edward Folliard of the *Washington Post* asks the key question.

Whittaker Chambers (far right) denounces Alger Hiss.

EARLY FIRSTS

On the second television show (November 13, 1947), Ruth Montgomery of the *New York Daily News* becomes the first woman reporter to appear on the *Meet the Press* television panel. The interviewee is Eric Johnston, president of the Motion Picture Association.

The first senator to appear on *Meet the Press*-TV is Sen. Claude Pepper (D-FL), on November 24, 1947.

The first female guest interviewed on *Meet the Press*-TV is Elizabeth Bentley, on September 12, 1948.

FOLLIARD: Mr. Chambers, in the hearings on Capitol Hill you said over and over again that you served in the Communist party with Alger Hiss. Your remarks down there were privileged; that is to say, you were protected from lawsuits. Hiss has now challenged you to make the same charge publicly. He says if you do he will test your veracity by filing a suit for slander or libel. Are you willing to say now that Alger Hiss is or ever was a Communist?

CHAMBERS: Alger Hiss was a Communist and may be now.

Chambers's on-air denunciation of Hiss made major headlines. Hiss sued Chambers for slander, and it looked as if he might win the case until Chambers produced the famous "pumpkin papers," microfilm of official documents stuffed in a hollowed-out pumpkin. Hiss was sentenced to five years. He proclaimed his innocence until his death in 1996.

Communist spies raise problems and passions on *Meet the Press* through the next five decades. On September 12, 1948, *Meet the Press* returned to NBC with a dramatic show featuring former Communist Elizabeth T. Bentley. The program has appeared continually on NBC-TV ever since.

Writing in the *Washington Times-Herald* in 1947, at the time of *Meet the Press's* television debut, Lawrence Spivak defined a liberal. "When I was a boy, a liberal was one who looked upon the state as . . . a necessary evil. Today, a 'liberal' is likely to be one who looks on the state as a panacea." The freedom and responsibility of the individual were central to Spivak's beliefs, but he was obsessively bipartisan and prided himself on being regularly accused of bias by all parties.

September 12, 1948

Elizabeth Bentley, "whose drawing power at the moment," according to the *St. Louis Post-Dispatch,* "must be second only to Betty Grable's," confessed before a Senate committee to being a courier for a Communist spy ring. She named a former Commerce Department export license officer, William Remington, as a Communist. In an echo of Chambers's sensational radio denunciation of Hiss on *Meet the Press,* Bentley accuses Remington on the air of being a Communist, reviving interest in the case and leading to Remington's eventual imprisonment.

The panel knew it was chasing a dramatic story, and its aggressive questioning disturbed some. The *St. Louis Post-Dispatch* reported that panelists Cecil Brown and Inez Robb "used a bullying technique which has been employed fairly successfully in ordinary newspaper interviews but which, I bet, will aggravate a lot of listeners."

Reviewing the Elizabeth Bentley show in the Cincinnati *Billboard,* Jerry Franklin wrote: "If succeeding victims of the *Meet* inquisitions stack up similarly, it should have a high-ranking video career."

After the show Remington informed Bentley:

On a Meet the Press *radio broadcast Elizabeth Bentley (far right) faces (left to right) May Craig, Nelson Frank, Lawrence Spivak, and Martha Rountree.*

"The cloak of immunity you wore before the Senate committee cannot be stretched to cover your remarks on the recent television program." After some hesitation he sued in the New York district court, naming Bentley, NBC, and the General Foods Corporation—sponsor of the program—as codefendants. The complaint quoted the contentious passage from the transcript:

QUESTION: What is this, Miss Bentley? You have made charges in your testimony before a congressional committee naming several people as Communists. Now, knowing very well here, Miss Bentley, you don't have congressional immunity, would you now identify William Remington as a Communist, or Alger Hiss, or anyone else that you have named?—knowing that you might open your way to a libel suit?

BENTLEY: Yes, I would certainly do that, but as long as I am under subpoena from a committee, I don't believe that I should go talking about these various matters until the committee has completed its hearings.

QUESTION: Well, you are talking about the matters here, and you've named these people as Communists, and I wish you'd do it out in the open.

BENTLEY: Certainly.

QUESTION: Will you now name William Remington as a Communist?

BENTLEY: Certainly. I testified before the committee that William Remington was a Communist.

QUESTION: And do you say that here and now?

BENTLEY: Yes, I said that before the committee, and I would certainly repeat my testimony before the committee.

QUESTION: And will you repeat here and now

OCT 7 1948

Remington Asks $100,000 in Suit

NEW YORK, Oct. 7—(AP)—William W. Remington, suspended Commerce Department employe, filed a $100,000 damage suit today against Miss Elizabeth T. Bentley and two other defendants.

He said Miss Bentley, admitted one-time Soviet espionage agent and former Communist party member, had falsely named him a Communist on a Sept. 12 "Meet the Press" radio program.

OCT 7 1948

Remington Sue[s] Ex-Spy, NBC, General Food[s]

NEW YORK — (U.P.) — W. Remington, former dep[artment] of commerce official, $100,000 libel suit in fede[ral]

REMINGTON SUES ELIZABETH BENTLEY FOR $100,000

New York, Oct. 6.—(AP)— [Willi]am W. Remington, susp[ended] Commerce Department em[ploye] filed a $100,000 damage su[it to]day against Miss Elizabet[h] Bentley and two other defen[dants]. He said Miss Bentley, adr[mitted]

Officers Elected For Symphony

(Please Turn To Page 4, Col. 1)

...r and gave th... ...wald, of El Mor... whenever they arrive. The song... Crazy. Period," and "Men Have Di... but Not for Love" . . . Salvador D... month with the completed manuscr... fisherwoman and her two mad chi... Elizabeth Bentley for her stateme... Press" program, will have a diff...

[C]hambers Faces [A]nother Slander [A]ction by Hiss

Is Named ... $100,000 S...

NEW YORK, Oct. 6— William W. Remington, s... commerce department ... filed a $100,000 damage s...

Remington, of Ridgewood, ... ficial of the U.S. Depart...

NEW YORK, Oct. 6 (AP) ... liam W. Remington, sus[pended] Commerce Department em[ploye] filed a $100,000 damage suit against Miss Elizabeth T. B[entley]

Remington, suspended ... Department employe, filed ... 000 damage suit agains[t]

> that William Remington is a Communist? Is that your charge? Did you make it—
>
> BENTLEY: I told you that I had. I told you that I testified before the committee that he was a Communist.
>
> QUESTION: Yes . . .
>
> BENTLEY: A member of the Communist party.

Remington's complaint then states: "By reason of such utterance and publication, plaintiff has been greatly injured and damaged in his employment, has been greatly injured and damaged in his profession as an economist, has been brought into public odium and contempt, and has suffered great pain and mental anguish in the sum of one hundred thousand dollars."

This would have been television's first libel suit but before the case could come to court, the in surance carrier for Press Productions, Inc.—the company established by Martha Rountree and Lawrence Spivak in 1947—made a settlement, details of which were not made public.

December 12, 1948

Menachem Begin, former commander in chief of the Irgun underground organization in Palestine, is in the United States on what he calls "a goodwill mission on behalf of those who fought for the liberation of Palestine from the British yoke." In six weeks the first elections will be held in the new state of Israel, and Begin will be elected to the Knesset.

> BEGIN: Well, the elections which are going to take place on January twenty-fifth will be elections to the Israeli Constituent Assembly, which will have the task to frame the constitution of our newly established state. . . . I myself will be one of the candidates of the list of candidates put forward by my movement, which is called the Freedom Movement.

William Hetherington (*Newark Evening News*) asks if he would propose armed action against Transjordan to depose King Abdullah.

> BEGIN: . . . [W]e certainly will strive for the realization of our national aim, which means the liberation of the whole of our country of Eretz Israel, which certainly comprises the territory on both sides of the Jordan. . . . [T]his partitioning of our country is an illegal act, and we are not going to recognize it.

He is scathing about the United Nations, asking rhetorically, "Do you think really that the United Nations are capable to solve the problem of Palestine or any problem in the world?"

> SPIVAK: Mr. Begin, your organization and you have been accused of many acts of violence and terror. Do you think that that is a good way to settle a dispute today?
>
> BEGIN: Well, I think, Mr. Spivak, your Washington was accused many years of acts of violence and also of terror. . . .
>
> BILL SLATER: No, not George Washington, acts of terror.
>
> BEGIN: No, not of terror, but just using form of fight.
>
> SLATER: But that was in a formally declared war.
>
> BEGIN: . . . We would have preferred to fight an open fight against the British. . . . We are a very small minority, and we had to fight an underground fight. . . . It is not true that our acts were acts of terrorism. It was a liberation war of our people against a foreign occupation. . . . I think it is a historic established fact that in Philadelphia there were a part of your population that called your fighters for freedom rebels.

And who, the panel wonders, is Israel's enemy now?

MOST GUEST APPEARANCES ON *MEET THE PRESS**

Bob Dole	56
Sam Nunn	29
George Mitchell	27
Richard Gephardt	25
Hubert H. Humphrey	25
Richard Lugar	24
Daniel Patrick Moynihan	24
Henry M. Jackson	23
James A. Baker III	21
George P. Shultz	20
Jesse Jackson	20
Al Gore	19
Thomas Foley	19
Howard Baker	19
Lloyd Bentsen	18
Caspar Weinberger	18
Leon Panetta	18
Newt Gingrich	17
Phil Gramm	16
Jack Kemp	16
J. W. Fulbright	15
Brent Scowcroft	15
Dick Cheney	15
Dick Armey	15
Christopher Dodd	15
Henry Kissinger	14
Bill Bradley	13
Walter W. Heller	13
Edmund S. Muskie	13
Nelson A. Rockefeller	13
William Bennett	13
Warren Christopher	13
Edward Kennedy	13

*As of June 30, 1997.

AGENCY Benton & Bowles
SALES CONTACT T C Shays
ORIGIN New York

information copied from contract card in file, pgms listed thusly:
"Try and Do It"
eff 9/12/48 "Meet the Press"
eff 5/29/49 "Leave It to the Girls"

STARTING OR RENEWAL DATE	NO. WEEKS	CLOSING DATE
July 4, 1948	52 wks	June 26, 1949
July 3, 1949	52 wks	June 25, 1950
	cancel Aug 21, 1949	

DATE OF CHANGE	NETWORK	DAY	TIME
July 4, 1948	WNBT WPTZ WNBW WRGB WBAL-TV WBZ-TV WTVR	Sunday	8:30-9:00pm
March 20, 1949	"	Sunday	8:00-8:30pm

eff 5/1/49 add WNBK, WBEN-TV, WWJ-TV, WSPD-TV, WTMJ-TV, KSD-TV, WNBQ
eff 6/5/49 add WICU
eff 7/3/49 WNBT, WPTZ, WDEL-TV, WBAL-TV, WNBW, WTVR, WJZR-TV WBZ-TV, WRGB, WBEN-TV, WWJ-TV, WSPD-TV, KSD-TV WNBK, WGAL-TV, WICU, WHAM-TV, WDTV,

BEGIN: The British still are our enemy, because they would like to bring their puppet King Abdullah into our country in order to come through him back into our country.

February 20, 1949

In the first of his twenty-five appearances on *Meet the Press*, Sen. Hubert H. Humphrey (D-MN)

addresses issues that will dominate American politics in the second half of the twentieth century: taxation, civil rights, and the role of federal government.

He proposes national legislation on civil rights.

HUMPHREY: [W]e cannot look—at least in the foreseeable future—for prompt state action in some areas of the country. That's why I want national fair employment practices legislation. . . .

MURRAY DAVIS (*New York World-Telegram*): If you force that on the southern states as a federal act rather than letting the states themselves determine it, what's going to happen to your Democratic majority in Congress?

HUMPHREY: Well, now I'll tell you. I am one of those persons that doesn't [*sic*] believe that a political party ought to just be a rallying ground for anybody that wants to get under the tent. . . . As a matter of fact, the best way in the world to strengthen the progressive elements in American politics, the liberal elements of American politics, is to permit people today who have been denied certain basic civil rights to have them.

. . .

GLENN NEVILLE (*New York Daily Mirror*): Senator, what I want to know is, is there anyone among you Democratic progressives who is interested in keeping the cost of government down instead of increasing it all the time?

HUMPHREY: . . . Money and the American national income comes [*sic*] from the people. People produce the goods and services. And I want to say that an educated child that develops, matures into manhood is a much better producer than one that has been denied the opportunities of education. A healthful child that grows healthily into healthful manhood or womanhood is a much more productive citizen. . . . Now, that isn't an expenditure of money in terms of what you call extravagance. That is an investment.

December 10, 1949

The role of women is an issue to which *Meet the Press* has returned repeatedly through its first fifty years, but one early show has a special place in the history of *Meet the Press:* Moderator, panelists, and guest were all women. Martha Rountree was the moderator, and one of the four panelists was a sharp young reporter for the *Washington Post,* Lawrence Spivak's daughter, Judy Spivak. Doris Fleeson (Bell Syndicate), May Craig (*Portland,* Maine, *Press Herald*) and Ruth Montgomery (*New York Daily News*) completed the panel questioning Democratic politician India Edwards.

December 10, 1949: Washington's leading males are at the men-only Gridiron dinner, so Meet the Press *presents an all-women program. From left to right: panelists Doris Fleeson, May Craig, Judy Spivak, Ruth Montgomery, moderator Martha Rountree, and guest India Edwards.*

IN THE NEWS

1950

- China takes over the American Consulate General in Peking.
- President Truman approves H-bomb production.
- Thirty-five American military advisers go to Indochina.
- Congressional hearings into organized crimes are televised.
- War breaks out in Korea when Soviet-backed North Korean forces cross the thirty-eighth parallel. American troops under General MacArthur land behind enemy lines at Inchon. The United Nations votes to unite Korea. MacArthur reaches the Chinese border, where U.S. troops are forced to make a winter retreat.
- Sen. Joseph McCarthy (R-WI) claims to have a list of 205 known Communists in the State Department. He never produces the list. Senate hearings investigate the charges.
- The army takes over the railroads to prevent a general strike.

1951

- President Truman rejects General MacArthur's request to invade Manchuria. MacArthur challenges the decision in public, and Commander in Chief Truman fires him. Calls for Truman's impeachment end only when the Senate supports the president.
- Julius and Ethel Rosenberg are arrested as spies, tried, and sentenced to death.
- Transcontinental television begins.

1952

- Elizabeth II accedes to the British throne.
- The U.S. Supreme Court rules Truman's proposed seizure of steel mills illegal.
- In the presidential election Republican Gen. Dwight Eisenhower defeats Adlai Stevenson by a landslide. Richard Nixon becomes vice president.
- The first hydrogen bomb is tested in the Pacific.
- President-elect Eisenhower goes to Korea and threatens China with atomic weapons.
- Eva Perón dies.

1953

- Soviet leader Joseph Stalin dies. Nikita Khrushchev wins the Kremlin power struggle, and international tensions ease.
- President Eisenhower announces the United States is funding France's war in Indochina.
- James Watson and F.H.C. Crick announce their discovery of the structure of DNA.
- Eisenhower refuses clemency. The Rosenbergs are executed.
- A cease-fire is signed in Korea. Fifty-four thousand Americans died in the war.
- In an American-backed coup the Mossadegh government is overthrown in Iran.
- Senator McCarthy makes an attack on the U.S. Army that leads to his downfall.

1954

- Five members of Congress are shot by supporters of Puerto Rico's independence.
- The televised Senate hearings into Senator McCarthy's allegations against the army are must-see TV, attracting daily audiences of twenty million. McCarthy's credibility lies in ruins. The Senate votes to censure McCarthy.

THE 1950s

- In Indochina Ho Chi Minh's forces are victorious at Dienbienphu.
- The U.S. Supreme Court rules that segregated schools are unconstitutional.

1955

- The United States agrees to help train the South Vietnamese Army.
- The U.S. Supreme Court orders the integration of schools with "all deliberate speed."
- The Geneva Summit Conference takes place.
- Argentinian leader Juan Perón is deposed in a coup.
- Bill Haley and the Comets release "Rock Around the Clock."
- Rosa Parks's refusal to give up her bus seat for a white in Montgomery, Alabama, leads to her arrest, conviction, and appeal. Dr. Martin Luther King, Jr., and others organize a bus boycott. Parks takes her appeal to the U.S. Supreme Court.

1956

- Russian tanks enter Hungary to crush a popular uprising. The West offers moral support.
- Egypt's Premier Gamal Abdel Nasser nationalizes the Suez Canal. Israel invades Egypt, and British and French troops seize the canal. After the UN calls for a cease-fire, Britain and France withdraw.
- In a historic ruling on the *Rosa Parks* case the U.S. Supreme Court declares segregated buses unconstitutional.
- Dr. Jonas Salk introduces a polio vaccine.

1957

- Sen. Joseph McCarthy dies.
- The Soviet Union launches the satellite *Sputnik I,* followed by *Sputnik II,* in which a dog orbits the earth for six months.
- President Eisenhower sends troops to Little Rock, Arkansas, to enforce integration at Central High School against objections of Gov. Orval Faubus.

1958

- Fulgencio Batista's government shows signs of collapse in Cuba.
- President Eisenhower creates the National Aeronautics and Space Administration (NASA). Its task: put a man in space.
- The space race begins, as *Explorer I* is launched.

1959

- Fidel Castro leads the revolution that overthrows the Batista regime. The revolutionaries seize American-owned cattle ranches and sugar estates.
- Alaska becomes the forty-ninth state of the Union.
- Hawaii becomes the fiftieth state of the Union.
- The postmaster general bans the mailing of *Lady Chatterley's Lover.*
- Soviet leader Nikita Khrushchev visits the United States.

Jukeboxes shake to the sound of rock and roll, marking the opening of the generation gap. James Dean embodies misunderstood youth; Elvis provides the sound track. Both are blamed for a new phenomenon, juvenile delinquency.

Teenagers are a rising economic force in an increasingly affluent America. A huge growth in car ownership encourages the spread of suburbia, and television is rapidly becoming the national pastime; thirty million television sets are sold in the 1950s. But the shadow of the H-bomb clouds the American dream. Bomb shelters sprout in suburban gardens, civil defense struggles to prepare for the day of destruction, and schoolchildren practice air-raid drills. Tensions with the Soviet Union ease after Stalin's death in 1953, but the risk of Soviet nuclear attack is destined to remain ever-present for forty years.

When war breaks out, it is in response to Soviet aggression, but it is not nuclear war. Soviet-backed North Korean forces move south across the thirty-eighth parallel on June 23, 1950, and within days President Truman dispatches American troops. He needs no congressional approval, because the United States is acting through the United Nations. In the same month thirty-five U.S. military advisers are sent to Indochina.

The Korean War leads to a political crisis at home. Gen. Douglas MacArthur skillfully repulses the North Korean advance and pushes north to the Chinese border. But Chinese troops pour over the border, forcing the United States to make a difficult retreat. MacArthur asks Truman's permission to attack Manchuria, and the president refuses. A public war of words breaks out between president and general, and MacArthur is replaced by Gen. Matthew Ridgway. MacArthur arrives home to a hero's welcome, and calls for Truman's impeachment are dampened only when the Senate ends the crisis by supporting the president.

The space race takes its first small leaps, as Russia's *Sputnik* satellites appear on the horizon. The skies turn frightening, UFO sightings increase, and fears of alien invasion parallel terrors of creeping communism. In 1950 Sen. Joseph McCarthy of Wisconsin claims to have a "list of 205 names," "known by the Secretary of State as being members of the Communist Party." Although the list is fictitious, the alarm it provokes is very real. America is enthralled by televised Senate hearings into McCarthy's accusations and his methods.

Other events feed the red scare in the 1950s. Julius and Ethel Rosenberg are executed as Communist spies, the American Consulate General in Peking is seized by China, and as the decade ends, the Batista regime is overthrown in Castro's Cuban Revolution. Fidel Castro's fatigues and cigar will become a familiar sight over the next thirty years.

One nation tries to free itself from Soviet domination. In October 1956 Hungary rises against its masters, smashing symbols of Stalin, freeing political prisoners, lynching secret police. But Russian tanks roll in, and the uprising is crushed, its leader executed. Despite Hungarian pleas to the free world, the West offers only moral support, preferring to avoid direct confrontation with the Soviet Union.

The Middle East remains a flashpoint. In 1956 Egyptian Premier Gamal Abdel Nasser nationalizes the Suez Canal. Britain and France respond with force, taking over the canal with the help of an Israeli incursion into the Sinai Peninsula. UN intervention leads to a Franco-British withdrawal, and Nasser becomes a heroic symbol to the Arab world.

The question of racial segregation reaches the U.S. Supreme Court in 1954, when the Court rules that segregated schools are unconstitutional. The ruling does not end the practice. At the start of the 1957 school year President Eisenhower sends thousands of soldiers to Little Rock, Arkansas, where Gov. Orval Faubus is opposing the enrollment of nine black students at Central High School. In Montgomery, Alabama, Rosa Parks refuses to give up her seat on a bus to a white person. She is arrested and fined. When she loses her first appeal against conviction, the case goes to the Supreme Court, and in 1956 the Court declares segregation on the buses unconstitutional.

Anti-Communist
Mme. Chiang Kai-shek (top); Communist revolutionaries Fidel Castro and Ché Guevara (middle); and moderator Martha Rountree (bottom).

By 1950 *Meet the Press*—America's Press Conference of the Air—was supplying a regular flow of headlines to the front pages of Monday morning's newspapers, none bigger than the story of Republican Gov. Thomas E. Dewey's on-air withdrawal from the 1952 presidential race and his endorsement of the still-undeclared Gen. Dwight Eisenhower. Governor Dewey would after all come no closer to the presidency than the famously false 1948 headline in the *Chicago Daily Tribune:* DEWEY DEFEATS TRUMAN.

Ned Brooks, veteran journalist and radio broadcaster, served as moderator of *Meet the Press* for twelve years, from November 22, 1953, to December 26, 1965.

A journalism graduate of Ohio State University, he was managing editor of the Scripps-Howard newspaper in Youngstown, Ohio, until coming to Washington in 1932 as the chain's political correspondent. He later became a highly respected fixture of Sunoco's *Three Star Extra*, a nightly news program heard on the NBC radio network.

After appearing frequently as a panelist on *Meet the Press* in the show's early television days, Brooks became the regular moderator in November 1953, a position he held until retiring as a result of illness at the end of 1965.

He died in April 1969 at age sixty-seven.

October 15, 1950

Leo Egan (*New York Times*) asks Governor Dewey if he is interested in the Republican nomination for president in 1952.

DEWEY: No, that one is out. I am definitely and finally removed . . . and that is beyond consideration.

EGAN: Governor, if you are not going to run, do you have any candidates in mind?

DEWEY: Well, it's a little early, but we have in New York a very great world figure, the president of Columbia University, one of the greatest soldiers of our history, a fine educator, a man who really understands the problems of the world, and if I should be reelected governor and have influence with the New York delegation, I would recommend to them that they support General Eisenhower for president if he would accept the draft.

EGAN: Governor, have you asked General Eisenhower if he is willing?

DEWEY: I have not.

EGAN: Do you know if he is a Republican?

DEWEY: Well, I have listened to some of his speeches, and I certainly should think that his philosophy would be in accordance with my own.

Following this sensational endorsement of Gen. Dwight D. Eisenhower, Dewey speaks about the post–world war world: "The cold war will last throughout your lifetime and mine. . . . I see no reason for believing that the Russians will attack us so long as they think we can retaliate with tremendous power. On the other hand, it is perfectly clear that they are determined to conquer the whole world, and nothing will ever disillusion them or deter them."

After Governor Dewey's stunning announcement on *Meet the Press,* Leo Egan told Lawrence Spivak that his editors were upset because he hadn't filed the Dewey story for the *Times*. He explained to them that he had asked the governor the same questions repeatedly on the paper's behalf but had elicited only evasive answers. Egan believed the bright focus of television inspired Dewey to let the answers flow, and Spivak saw the incident as an early indication of the psychological impact that facing large television audiences could have on guests. It encouraged truthfulness.

I think it is setting a low level if our only goal for official conduct is that it be legal instead of illegal.

—Sen. J. William Fulbright (D-AR), February 25, 1951

This statement on influence peddling in Washington, D.C., highlights an issue that resonates through fifty years of *Meet the Press.*

August 7, 1951

Sen. Joseph McCarthy, the controversial Communist hunter from Wisconsin, is dedicated to unearthing Communist sympathizers. At the time of his fifth *Meet the Press* appearance, he is threatening to name card-carrying Communists in the State Department. Word reaches NBC that an audience member is carrying a gun and will shoot McCarthy if he carries out his threat. Moderator Martha Rountree, sitting alongside Senator McCarthy, is alarmed to see him take a gun out of his briefcase and place it on his lap, where it remains throughout the show. McCarthy names no names, and there is no shoot-out.

John L. Lewis, president of the United Mine Workers of America, appears on Meet the Press *on July 15, 1951. Before the show he said to Lawrence Spivak, "I suppose you have some of those 'have-you-stopped-beating-your-wife' questions."*

December 2, 1951

French colonialists are fighting Communist forces in Indochina. Just back from Indochina, the young Massachusetts congressman John F. Kennedy makes his first national television appearance and the first of his eight appearances on *Meet the Press.*

The panel asks him about the lessons he brought back.

> KENNEDY: You can never defeat the Communist movement in Indochina until you get the support of the natives, and you won't get the support of the natives as long as they feel that the French are fighting the Communists in order to hold on to their power there. And I think we shouldn't give military assistance until the French clearly make an agreement with the natives that at the end of a certain time when the Communists are defeated the

December 2, 1951: Revere Ware—founded by Paul Revere—was the regular Meet the Press *sponsor when Massachusetts Congressman John F. Kennedy made his first appearance on the show.*

French will pull out and give this country the right of self-determination and the right to govern themselves. Otherwise this guerrilla war is just going to spread and grow, and we're going to finally get driven out of Southeast Asia.

The congressman is remarkably open about the need to clean up influence peddling in the Democratic party, stating that the president must take the lead. "I don't think the Democratic party should win an election unless it does clean up. . . . I think efforts are being made to clear it up, but unless we are successful, then I think we should lose the election."

A year after Republican Governor Dewey's endorsement of General Eisenhower on *Meet the Press,* Ike has still not declared his intentions. Ernest Lindley (*Newsweek* magazine) asks Kennedy about the Democratic ticket.

KENNEDY: [I]f President Truman is a candidate for reelection, he would receive the nomination. I would say he would probably be the strongest. Now there's been some talk of General Eisenhower running. I don't know whether General Eisenhower is a Republican or Democrat.

. . .

LINDLEY: If General Eisenhower were the Democratic nominee, do you think any Republican could defeat him?

KENNEDY: Once General Eisenhower took a position on civil rights and labor legislation and endorsed the Democratic program, then I think that perhaps he would be weakened. Regardless of what side he takes, he's going to be weaker than he is today. . . . I think that's the difficulty in politics. You are always bound to lose supporters once you take a stand on an issue.

More than forty years later the same concerns would be raised about Gen. Colin Powell's possible candidacy for political office.

Of John F. Kennedy, Spivak said: "From the beginning he knew how to handle a press conference, and you didn't force him to say anything he didn't want to say."

James Reston of the *New York Times* was on the panel interviewing Congressman Kennedy, and he was smoking. This was bold behavior, as Lawrence Spivak was an implacable campaigner against tobacco. He would never permit smoking in his office, and he normally allowed no smoking on the *Meet the Press* set, even during commercial breaks. This unbreakable rule led to Randolph Churchill's accusing Spivak of being "a goddamned dictator," while Ed (four-packs-a-day) Murrow, deprived of his cigarettes for the duration of the show, gave a sorry performance when he was the guest on *Meet the Press* on June 4, 1961, as director of the United States Information Agency. The crew could see Murrow's legs twitching furiously under the chair, apparently not from nervousness but because of nicotine deprivation. Skeleton artwork hung in the *Meet the Press* office to warn people of the dangers of tobacco, and there were No Smoking signs in several languages. Even Spivak's frequent poker games were smoke-free, with Spivak paying his fellow players for every cigarette they didn't smoke. Oddly enough, his wife was a smoker. Charlotte Spivak—an artist and sociologist—was quite unlike her husband in interests and disposition, but they were an unusually devoted couple. Neither daughter Judith nor son Jonathan, a *Wall Street Journal* reporter, smoked cigarettes.

January 27, 1952

Presidential adviser W. Averell Harriman gives a robust defense of aid to Europe.

HARRIMAN: I don't like this word "aid" because that sounds as if we're giving something to somebody else. This is a mutual business. We are helping them with a contribution of arms. They supply the troops, the manpower and training. . . . I'm satisfied that the money we are spending to help arm our allies is the cheapest form, the most security for the minimum amount of money.

Averell Harriman later told Lawrence Spivak that his *Meet the Press* appearance had changed his life. He had been very reluctant to face the panel, but he enjoyed the experience, and the gratifyingly positive response to the program was what led him to politics and running for governor of New York.

March 30, 1952

The name on the Democratic ticket was not a foregone conclusion. There was a great deal of speculation on whether or not President Truman would run again, and there were some indications that Gov. Adlai Stevenson might be his favorite if he withdrew from the race. Lawrence Spivak decided to bring Stevenson to the microphone the day after a big Democratic gathering where Truman was the major attraction. "No matter what Truman said or did," Spivak explained, "Stevenson was certain to be highlighted because of the occasion. When the thing that nobody expected to happen did happen—when Truman irrevocably took himself out as a candidate for reelection—Stevenson became the 'hottest news in America.' His appearance on *Meet the Press* the next day created great excitement." Spivak remembered Stevenson's appearance as one of the most significant in the show's history.

RICHARD WILSON (*Des Moines Register*): What do you think the attitude of the people is today? What do they want? What are they dissatisfied with?

STEVENSON: . . . I think they are very much concerned about the level of morals in public life. I think naturally they are concerned about the level of taxes. I think the long, frustrating ordeal in

Korea has been a source of both bewilderment and confusion, anxiety.

. . .

EDWIN LEAHY (*Chicago Daily News*): You have said that you don't want a place on the ticket, haven't you, that you aren't seeking it?

STEVENSON: Yes, I have said that I was a candidate for governor of Illinois and that's all.

LEAHY: Wouldn't your grandfather, Vice President Stevenson, twirl in his grave if he saw you running away from a chance to be a Democratic nominee in 1952?

STEVENSON: I think we will have to leave grandfather lie.

LAWRENCE SPIVAK: President Truman said yesterday that he will not be a candidate for the Democratic nomination, nor will he accept a draft. Does that describe your position, sir?

STEVENSON: My position, Mr. Spivak, and perhaps I should take this opportunity to try to make it clear if it's not, is that I'm an announced candidate for governor of Illinois. I do not seek, I will not seek the Democratic nomination for the presidency.

. . .

MAY CRAIG (*Portland*, Maine, *Press Herald*): President Truman said a very simple thing last night. He said, "I shall not accept the nomination." Will you say that or will you not say that?

STEVENSON: I will not say that.

He said enough. On the following day the headline covered the front page of the *New York Post:* BOOM ON TO DRAFT STEVENSON.

Jacob Arvey, Democratic national committeeman from Illinois, said later that year on *Meet the Press* (October 26, 1952): "Were it not for this program, he would never, in my opinion, have been considered as a candidate for the presidency."

After the election *Look* magazine wrote (February 10, 1953): "When American voters went to the polls last November to choose between Gen. Dwight D. Eisenhower and Gov. Adlai E. Stevenson, a radio and television program was at least partially responsible for their names appearing on the ballots." *Meet the Press* had become a recognized political player.

April 4, 1952: NBC begins broadcasting the audio of *Meet the Press* over the NBC radio network. The radio version was discontinued on July 27, 1986.

Somehow this show about three times out of four inspires us to write an editorial.
—*New York Daily News* editorial, April 8, 1952

Alben W. Barkley becomes the first vice president of the United States to appear in a *Meet the Press* interview, on July 20, 1952. Every succeeding vice president has appeared on *Meet the Press*.

September 14, 1952

Breaking major news was becoming a matter of course for *Meet the Press,* but occasionally a story got away. When General Eisenhower's vice presidential running mate—California Republican Sen. Richard M. Nixon—made the first of his seven *Meet the Press* appearances, Lawrence Spivak let a story slip through his fingers. Before the show, panelist Peter Edson (Newspaper Enterprise Asso-

The four *Meet the Press* panelists were chosen with care. Writing ability was clearly less important than the ability to ask good, quick, revealing questions. Panelists also had to adapt to the guest's answers and know when a follow-up question would advance the discussion.

Lawrence Spivak liked to mix specialists and generalists on the panel. While an expert could pursue the guest on factual details, an overdose of experts might miss the obvious questions that the program's audience would want to ask. Spivak also liked to stay with familiar faces, believing the

audience considered the journalists personalities and found constant change unsettling. New panelists were blended in slowly.

Variations in the panelists' ages, looks, and personalities were considered desirable, and Spivak would, as far as possible, choose journalists from a wide geographical range. This could present problems since the best journalists tended to gravitate to a few prestigious publications.

Since the early days of *Meet the Press* guests have been told which reporters they will face, but only after the guests accept the invitation to appear. Producers never deliberately select a reporter a guest would find intolerable, largely because the guest would probably cancel the interview. Two notable hostilities: Eleanor Roosevelt v. Hearst columnist Westbrook Pegler and Robert McNamara v. lawyer-journalist Clark Mollenhoff.

Guests may be told what general areas of questioning to expect but are never warned of specific questions. (This strict rule became flexible in the case of first lady Nancy Reagan, who agreed to be interviewed only if questions were limited to her antidrug campaign.)

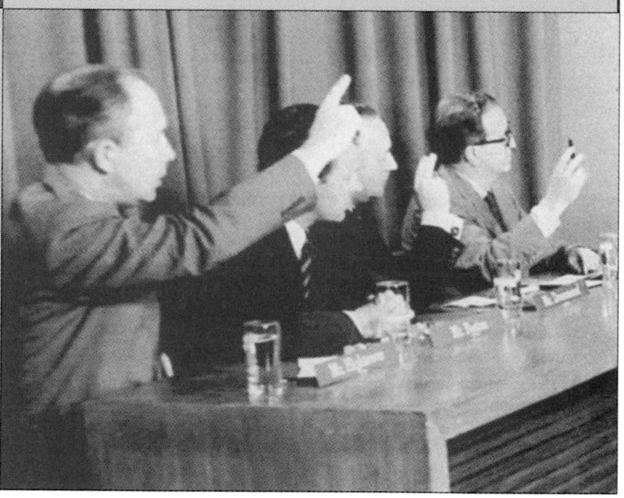

ciation) informed Spivak of rumors concerning a special fund paying Nixon's campaign expenses. Spivak told Edson not to question Nixon about it, a rare departure from his rule not to edit the reporters' questions. The vice presidential candidate was asked about a five-thousand-dollar campaign contribution from reputed influence peddler Henry ("the Dutchman") Grunwald, but it was not until after the show that Edson talked to Nixon about the fund. Nixon spoke surprisingly freely about it and even gave Edson a contact in California. The story broke in the press, and Nixon delivered the famous "Checkers" speech on television a week later, defending his behavior. Spivak thought his veto was honorable and fair, and he believed the story would not have come out if Nixon had been questioned about the fund on air.

November 9, 1952

As Richard Nixon is elected vice president, his future presidential nemesis enters the Senate. Lawrence Spivak, acting as moderator, introduces Sen.-elect John Kennedy, "whose sensational victory in Massachusetts in the face of General Eisenhower's landslide has brought him to national attention as the most important Democratic figure in New England." Senator Kennedy repeats his concerns about involvement in Indochina, saying that "we take the chance of financing a war which in the end we are going to eventually lose, unless we can win the support of the natives of that area."

He backs President-elect Eisenhower's plan to go to Korea: "I agree with Governor Stevenson that the right address to end the Korean War is not Korea but Moscow, but there are a number of things which he can do."

June 7, 1953

French statesman Jean Monnet, often called the father of Europe, talks of his faith in a united Europe. Moderator Martha Rountree welcomes Monnet as "the man who has done more than almost any other European statesman toward the unity of the free nations of Europe." Monnet's

September 14, 1952: Richard Nixon (far right) shares the raised podium with moderator Martha Rountree.

European vision shines through his first reply, about the coal and steel community newly formed by six European nations. It is, he says, "the first federation of Europe."

MONNET: They didn't only pool their coal and steel, they in fact delegated the powers that had been exercised by every one of these nations separately, to institutions which are now the first federal institution of Europe, and it stands to reason that if you do that and if you eliminate the barriers and the frontiers and have a common market of one hundred and fifty million people, you improve the production and therefore improve the prices. . . . For the first time in the history of Europe the market is free and prices are free, and whether they come down depends now on the supply and demand in the market itself.

. . .

ROSCOE DRUMMOND (*Christian Science Monitor*): Do you think that this has serious prospects of leading substantially toward a European federation or a European parliament?

MONNET: Mr. Drummond, it not only has the prospects but is leading towards the European federation. . . . [W]e are on the way to having a United States of Europe.

. . .

MARTHA ROUNTREE: Speaking of frontiers and boundaries, what future do you predict for East Germany now in relation to your federation?

MONNET: That does not rest with me and with us to predict only. You know the conditions that exist, but I do think that the Germans of East Germany should one day peacefully rejoin the Germans of Western Europe in a united Europe.

July 26, 1953: Almost forty years before Ross Perot, Postmaster General Arthur E. Summerfield brings a chart to the studio to make his point.

The idea of peaceful reunification with Communist countries is almost unthinkable in the anti-Communist atmosphere of the 1950s, when fears of red spies are at their height. On November 22, 1953, spy hunter Robert Morris, counsel to the Senate Internal Security Subcommittee, says on *Meet the Press* that only two of the four spy rings cited by ex-Communist Elizabeth Bentley (see *Meet the Press*, September 12, 1948) have been exposed, so two red rings could still be active in the U.S. government. Three weeks later Sen. Joseph McCarthy is back on the program to report on the hunt for Communists.

September 10, 1953. Press Productions, Inc., buys Martha Rountree's fifty shares, and Lawrence E. Spivak becomes sole stockholder. In December, Press Productions, Inc. sells about fifteen shares of Treasury stock to James, Evelyn, and Edgar Kobak (the Mutual president responsible for bringing *Meet the Press* to radio), and J. K. Lasser (the accountant).

December 13, 1953

Lawrence Spivak introduces Sen. Joseph McCarthy (R-WI) as "America's most controversial figure," and his performance justifies the description. When panelist John J. Madigan of Hearst Publications raises Adlai Stevenson's proposal for "a crusade wherein Communist tactics would not be used to get rid of Communism in this country," McCarthy is dismissive: "All those who seem to have a special fondness toward the Communist philosophy, repeat over and over like a broken record, let's get rid of Communists but let's not get rough with them."

. . .

MADIGAN: Do you know how many of those [fired for security reasons in the Eisenhower administration] were actually loyalty risks and how much involved human frailty?

McCARTHY: . . . It varies. You take those discharged for Communist connections and perversion, add the two together, it runs over ninety percent.

SPIVAK: Ninety percent for what?

McCARTHY: Ninety percent of the total of one thousand four hundred and twenty-seven.

SPIVAK: Ninety percent for perversion or ninety percent for loyalty?

McCARTHY: The combination of Communist activities and perversion.

SPIVAK: But what part of that is Communist activity?

McCARTHY: I couldn't break that down for you.

February 14, 1954

John F. Kennedy is the guest as *Meet the Press* becomes the first news program to be broadcast in color. Before one of his eight *Meet the Press* appearances, Kennedy said to Lawrence Spivak, "I suppose you're going to throw some sharp curves at me."

SPIVAK: We have too high a regard for you to pull our punches.

KENNEDY: Well, I wouldn't mind if you lowered your regard a bit.

On air Kennedy repeats his belief, stated on previous *Meet the Press* performances, that "without the support of the native population, there is no hope of success in any of the countries of Southeast Asia." The doomed French effort in Indochina illustrates his point. "Westerners are fighting natives even though they are Communists. For the United States to intervene as Westerners against natives, particularly when the population has not supported the struggle in the past, I think would not guarantee the prospects of victory, and therefore it would be a mistake for us to go in."

. . .

MAY CRAIG (*Portland*, Maine, *Press Herald*): President Truman took us into the Korean War without asking Congress. Do you think, as Senator [John] Stennis says, that Eisenhower is inching us into a war in Indochina now?

KENNEDY: No, but I do think that the technicians were probably unnecessary. . . . [I]t is a step forward in involvement in French Indochina. I

This is not the difficulty of the eighty-third Congress. This is not the difficulty of this Administration. This is not the difficulty of this century. It goes back over the last fifteen hundred years to when Western civilization began. That is the stage upon which this little incident is being played. Anyone who cannot see this as the crisis of this civilization is blind.

—Sen. Ralph E. Flanders (R-VT) on Sen. Joseph McCarthy, June 13, 1954

don't think we should continue that involvement until the political conditions are present to secure us victory.

Despite his understanding of the political complexity of Indochina, Kennedy would later increase the number of troops there during his presidency.

March 14, 1954

In the months since his last *Meet the Press* appearance, Senator McCarthy and his assistant Roy M. Cohn have been accused of having sought to obtain a commission and special privileges for G. David Schine, drafted heir to a hotel fortune and unpaid subcommittee consultant. On the day following Cohn's appearance on *Meet the Press*, the *New York Times* has a page one report: COHN AGAIN DENIES HE ASKED FAVORS AND ACCUSES ARMY/Says That He Never Sought Special Status for Schine—Charges Deal on Inquiry/LOYALTY PLEDGE IS CITED.

Cohn acknowledges on air that the staff of the Senate Permanent Subcommittee on Investigations is being asked to sign a loyalty pledge to him.

The confrontation with the army was to lead to McCarthy's downfall.

April 11, 1954

When Eleanor Roosevelt appears on *Meet the Press*, Senator McCarthy is, almost inevitably, the first subject raised by the panel, and Mrs. Roosevelt is hostile toward McCarthyism.

ROOSEVELT: I object very strongly to the methods that have been used, not to trying to deal with the issue. I object to trying to use the same methods that you object to in communism and in fascism. . . . I think that one's opposition is to the use of a committee of the Congress in ways that I do not think are legitimate and which have endangered, I think, the freedoms and the rights of some of our people.

She also denies that her husband, President Franklin D. Roosevelt, had had advance knowledge of the Japanese attack on Pearl Harbor and had exploited the situation to hasten America's involvement in World War II.

May 30, 1954

Sen. Guy M. Gillette (D-IA) talks about McCarthy's increasing unpopularity since the start of the wildly popular televised Senate hearings into his accusations of communism in the army.

October 3, 1954

Sen. Joseph McCarthy makes his first public comments since publication of the Watkins Committee report, which recommends that the Senate censure him. McCarthy defends his actions and attacks the objectivity of the committee. He blames his involvement in the first Senate censure motion in twenty-five years on his all-out fight against communism.

Meet the Press *showed America the rise and fall of Sen. Joseph McCarthy and his anti-Communist campaign.*

November 14, 1954

Sen. Sam Ervin (D-NC), one of the six men on the Senate committee at the center of what *Meet the Press* moderator Ned Brooks calls the "stormy debate over the proposed censure of Senator McCarthy, now moving into its second week," is questioned about the committee's report and Senator McCarthy's allegations of the Democratic committee members' bias against him. After declaring himself in favor of censure, Ervin says, "I think it is apparent to everybody that Senator McCarthy intends to besmirch throughout the nation every senator who dares to oppose his will or to express disapproval of his disorderly behavior."

ERVIN: [I] cannot conceive of McCarthy ever admitting that he ever did anything wrong. . . . He made a statement in which he said that the members of the committee were unwitting handmaidens and involuntary agents and attorneys in fact of the Communist party, that they expressed and distorted truth in order to bring in this report. If Senator McCarthy did not believe those things when he said them about the Senate committee, then there is a pretty solid ground to say that he ought to be expelled from the Senate for moral incapacity. . . . On the contrary, if he put those things in there honestly believing them to be true, then he has evidently suffered gigantic mental delusions, and it may be argued with much force that he should be expelled from the Senate for mental difficulty.

November 21, 1954

Pierre Mendès-France, premier of France, is the first head of government on *Meet the Press*. "The excitement was unbelievable," Spivak told the *Jackson Clarion-Ledger* later. "When I drove up to the studio with him in New York, the streets were lined with hundreds of cheering admirers, and the climate inside was one of extraordinary excitement." Before an audience estimated at ten million, Mendès-France causes a storm at home by appearing in photographs drinking *milk*, which deeply offends the patriotic sensibilities of France's wine industry. Throughout the interview he sits with a glass of milk in front of him.

Mendès-France is so fluent in English that his interpreter, Roger Vaurs, does not have to put in one word.

May 7, 1950: The White House provides a backdrop for the Meet the Press *panel and studio guest Congressman Emanuel Celler (D-NY). Moderators-to-be Ned Brooks and Lawrence Spivak are on the left.*

Lawrence Spivak asks him about one of his most extraordinary achievements:

> SPIVAK: I understand that you have been successful in getting the French taxi drivers to stop using their horns.
>
> MENDÈS-FRANCE: That's a very important reform.
>
> SPIVAK: We'd like to know what magic you used, so that we might be able to use it here on the taxi drivers.
>
> MENDÈS-FRANCE: There was no magic. We asked them very strongly, and we explained why it was necessary. Here, again, I come to what I said a few minutes ago: No reform is ever accepted in a democratic country if the people don't understand the necessity of it. Each time we are doing something, each time we are making a decision, we always feel it necessary for the people to understand very well. That's the reason for which I am speaking to my countrymen by radio each week.

French wine growers were appalled to see photographs of their premier, Pierre Mendès-France, drinking milk on American television. It seemed like treachery.

December 12, 1954

Senator McCarthy's Communist threat was in large measure a work of the imagination, but Red China was real and threatening. On *Meet the Press*, Anthony Nutting, head of the British delegation to the United Nations, declares that Great Britain would be "involved" if red China attacks Chiang Kai-shek's Formosa. "We are fairly and squarely in your corner." Next day the British Foreign Office takes the unusual step of qualifying his statement, implying that he has overstepped the mark on *Meet the Press*. The *Daily Express*, London, reports (December 14): "The Foreign Office has sent urgent signals to New York for an official transcript of the interview given by Mr Nutting—in a program called 'Meet the Press.' Peiping (Beijing) radio says Nutting is 'clamoring for war.'"

Anything that makes any race feel inferior or makes second-rate citizens out of them is not only un-American but un-Christian.

—Billy Graham, March 6, 1955

March 20, 1955

Some politicians were working to break through ideological divisions rather than exploit them. *Meet the Press* has reported on many major political developments in its fifty-year history. In March 1955 the course of history is changed on *Meet the Press* when Sen. Walter George (D-GA), chairman of the Senate Foreign Relations Committee, calls for a meeting of the heads of state of the four leading powers, a call quickly taken up by the president and culminating in the 1955 Geneva Summit

Conference with President Eisenhower, Nikita Khrushchev, Nikolai Bulganin, and Georgi Zhukov. As moderator Ned Brooks makes clear in his introduction, presidents listen when Senator George speaks on foreign relations.

After speaking on a range of international problems, George makes his dramatic call.

> GEORGE: I think we have reached a stage in our international relations at this moment when the real hope of avoiding war is through some high-level conferences between the leading powers.
>
> . . .
>
> JOHN HIGHTOWER (Associated Press): Senator, do I understand you to mean by what you just said you think it would be wise within the next few months to have a meeting which brought together the heads of the American, British, Russian, and, say, French governments?
>
> GEORGE: Well, I think the great nations who are vitally interested in world peace and the stability of governments ought to be brought together as soon as it is practical.

As Spivak said later, "No American in a responsible position had suggested such a move out loud before, but the voice of the chairman of the Senate Foreign Relations Committee carried such authority that the whole world heard the suggestion within hours—by cable, diplomatic channels, radio and television, and headlines from here to Moscow.

May 2, 1955: Resisting offers from William Paley at CBS, Press Productions, Inc., authorizes Lawrence Spivak to sell rights title and interest in *Meet the Press* to NBC for a seven-figure sum. It is voted to liquidate the company within twelve months. Spivak retains complete control over *Meet the Press,* picking guests and panelists.

September 18, 1955: Dag Hammarskjöld, the second secretary general of the United Nations, is the guest on Meet the Press.

The president commented favorably on it; Churchill and Eden urged it; and Bulganin replied to it. As the *Atlanta Journal* put it, George's statement 'favoring American initiation of a top-level conference on major East-West problems . . . quickly skyrocketed into the story of the week. It may become the story of the year.'" It did; before the year was out, Eisenhower and Khrushchev met in Geneva at the first big peacetime summit conference.

December 11, 1955

Before the end of the year *Meet the Press* is once again a vehicle for a headline-making announcement, when former President Herbert Hoover calls for the creation of a new office of administrative vice president to help operate "the biggest business in the world."

> LAWRENCE SPIVAK: Mr. Hoover, for many years there has been, or at least recently there has been talk of increasing the power of the vice presidency in order to lessen the load of the president. Do you favor that?
>
> HOOVER: Well, I just can't deal with that in one sentence.

SPIVAK: We'll let you have four or five, Mr. Hoover.

HOOVER: The vice president is an elective officer. He has certain constitutional duties, and gradually the vice presidents have been brought more and more into the administration by way of assisting the president in policy-making questions and social relations and speechmaking, et cetera. That, I think, is probably the only field that could be occupied by the vice presidency as it is presently set up. If the vice president were placed between the president and the Cabinet officers and the heads of important agencies, I think we'd have utter confusion. My suggestion, if I may go on, is that what we need is a new administrative vice president to be selected by the president and assigned such duties as he may wish. In that fashion he could take away a tremendous amount of detail work.

The poet Robert Frost appeared on Meet the Press *on Christmas Day 1955 and returned on December 23 the following year. A Christmas 1958 appearance was preempted for an NBC space special on the development of the Atlas rocket. In early December the Defense Department had announced Project Discoverer, a long-range satellite program aimed at placing mice, monkeys, and eventually humans in space and bringing them back alive. The Frost interview was recorded and rescheduled in March. Frost declared later that "when I come to the Pearly Gates and am asked severely, 'Have you lived modern?' I shall be able to say in my defense one important thing—'Yes, I have been on television several times with Larry Spivak on* Meet the Press.*' That's my hope of getting by."*

This program had real and instant political repercussions. Sen. John F. Kennedy—who was well aware of television's growing influence—asked for a transcript of Hoover's comments on *Meet the Press* and announced that he would follow up the former president's proposal by presenting legislation in the coming Congress to authorize the appointment of an administrative vice president. Television and *Meet the Press* have become an established part of the democratic process.

WEDNESDAY, JUNE 6, 1956

Newspaperman Victor Riesel's long crusade against corruption in labor unions led to a violent response by New York labor racketeers. Two months before his *Meet the Press* appearance, he was permanently blinded when acid was thrown in his face. Waterfront gangsters were linked to the violence, but as Riesel tells panelist Murray Davis (*New York Telegraph and Sun*), "The throwing of acid is a traditional weapon of the jungle of garment and trucking area racketeers."

President Eisenhower saw Victor Riesel on *Meet the Press* and was much impressed by his demands for federal action against union racketeers, and he announced plans for White House action against underworld infiltration of unions.

August 5, 1956

An internal problem more troubling than communism is entering a new phase in the 1950s: race. In 1954 the U.S. Supreme Court rules that segregated schools are unconstitutional, but the fight for equality continues on many fronts.

NED BROOKS: Our guest is the executive secretary of the National Association for the Advancement of Colored People, Mr. Roy Wilkins. The initials NAACP have come to symbolize the battle now being waged to end racial discrimination. The organization was founded nearly fifty years ago, but many people were only vaguely aware of its existence until it took the leadership in bringing the school segregation cases before the Supreme Court. Since winning that important victory, NAACP has carried most of the legal burden for translating the court ruling into action, and in so doing it has aroused intense opposition in the South.

The panel soon turns to the question of desegregation.

THOMAS R. WARING (*Charleston,* South Carolina, *News and Courier)*: After exhaustion of the legal procedures, would you advocate military force to enforce the Supreme Court's [desegregation] orders?

WILKINS: Up to this point we have never mentioned military sanctions or the use of federal troops, and I am not able at this point to say whether we ever would advocate it. Certainly it seems to me that a government is obligated to enforce the law in this case just as it would with respect to antitrust violations or traffic laws.

Frank Van Der Linden (*Nashville,* Tennessee, *Banner*) asks Wilkins about the NAACP's defiance of an Alabama court order to produce its records.

WILKINS: We declined to submit our list of members, their names and addresses in the state of Alabama. And we've done this because it has been

August 5, 1956: Lawrence Spivak (left), moderator Ned Brooks (center), and guest Roy Wilkins, executive director of the NAACP (right).

our experience that our members have been subjected to persecution, to denial of credit, to the loss of their jobs, to physical threats and violence. . . . In Selma, for example, sixteen out of twenty-nine of our people lost their jobs within twenty-four hours after their names became known and were published in the newspaper.

September 16, 1956

As the presidential election approaches, the Republican vice presidential nominee becomes an issue. Eleanor Roosevelt attacks Richard Nixon on *Meet the Press,* saying he called Helen Gahagan Douglas a Communist in the 1950 Senate race.

> ROOSEVELT: I happen to remember very clearly his campaign for the senatorship. I had no respect for the way in which he accused Helen Gahagan Douglas of being a Communist because he knew that was how he would be elected, and I have no respect for the kind of character that takes advantage and does something they know is not true. He knew that she might be a liberal, but he knew quite well—having known her and worked with her—that she was not a Communist, and I've always felt that anyone who wanted an election so much that they would use those means did not have the character that I really admired in public life.

Mrs. Roosevelt's attack on Nixon was widely reported and widely contested. Weeks later she said she had perhaps gone too far and admitted that Nixon had merely implied the slur. At the same time Sen. John F. Kennedy declares on *Meet the Press* (October 28, 1956) that Richard Nixon represents the future of the Republican party.

Some issues have proved to be as durable as *Meet the Press:* civil rights, the confrontation with communism, and strife in the Middle East. In 1956 there are fears that the Middle East might draw the major powers into war. The problem begins when Egyptian Premier Gamal Abdel Nasser nationalizes the Suez Canal, a vital waterway linking the Red Sea and the Mediterranean. Britain and France respond with a military takeover of the canal. Their plan involves an invasion of Egypt's Sinai Peninsula by Israel, followed by a Franco-British attack on the canal.

September 23, 1956

John Foster Dulles, secretary of state, asked about the Suez crisis, warns that war over the canal would bog the West down "for almost an indefinite time." Three days later Britain and France put the crisis in the hands of the United Nations. But the invasion plan goes ahead on October 29. It is condemned by the United States, and the United Nations demands withdrawal.

November 11, 1956

Senate Republican leader William F. Knowland says he would recommend UN sanctions against

Britain, France, and Israel if they fail to withdraw their forces from Egypt speedily, in accordance with a UN resolution.

He also rejects Russia's offer to send "volunteers" to help Egypt as "detrimental to the peace of the world." He says the United States wants "peace with honor."

The British and French comply, leaving Nasser the canal and the glory.

November 25, 1956

Dr. Mahmoud Fawzi, Egyptian foreign minister, claims Egypt's takeover of the Suez Canal "is our own business." He evades questions on whether Egypt would negotiate with Israel to settle disputes. A week later, Israel's foreign minister is the guest on *Meet the Press.*

December 2, 1956

NED BROOKS: Our guest is the foreign minister of Israel, Mrs. Golda Meir. The nation she represents is one of the smallest and the newest, and almost from the time of its birth in 1948 Israel has been the center of Middle Eastern disputes threatening to explode into war. The tensions between Israel and her Arab neighbors reached the breaking point a few weeks ago. It was then that Israel moved armed forces into Egypt. Mrs. Meir is now in this country attending sessions of the United Nations as Israel's chief delegate. She was appointed foreign minister last June, and she is the only woman in the world holding that office.

. . .

LAWRENCE SPIVAK: Mrs. Meir, just what did Israel hope to gain by her attack on Egypt?

MEIR: In one word, security. We went into the Sinai Desert for one purpose and one purpose only, certainly not for territorial annexations. We went to drive the danger that was facing us from the Egyptian forces in the Sinai Desert farther away from our borders.

SPIVAK: Now as you review world events since October 29, when you marched on Egypt, do you really think the attack has accomplished anything of real value either for Israel or for the world?

MEIR: I think it has. There are no fedayeen gangs now in the Sinai Desert nor in Gaza. There's no Egyptian Army in the Sinai Desert; there are no bases there for tanks and guns. Our boats are now free to sail through the Straits of Aqaba. That is all we wanted.

. . .

We are withdrawing our forces in negotiations with the United Nations, I think to the satisfaction of the United Nations.

PAULINE FREDERICK (NBC News): Does that include withdrawing from the Gaza Strip?

MEIR: Gaza Strip is one of the items about which we are now negotiating with the United Nations.

. . .

FREDERICK: Madam Minister, Ambassador Eban has suggested that a buffer zone be set up between Egypt and Israel. Would you agree with that?

MEIR: Yes . . . If you see the peninsula of Sinai—if you can visualize a map for a moment—then it's as though a peninsula there was created to be the natural buffer zone between Israel and Egypt. Since it is not a populated area at all, it would not inconvenience anybody to have that territory used as a buffer zone.

. . .

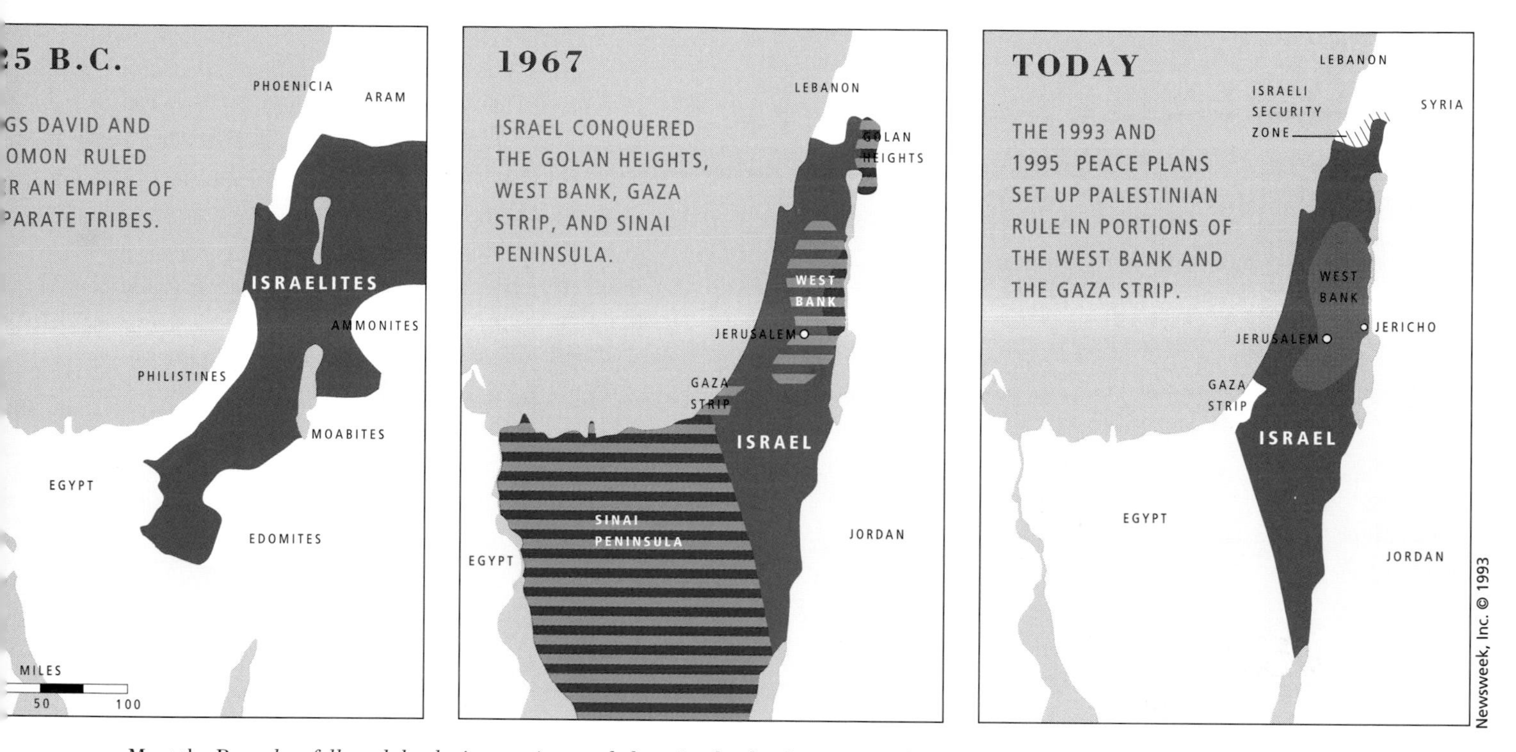

Meet the Press *has followed developing tensions and changing borders between Israel and her Arab neighbors since Menachem Begin appeared on the program in 1948, the year of Israel's birth.*

MAY CRAIG (*Portland*, Maine, *Press Herald*): Madam Minister, do you believe that the Arab nations wish to destroy Israel as a state?

MEIR: To my sorrow, yes.

. . .

CRAIG: How do you think Israel can be maintained in the midst of a hostile population on all sides?

MEIR: Mrs. Craig, maybe it is easier for us to understand it than for others, because throughout our Jewish history, if the Jewish people went out of existence just because other people wanted them to go out of existence, there wouldn't be a Jewish people and there wouldn't be an Israel today, but there is a certain stubbornness about our people that we just want to live the same as other people do, so we have lived among nations that didn't like us and now we live in an area as an independent state where people don't like us. We hope temporarily.

Mrs. Meir also expresses Israel's alarm at Syria's growing military might and its increasingly threatening posture toward Israel. "[W]hen these threats are supported according to our information with planes and tanks and heavy guns that are being massed in Syria, we at least think that there is reason for our fear." The following day Meir's statement on *Meet the Press* dominates the front page of the *New York Post*, where the headline SYRIA BUILDUP ALARMS ISRAEL knocks all other news off page one.

Dexter Avenue Baptist Church
DEXTER AVENUE AT DECATUR STREET
MONTGOMERY, ALABAMA
PHONE 3-3970

MARTIN L. KING, JR., *Minister*
309 South Jackson Street

March 29, 1957

Mr. Lawrence E. Spivak, Producer
Meet the Press
NBC Television
528 Lexington Avenue
New York 17, New York

Dear Mr. Spivak:

On my return to the country I found your letter of March 4, on my desk making inquiry concerning my availability for an interview on "Meet the Press." I will be more than happy to accept the invitation for such a significant interview. I am quite familiar with "Meet the Press," having seen the program several times on television. I would appreciate it very much if you could give me some idea of the Sunday that this interview would take place so that I can immediately begin setting up my schedule in the light of this program.

If it is at all possible please send additional information on "Meet the Press." Thanks again for the invitation, and I will be looking forward to hearing from you concerning further details.

Cordially yours,

Martin L. King Jr.
Martin L. King, Jr.
Minister

MLK:mlb

In March 1957 Dr. Martin Luther King, Jr., accepts Lawrence Spivak's invitation to appear on Meet the Press, *but arrests and imprisonments delay his first appearance for more than three years.*

April 14, 1957

On the eve of the new baseball season Jackie Robinson is the first athlete to appear on *Meet the Press*. The first man to break the racial barrier in the major leagues, Robinson helped the Brooklyn Dodgers win six pennants in ten years, and in 1949 he was voted the National League's Most Valuable Player. He has devoted much of his time to the National Association for the Advancement of Colored People (NAACP), which prompts a question from Lawrence Spivak:

SPIVAK: How do you answer those people who insist that the NAACP is moving very, very fast to get the rights for the Negro but seems to be doing not enough to impress upon the Negro his own responsibility as he gets these rights?

ROBINSON: When they say that the NAACP is moving too fast—you know, I heard that, Mr. Spivak, when I was out in Pasadena, California, trying to get into the YMCA: "Take your time; be patient." Patience is fine. I think if we go back and check our record, the Negro has proven beyond a doubt that we have been more than patient in seeking our rights as American citizens. "Be patient," I was told as a kid. I keep hearing that today, "Let's be patient; let's take our time; things will come." It seems to me, the Civil War has been over about ninety-three years; if that isn't patience, I don't know what is.

September 8, 1957

A year after the Suez crisis, another invasion brings the world closer to war. Soviet tanks roll into Hungary to crush a popular uprising. The West offers the Hungarians only words of encouragement. Henry Cabot Lodge, the U.S. ambassador to

On April 28, 1957, Robert F. Kennedy makes the first of his nine Meet the Press *appearances. As chief counsel to the Senate Select Committee to investigate improper activities in the labor or management field, he talks about labor racketeering, and accuses Dave Beck of the Teamsters, of theft.*

the United Nations, explains the U.S. government position on *Meet the Press.*

> LODGE: We will help all the forces that are working in the long pull for liberation. That does not mean that they [the Russians] will get out tomorrow, but neither will they remain forever. There will be an ultimate liberation. . . .
>
> We have done everything we could short of force. The UN has done everything we asked of it. But we don't think force practical. You are dealing with a major military power with total contempt for public opinion when it goes against its wishes.
>
> We can help Hungary by moral pressure; we cannot help it by armed force.

November 10, 1957

Moscow's brutal intervention in Hungary fueled fears of Soviet aggression and Communist dreams of conquest. As the Soviet Union celebrates the fortieth anniversary of the Communist Revolution, Alexander Kerensky appears on *Meet the Press.* Ned Brooks introduces Kerensky as "the head of what has been called the only democratic government the Russians ever had. He is the only living member of the provisional government which took over following the collapse of the czar's regime. The Kerensky government in turn was overthrown by the Bolsheviks under Lenin and Trotsky." After hearing Kerensky explain conditions surrounding

I don't accept this term "terrorist," because freedom fighters cannot be called terrorists.

—Archbishop Makarios of Cyprus, on the struggle to force the British out of Cyprus, September 15, 1957

the revolution, Lawrence Spivak asks him whether the United States is in danger of attack from the present Soviet leaders.

KERENSKY: No, no. I might tell you a paradox. I think we have now a very important new factor in the political life: the H-bomb. The H-bomb changed completely all international relations, and the possibility of a supposed Third War and attack from Moscow to the United States or from the United States to Moscow—I think it excludes it completely.

SPIVAK: You think that war at the present time is not possible?

KERENSKY: It is not possible. Little wars, yes, but not the big war between big powers.

. . .

I think the time has changed. I think the restoration for a totalitarian terrorist dictatorship [in Russia] now is impossible. Why? Because you have a new generation. You have a new psychology. You have the restored intellectual classes.

November 10, 1957: Alexander Kerensky was introduced on Meet the Press *as "the head of what has been called the only democratic government the Russians ever had," a government overthrown by the Bolsheviks. Thirty years after Kerensky's appearance, the program followed the collapse of communism and the growth of democracy in the Soviet Union.*

May 26, 1957: Lewis L. Strauss, chairman of the Atomic Energy Commission, says nuclear tests do not present a radiation hazard.

April 28, 1958

The H-bomb—the nuclear deterrent—is, as Kerensky said, a major new factor in international relations and a very controversial one. Ban the Bomb movements sprout on both sides of the Atlantic. On *Meet the Press* former Secretary of Agriculture Sen. Clinton Anderson (D-NM) says that America's military leaders want "dirty bombs." They have "pulled bombs out of the stockpile and inserted something that makes them dirty," claims the ranking member of the Joint Atomic Energy Committee.

May 11, 1958

Nobel Prize-winning scientist Dr. Linus Pauling was a prominent campaigner against the testing of nuclear weapons. He is given a very rough ride by Lawrence Spivak, who attacks him for Communist links. Before the broadcast the president of the Beverly Hills Freedom Club sent Spivak "a record of his [Pauling's] Un-American history with the Senate Subcommittee," and this information emerges as the broadcast reaches its climax.

PAULING: Every nation in the world, every person in the world is in great danger now, danger of destruction, annihilation by a nuclear war. . . . I am interested in individual human beings. That is why I keep talking about the number of human beings who die of leukemia as a result of the bomb tests.

SPIVAK: Is that why you came to the aid of convicted spies who were executed?

PAULING: Convicted spies?

NOBEL PRIZE-WINNING SCIENTISTS ON *Meet the Press*

Dr. Linus Pauling (Chemistry)
Dr. Norman Ramsey (Physics)
Dr. Glenn T. Seaborg (Chemistry)
Dr. Harold C. Urey (Chemistry)

May 11, 1958: Many viewers felt Lawrence Spivak's attack on Linus Pauling's Communist sympathies went too far.

SPIVAK: Yes, the Rosenbergs.

PAULING: I am not sure that it is right to call them convicted spies.

SPIVAK: They were convicted as spies, and they were done away with as spies.

PAULING: Yes, but what for?

SPIVAK: They were executed as spies.

PAULING: Executed for what?

SPIVAK: So far as I know for treason, for giving away secrets of the United States. . . . And you came to their aid. Because you are interested in human beings?

PAULING: That is right. I am interested in human beings. I am interested in the Constitution of the United States. I am interested in the individual.

SPIVAK: Why do you always seem to be interested in Communist human beings?

Pauling's wife was outraged by Spivak's hostility and accosted him in the studio after the show to complain about the "unfair" treatment. Many viewers agreed, writing to complain of the "wolfish instincts" of the panel and its "vicious, degrading, personal smear attack perpetrated against Dr. Pauling." The attack was, many thought, in the spirit of McCarthyism.

ATOMIC ENERGY COMMISSIONERS ON *Meet the Press*

Gordon Dean
David Lilienthal
John A. McCone (before heading the CIA)
Dr. Glenn T. Seaborg
Lewis L. Strauss

Twenty viewers' descriptions of Lawrence Spivak: rude, unfair, vicious, aggressive, tenacious, challenging, probing, nagging, waspish, hounding, tart-tongued, autocratic, dictatorial, spunky, merciless, and impolite, with the humorless vindictiveness of a dyspeptic owl.

I find Mr. Spivak a thoroughly objectionable, offensive, intrusive, abrasive, tactless, and generally insufferable newsman. He has a monumental impertinence. In short, Mr. Spivak is the kind of newsman most of us out here would like to be. —Jacob Hay, television critic for the *Baltimore News-American*

And President Lyndon Johnson described him as "the toughest of the tough."

Spivak was not one to take such slurs without comment. He wrote back to his detractors, enclosing a transcript of the broadcast. The following reply is typical: "I find it hard to understand why you write so feelingly against 'smear by association,' but resort to it. Is nobody ever to ask anybody a question about Communist or Communist front associations without being branded openly or by indirection a 'McCarthyite'?

"It was necessary and proper for us to investigate whether he had the same competency to speak in the fields of fall-out, nuclear physics, military security and genetics, as in his own special field of biochemistry."

September 7, 1958

The nation was understandably alarmed by estimates that a full-scale nuclear attack on the United States could wipe out 90 percent of the population. As the first director of the Office of Defense and Civilian Mobilization, Leo Hoegh has advice for coping with a nuclear war. He has a list of five things everyone should know. First, people should know the warning signals and what they mean.

> HOEGH: Secondly, they should know their community plans. Third, they should know first aid and home preparedness. Fourth, they should know how to take care of themselves in case of radiological attack. And fifth, they should know six forty and twelve forty on their radio dial, CONELRAD, for official directions and instructions. If people know these five points, they are going to have a good opportunity of surviving any type of nuclear attack.

Hoegh also urges every citizen to install a fallout shelter.

> HOEGH: It's not expensive. It's something that by a little ingenuity and following our instructions they can do in their own homes.

He advises sandbagging the basement to keep out radioactive fallout and recommends reading the office's new handbook, soon to be distributed to forty million homes by the Boy Scouts of America.

Lawrence Spivak has an advance copy and sounds bemused by the illustration of decontamination, which shows a woman with a carpet sweeper and a man taking a shower.

> SPIVAK: And if one hundred and fifty of our big cities were attacked by nuclear weapons, you expect the women of this country to get their carpet sweepers out and the men to take showers?
>
> HOEGH: Now remember this: If there are particles blown into the home, pick them up, get them up and do it with a machine, and then throw it outside after you've done it. But you must not leave the radioactive particles next to you or within your home. That's sound advice to you.

December 7, 1958

The space race brought a new dimension to the arms race in the 1950s, and space-based military systems become an issue. In the year of the launch of the free world's first scientific earth satellite, *Explorer I*, rocket expert Dr. Wernher von Braun is interviewed about the space race in the military and civilian fields.

> VON BRAUN: I believe that unless we want to fall back against the Russians in the long run, we have to have an aggressive space program also. I think that utilizing the same missiles or similar missiles as will emerge from the military programs, we can afford to do many of these things at the same time, for example, pursuing an active man-in-space program while at the same time launching probes to the moon or even the nearer planets.

. . .

LAWRENCE SPIVAK: Earlier this year you were quoted as saying that it would take the United States five years to catch up with the Soviet Union in rocketry. . . . In view of what we have learned recently and what we have done recently, does that estimate still hold?

VON BRAUN: The great unknown in this whole problem complex is that it is very difficult to appraise the working speed of the Russians in their missile program. My estimate was based on the demonstrated fact that the Russians have a very aggressive missile program which at least a year ago seemed to exceed ours.

. . .

ERIK BERGAUST (*Missiles & Rockets* magazine): You are known as an advocate of transporting army troops by ballistic rockets. Could you elaborate a little on the army thinking along these lines?

VON BRAUN: The basic idea is the following: In a nuclear war you have to think not only in great depth of the battlefield but also in terms of units operating in isolated areas that must be completely independent in supplies and in their movements. To supply such ground units by air in the old-fashioned way with propeller airplanes has become quite a little bit risky due to the event of effective ground-to-air missiles. For that reason you have to think of other means of transportation to get the ammunition and fuel supplies and whatever military units need, even food and blood plasma, maybe occasionally even a new commanding officer, in there. . . .

BERGAUST: How far advanced are you in this kind of program, if you do have a program?

VON BRAUN: The program isn't too active yet.

. . .

SPIVAK: [How] soon do you think we can now get a manned rocket around the moon?

VON BRAUN: To send a manned rocket around the moon without a landing on the moon's surface—this I think could be done within maybe a little more than five years and a little less than ten years, depending on how we go about it.

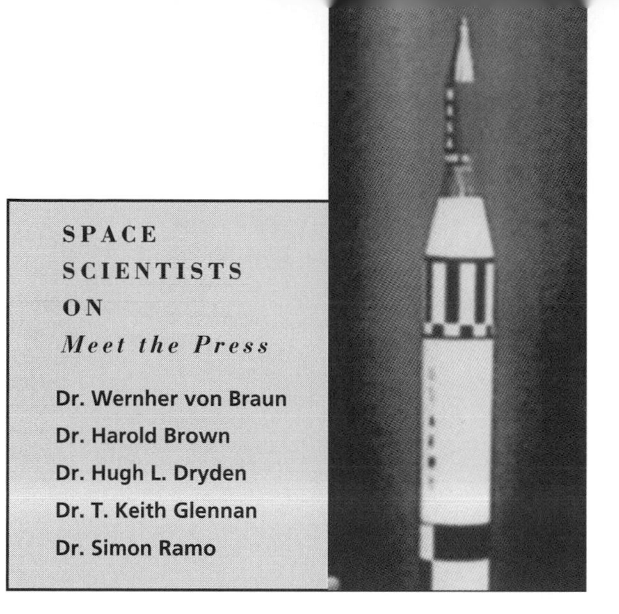

SPACE SCIENTISTS ON *Meet the Press*

Dr. Wernher von Braun
Dr. Harold Brown
Dr. Hugh L. Dryden
Dr. T. Keith Glennan
Dr. Simon Ramo

January 18, 1959

Suspicions of the Soviet Union were reduced by the two-week visit to the United States of Anastas Mikoyan, the first deputy premier of the Soviet Union. He faced the press at the end of a successful tour. This show drew one of the largest audiences in the history of *Meet the Press* and was one of the program's biggest-ever newsmaking events. Requests were received for more than ten thousand transcripts.

Initially the Russians wanted the program to be filmed on the Wednesday before broadcast, then agreed to a live Sunday interview when Mikoyan's appointment with Eisenhower was changed from Monday to Saturday.

On the day of the broadcast some seventy-five policemen were scattered around the NBC building and patrolling the surrounding blocks. Two dozen security and intelligence officials were inside the studio, which was packed with overseas and American reporters and photographers, every one cleared by official security channels.

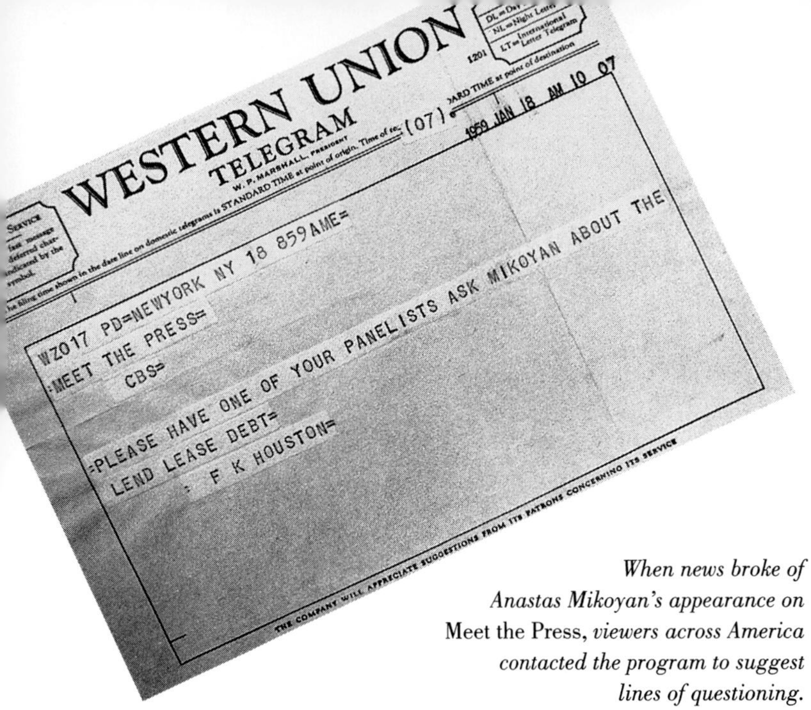
WESTERN UNION
TELEGRAM
W. P. MARSHALL, PRESIDENT
1959 JAN 18 AM 10 07
WZ017 PD=NEWYORK NY 18 859AME=
MEET THE PRESS=
CBS=
=PLEASE HAVE ONE OF YOUR PANELISTS ASK MIKOYAN ABOUT THE
LEND LEASE DEBT=
F K HOUSTON=
THE COMPANY WILL APPRECIATE SUGGESTIONS FROM ITS PATRONS CONCERNING ITS SERVICE

When news broke of Anastas Mikoyan's appearance on Meet the Press, *viewers across America contacted the program to suggest lines of questioning.*

NED BROOKS: Our guest is first deputy premier of the Soviet Union, Mr. Anastas Mikoyan. . . . Mr. Mikoyan is the highest-ranking Soviet official ever to visit the United States.

In the course of the hourlong interview Mikoyan voices Russian concern over German rearmament and outlines his country's position on the divided city of Berlin:

MIKOYAN: We want to do away with this city being a center of indirect aggression at the present time and a possible hotbed of war. And we want the city of West Berlin to be guaranteed not by foreign bayonets but rather by international organizations and the great powers, including guarantees of free access to the city, both from the East and the West.

MARQUIS CHILDS (*St. Louis Post-Dispatch*): And that being the case, you would include East Berlin with West Berlin as a free city?

MIKOYAN: That is impossible, because East Berlin is the capital of the German Democratic Republic.

Asked about the absence of criticism of officials in the Soviet press, he says, "One shouldn't criticize for the sake of criticism. As long as we are working well, there is no reason for us to be criticized." The compliant Russian press has not prepared him for Lawrence Spivak. As the program enters its final minute, Spivak asks a lengthy question that leads to a diplomatic incident.

SPIVAK: Mr. Minister, as long as words do not mean the same thing to us, how can we come to meaningful agreements? You say you came to Hungary's defense. The rest of the world said you attacked Hungary. You call our society capitalistic slavery. We know it is a free society, who live here. You call your government democratic. The rest of the world calls it a police state. How can we come to meaningful arrangements if there is this kind of disagreement?

BROOKS: Gentlemen, I am afraid we are not going to have time to translate the question, much less get an appropriate answer. Our hour has gone very rapidly. I am sorry to interrupt, but our time is up.

The Russian ambassador, Mikhail A. Menshikov, was watching in the studio, and he was furious, believing that Mikoyan had deliberately been cut off to stop him from answering Spivak. The following day Mikoyan blasted Spivak at a National Press Club luncheon: "Mr. Spivak did not behave in a proper fashion yesterday. . . . Before the press conference came to an end, the moderator told him there is only one minute left, and at that very moment he began a question which in the *New York Times* takes up seventeen lines, full of attacks in regard to the Soviet Union. He took up the whole of the remaining minute."

The *New York Times* gave the interview its lead front-page position, reprinted the whole transcript, and stated in an editorial that Mikoyan "lost much of his earlier gain in public relations by his disingenuousness in his television interview." In

Deputy Premier Mikoyan claimed that the heat of the studio lights made him perspire, but many believed the panel's aggressive questioning was the cause of his discomfort. This photograph was reproduced around the world.

Germany *Die Welt* devoted its front page to the story. Within three days films of the program were shown in Germany, France, the U.K., Japan, Mexico, Australia, and Luxembourg, and mail was landing on Spivak's desk. Some hailed his performance ("never was I so proud of our free and untrammeled press," "you are a credit to America") while others asked: "Did it ever occur to you that the man you were being insolent to could start the bombs flying?" Most agreed with the *Washington Post* and *Times-Herald* that "whether or not the questioning in his television interview was unfair, as he claimed, one result was to emphasize to viewers the sinister quality of their able adversary."

Even Bob Hope became involved in the controversy, commenting that Mikoyan "came on a passport listing him as a politician, then he went on television and became a comedian." Writing in the *New York Mirror*, Hope—who had watched the program—said he had heard that the plane flying the Russian leader home had conked out over Newfoundland, but that there was no truth in the rumor "that the pilot was Lawrence Spivak."

Spivak has the last word on the controversy: "It was one of the most exciting programs in recent years." Chastened by Mikoyan's experience, the Russians allowed no official to appear on American television for years. Long after passions had subsided, Spivak met the Russian ambassador at the United Nations. "I later realized," Menshikov admitted, "that you are equally mean to everybody."

On January 19, 1959, Spivak wrote to Mikoyan, apologizing for the final question: "We might really begin to make progress if we both realize once and for all that neither country can conquer the other by force of arms, that the result of a military attempt can only destroy everybody. Nobody wins

Mr. Spivak speaking to Mr. Mikoyan

Mr. Mikoyan meets the press

Makes news in New York ...beats a deadline in London

On Sunday, January 18, Anastas I. Mikoyan, Soviet diplomat, was a guest on National Broadcasting Company's popular "Meet the Press" TV program in New York 6:00-7:00 P.M. A film version was made for British Broadcasting Co. which planned to show it over the British network two days later.

Right after the New York telecast, with the cooperation of NBC International, the film was rushed to Idlewild by Emery and shipped out on BOAC's new Comet jet at 9:00 P.M. that evening. Emery met the shipment at London Airport and, just nine hours after the film left New York, delivered it to BBC in London for televising on Monday, a day ahead of scheduled showing.

Only Emery gives you pickup 24 hours a day...first flight out departures ... and seeing your shipment through all the way. Emery's coordinated air and ground handling operations make the most out of jet air speed ... *at competitive prices too.* This is why NBC also makes hundreds of *domestic* shipments every month via Emery.

Find out how Emery can help you. Call or write us. We have offices in all major cities.

EMERY AIR FREIGHT CORPORATION

General Offices: 801 Second Avenue, New York 17 • Domestic and International Service

EAF 208
Business Publications—1959

There were no satellites to beam Anastas Mikoyan's performance around the world. Film was rushed to Europe by air from New York's Idlewild (JFK) airport.

an earthquake, and a nuclear war would be an earthquake that would shatter the whole world. If your economic system can bring more freedom and more good things of life than ours, you can easily prove it, and you can conquer all of us without firing a shot. On the other hand, if in fair, free and friendly competition our system can do it better, I think we must eventually win you over to our way. The probabilities are, of course, that each system has something to offer the other and that eventually each will be molded and changed by the other."

To avoid any repetition of the Mikoyan incident, *Meet the Press* began the practice of issuing a two-minute warning to guest and panel when the end of the program was nearing.

One letter of congratulation came from Spivak's daughter Judy in Bonn, Germany, with her husband:

> *Dear Pa,*
>
> *To our great joy and delight, we saw the Mikoyan broadcast on German TV tonight. It was terrific—and that face Mikoyan made was enough to scare the little children. He looked a good deal like Hitler, as a matter of fact.*
>
> *The program was introduced as "one of the most interesting regular programs on American television," with full credits and comments on the size of the audience. The announcer also said he "wanted to call your special attention to the sharp questions of Mr. Spivak" and at one point during the program, he interrupted to say, "Watch out—he's pulling out his dagger now."*

Three years later, Judy Spivak Frost died of cancer.

April 19, 1959

The Soviet menace seemed frighteningly close to home when Fidel Castro led the revolution that overthrew Cuba's pro-American president Batista. Appearing on *Meet the Press* during his first visit to the United States since the revolution three and a half months earlier, Cuban Prime Minister Fidel Castro arrived at the studio with a fifty-strong entourage, throwing the State Department security operation into instant disarray since the Cubans had supplied them with a list of only twenty names. Antismoking crusader Spivak would not allow the Cuban to smoke his famous cigars in the studio, but even Spivak could not persuade Dr. Castro to change out of his army fatigues or wear a tie. Castro was fascinated by television technology and seemed more interested in discussing NBC's cameras than appearing on them, but he was seated between his interpreter and moderator Ned Brooks in time for the opening of the show.

Much of the questioning concerns Castro's Communist links. He flatly denies being a Communist.

> CASTRO: Democracy is my ideal, really. . . . I am not Communist. I am not agreed with communism.
>
> . . .
>
> MAY CRAIG (*Portland,* Maine, *Press Herald*): An American magazine published here this week says, after a survey of Cuba, that your brother is a Communist and his wife also. Do you believe that?
>
> CASTRO: Who is going to know better than myself? That is my brother and my sister-in-law. I can tell you they are not Communists.
>
> . . .
>
> CRAIG: We have been deceived in this country and have had Communists in our government. Are you sure you have none in your government?
>
> CASTRO: . . . [T]heir influence in government is nothing, not exists at all. And to prove this what you ought to do is to see what we are doing in Cuba and if we are helping the Communist idea, or if we are helping the democratic idea.
>
> . . .

April 19, 1959: May Craig's determined questioning of Fidel Castro made her a cult figure in Cuba.

May Craig, who appeared on the show 243 times, holds the record for the second most appearances by a non-NBC panelist, behind David Broder. She made her *Meet the Press* debut on January 30, 1949, when the guest was John McCormack, who later became Speaker of the House. Her final appearance was August 1, 1965, when she questioned Sen. John Stennis (D-MS).

A feminist who fought the male-dominated world of journalism, she broke barriers with a number of firsts: first woman correspondent allowed on a battleship at sea; first woman civilian to fly over the North Pole; first woman journalist accredited by the U.S. Navy. She covered the London bombings of World War II and the liberation of Paris.

"She looks like a sweet little old Maine grandmother. But her mind is as tough as a very old down East lobster," commented one anonymous Washington official.

She was part of the Washington press corps and counted the winning of a Senate appropriation for the outfitting of a ladies' rest room in the Senate press gallery as one of her major triumphs. From her home near the Capitol she wrote a daily column for the *Portland,* Maine, *Press Herald* and always had it finished before her 8:30 A.M. breakfast. She wore suits, and whether at press conferences or on television, she would not be seen without a hat, selected from her collection of forty, many alarmingly busy.

"Well, there you are, Senator. You would snap back at May Craig!"

As *Look* magazine reported in 1962, "In the 38 years that she has been reporting in the capital, May Craig has never appeared by daylight without a gaily colored hat." She wore hats partly to be noticed and remembered at press conferences, and the ploy worked. "Don't forget there are brains under the hat," she warned. Her appearance was carefully crafted. When she was considering her television persona, "I made up my mind I'd rather be grim than giggly." The contrast between the flamboyant hats and the granite face made May Craig an instantly recognizable television star.

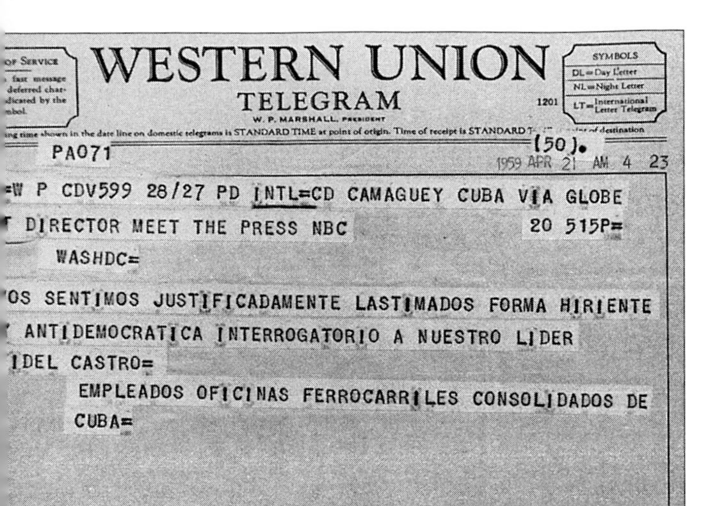

WESTERN UNION
TELEGRAM
W. P. MARSHALL, PRESIDENT

SYMBOLS
DL=Day Letter
NL=Night Letter
LT=International Letter Telegram

PA071
(50).
1959 APR 21 AM 4 23

=W P CDV599 28/27 PD INTL=CD CAMAGUEY CUBA VIA GLOBE
DIRECTOR MEET THE PRESS NBC 20 515P=
WASHDC=
OS SENTIMOS JUSTIFICADAMENTE LASTIMADOS FORMA HIRIENTE
ANTIDEMOCRATICA INTERROGATORIO A NUESTRO LIDER
IDEL CASTRO=
EMPLEADOS OFICINAS FERROCARRILES CONSOLIDADOS DE
CUBA=

RICHARD WILSON (Cowles Publications): When do you intend to have an election in Cuba?

CASTRO: You can be sure I am the man most interested in one election, because for me, and for our ministers, power is only a sacrifice. Power is only a job. What we want is to get as soon as possible a condition for free election.

WILSON: How long will that take?

CASTRO: Not in any condition more than four years, in any condition.

May Craig's cult status spread to Cuba, where *La señora del sombrerito* was attacked. ("*La impertinente 'newswoman'—helada, discutida, desdeñosa*" was "*la figura más impopular para los cubanos.*")

After the show Spivak wrote a letter of thanks to Dr. Castro, signing off, "With best wishes for the success of your regime."

August 9, 1959

On the eve of Soviet Premier Khrushchev's visit to the United States and a day before his own eighty-fifth birthday, President Herbert Hoover makes his second appearance on *Meet the Press*. An eighty-five-year-old former president has the right to break even Lawrence Spivak's rulebook, and Hoover begins not by answering a question but by reading a statement.

HOOVER: I have a little script that will just take two minutes, and after that we'll do the usual ad lib job.

NED BROOKS: That's all right.

HOOVER: The Soviet premier on this visit could bring the greatest, most generous gift which mankind has received in a thousand years. He could interpret his oft-repeated statement as to peaceful coexistence as eliminating all international demands, all warnings, all threats and all conspiracies against free people. He could, to make peaceful coexistence effective, agree to cooperate in the United Nations and upon the abolition of nuclear warfare, accompanied by subsequent sessions on disarmament in general; and all of this would require international inspections as a guarantee for which we should be willing to submit also. All the people of the world, after this forty years of death and destruction and famine and pestilence, want peace. Peace would give civilization a greater impulse forward than we have seen in two centuries. It would end the world's problems of hunger and poverty. Thus it is Mr. Khrushchev's opportunity to win immortality among the leaders of all men.

But this is unlikely to be the result of this visit. The tactics of the Communists may change, but their determination to dominate the world continues.

After the show Meet the Press *presents Mr. Hoover with an eighty-fifth-birthday cake.*

IN THE NEWS

1960

- The Russians shoot down U.S. pilot Gary Powers in a U-2 spy plane.
- The Russians send a live dog into space.
- The Pill becomes available by prescription.
- Dr. Martin Luther King, Jr., is arrested for protesting segregation at an Atlanta lunch counter and is imprisoned for parole violation.
- Presidential candidates Nixon and Kennedy take part in the first televised debates, on NBC.
- Sen. John F. Kennedy is elected president.

1961

- Russian cosmonaut Yuri Gagarin orbits the earth.
- An invasion of Cuba by anti-Castro Cubans ends in fiasco at the Bay of Pigs.
- President Kennedy asks Congress for money to put a man on the moon before the end of the decade.
- President Kennedy creates the Peace Corps.
- Alan Shepard flies three hundred miles and fifteen minutes into space.
- To stop flight to the West, East Germany erects the Berlin Wall, dividing a city.
- The first U.S. military companies are sent to Vietnam.

1962

- President Kennedy says U.S. military advisers in Vietnam will retaliate if attacked.
- John Glenn orbits the earth in his Mercury capsule.
- Pope John XXIII's Vatican II begins.
- President Kennedy demands removal of Russian missiles on Cuba. Soviet Premier Khrushchev backs down.
- Marilyn Monroe dies in an apparent suicide.

1963

- Antisegregation campaigners in Birmingham, Alabama, are dispersed by dogs and cattle prods. The nation sees the brutality on television.
- President Kennedy sends a civil rights bill to Congress.
- The U.S. Supreme Court rules unconstitutional laws requiring recitation of the Lord's Prayer in public schools.
- A treaty among the United States, the USSR, and Great Britain bans all but underground nuclear testing.
- Dr. Martin Luther King, Jr., speaks to more than two hundred thousand pro-civil rights marchers in Washington, D.C. His "I have a dream" speech is heard around the world.
- President John F. Kennedy is assassinated in Dallas, Texas, and Vice President Lyndon Johnson is sworn in as president. Lee Harvey Oswald is arrested for the killing and is shot dead by Dallas nightclub owner Jack Ruby.

1964

- The Civil Rights Act outlaws discrimination in employment and public housing.
- Two days after the U.S. destroyers *Maddox* and *C. Turner Joy* are attacked by North Vietnamese patrol boats in the Gulf of Tonkin, the *Maddox* reports a second attack. President Johnson immediately orders a major air strike on North Vietnam.
- In a Kremlin power struggle Khrushchev is ousted; Aleksei Kosygin and Leonid Brezhnev take over.
- The Beatles land in the United States.
- Lyndon Johnson defeats Barry Goldwater in the presidential election.

THE 1960s

1965

- Malcolm X is assassinated.
- President Johnson sends over eighty thousand troops to Vietnam. Congress grants his request for more money for the war. The death toll rises.
- President Johnson sends the marines to the Dominican Republic. Television cameras show them participating in the overthrow of the government.
- Riots rip cities throughout the summer.
- The first antiwar protester burns his draft card.

1966

- The Black Panthers appear on the scene.
- Antiwar protesters picket the White House.
- Medicare begins.
- The National Organization for Women is founded.

1967

- Boxer Muhammad Ali is stripped of his WBA heavyweight crown after his refusal to join the armed services.
- Three astronauts die when *Apollo I* burns before takeoff.
- When Arab countries call up their reserves, Israeli planes attack airfields in Egypt, Jordan, and Syria, destroying grounded planes. The war is over in six days, leaving Israel in control of the West Bank, the Gaza Strip, the Golan Heights, and the Sinai.
- Summer sees race riots in more than thirty states.
- It's the "Summer of Love" in San Francisco.
- Dr. Christiaan Barnard performs the first successful heart transplant operation.
- By year's end there are five hundred thousand U.S. troops in Vietnam.

1968

- North Vietnam mounts the Tet offensive.
- In a television appearance President Johnson withdraws from the 1968 presidential race.
- The Paris Peace Conference opens.
- Dr. Martin Luther King, Jr., is shot dead in Memphis.
- Sen. Robert F. Kennedy is killed by Sirhan Bishara Sirhan at the Ambassador Hotel, Los Angeles.
- In the "Prague Spring," Czech leader Alexander Dubček introduces liberal reforms. Soviet tanks roll in and crush the initiative.
- At the Democratic National Convention in Chicago, Vice President Hubert Humphrey is nominated for president, but the convention is remembered for violent police attacks on antiwar demonstrators.
- Richard Nixon, representing the "silent majority," is elected president of the United States.

1969

- President Nixon orders the bombing of Cambodia.
- U.S. troop reductions begin.
- *Apollo 11* lands, and Neil Armstrong walks on the surface of the moon.
- The three-day Woodstock music festival draws five hundred thousand people to upstate New York.
- A quarter of a million people protest the Vietnam War in Washington, D.C.

Russia holds an early lead in the space race. Cosmonaut Yuri Gagarin completes an orbit of the earth in April 1960, followed by American John Glenn, whose *Friendship 7* capsule circles the planet in February 1962. Meanwhile, back on earth, Cuban-based Russian missiles threaten the United States. In a showdown with Khrushchev's Soviet Union, President Kennedy demands that the Russians withdraw the missiles. The world teeters on the brink of nuclear war until the Kremlin backs down in October 1962.

The Beatles land in 1964. They are followed by flower power, Indian gurus, hippies, love-ins, cults, and music festivals. Drug use becomes widespread on college campuses. Marijuana is the drug of choice, until Timothy Leary promotes the new psychedelic LSD with his slogan "Turn on, tune in, drop out." Some users claim to be enlightened by LSD's "acid" experience; others are damaged. "Make love not war" is taken up as the key mantra of the decade. Many see it all as proof of the moral pollution of the "permissive society."

It is the decade of Camelot, the glamorous Kennedy years at the White House, when anything, even sending a man to the moon, seems possible. President Kennedy sets NASA a deadline: a moon landing before the decade's end. There are setbacks. In January 1967 three astronauts die as *Apollo 1* burns on the launchpad. But in July 1969, watched by a global television audience, Neil Armstrong beats the deadline and steps from *Apollo 11* onto the surface of the moon, "one small step for man, one giant leap for mankind."

The assassin's bullet punctuates the decade and shatters America's innocence. On November 22, 1963, the president is killed in Dallas, Texas. Lee Harvey Oswald is quickly arrested as the killer, but he is shot dead on November 24 by Dallas nightclub owner Jack Ruby. Many believe the mystery surrounding the Kennedy murder remains unsolved, in spite of the assurances of the Warren Commission that a lone assassin was responsible for the crime that put the free world in mourning.

Three months before the Kennedy assassination, civil rights leader Dr. Martin Luther King, Jr., addresses a huge crowd gathered in Washington, D.C., to demand equal rights. Two hundred thousand hear him deliver one of the most inspiring speeches of all time. "I have a dream," he begins. On April 4, 1968, in Memphis, Tennessee, Dr. King is shot dead. James Earl Ray is convicted of the killing.

Three months after the murder of Martin Luther King, Jr., the late John F. Kennedy's brother New York Sen. Robert F. Kennedy is running for president when he is shot at the Ambassador Hotel in Los Angeles by the Palestinian Sirhan Bishara Sirhan and killed.

Dr. King preached nonviolent protest, but the struggle for equal rights grows more militant in the 1960s, with black power a potent new rallying call, and Malcolm X a charismatic leader. But he too is killed by an assassin in 1965. Racial violence breaks out as city neighborhoods burn from coast to coast: Harlem, Watts, Newark, Chicago, Detroit. Americans watch their cities burning on television. A special commission reports to President Johnson: "Our nation is moving toward two societies, one black, one white."

The Vietnam War is an increasingly divisive force in the land, as the United States becomes more deeply immersed in the war under President Lyndon Johnson. President Johnson's dream of a Great Society is swamped by war. The mysterious 1964 Tonkin Gulf incident triggers a major escalation, and by the end of 1967 there are five hundred thousand U.S. troops in Vietnam. Antiwar protesters take to the streets, as the nation divides between doves and hawks. Lyndon Johnson withdraws from the 1968 presidential race, leaving "dove" Eugene McCarthy to challenge "hawk" Hubert Humphrey. The streets surrounding the 1968 Democratic National Convention in Chicago degenerate into a riot as Mayor Richard Daley's Chicago police battle protesters in front of the world's television cameras. Richard Nixon wins the election, promising to end the war.

Racial problems and the war in Vietnam divide the nation throughout the 1960s, but America unites at the end of the decade to celebrate the moon landing.

Sen. John F. Kennedy's January 1960 appearance is the first edition of *Meet the Press* sponsored by King Sano cigarettes, whose spokesman is Rod Serling, creator of another long-running television series, *The Twilight Zone*.

January 3, 1960

On Saturday, January 2, 1960, Sen. John F. Kennedy appeared before a packed press conference in the Caucus Room to announce that he would be seeking the Democratic presidential nomination. Competition for the first television interview with the candidate was understandably hot, and Lawrence Spivak beat the competition. On *Meet the Press* Senator Kennedy makes a chillingly prophetic statement about the death of a president.

JOHN STEELE (Time-Life, Inc.): You have defined the job of the vice president as that of breaking ties and watching the president's health. Does that mean if you are the presidential nominee of the Democratic party, you will select a "Throttlebottom" as your vice presidential running mate?

KENNEDY: No, I will select the best man I could get. If my life expectancy was not what I hope it will be—but that really is not, I wouldn't think, an enviable prospect for the second man, whose only opportunity to exert influence in the course of events would be if I should die.

Vice Adm. Hyman G. Rickover's criticism of American education on January 24, 1960 brings the biggest audience response in the program's fourteen-year history, with more than ten thousand requests for transcripts. He says that education is the biggest problem facing the United States, that we are falling seriously behind the Russians, and that we can't win the arms race without winning the education race. "Unless we have a thoroughly educated citizenry, we will not be able to solve either our military problems or the many other problems that are facing this country."

Rickover sees federal standards as part of the remedy. "We don't have to run our schools federally, but we can set up federal standards. Education has not been improved anywhere else in the world without first setting up standards. We have standards for airplane travel, for lipstick colors, for the size of socks, but we have no standard for education."

Almost every letter praised Admiral Rickover's remarks.

March 20, 1960: As cold war tensions mount in Berlin, German Chancellor Konrad Adenauer discusses the crisis on Meet the Press.

Cordially yours,

Martin L. King, Jr.
Minister

On April 17, 1960, Dr. Martin Luther King, Jr., makes his first *Meet the Press* appearance, three years after accepting an invitation from Lawrence Spivak.

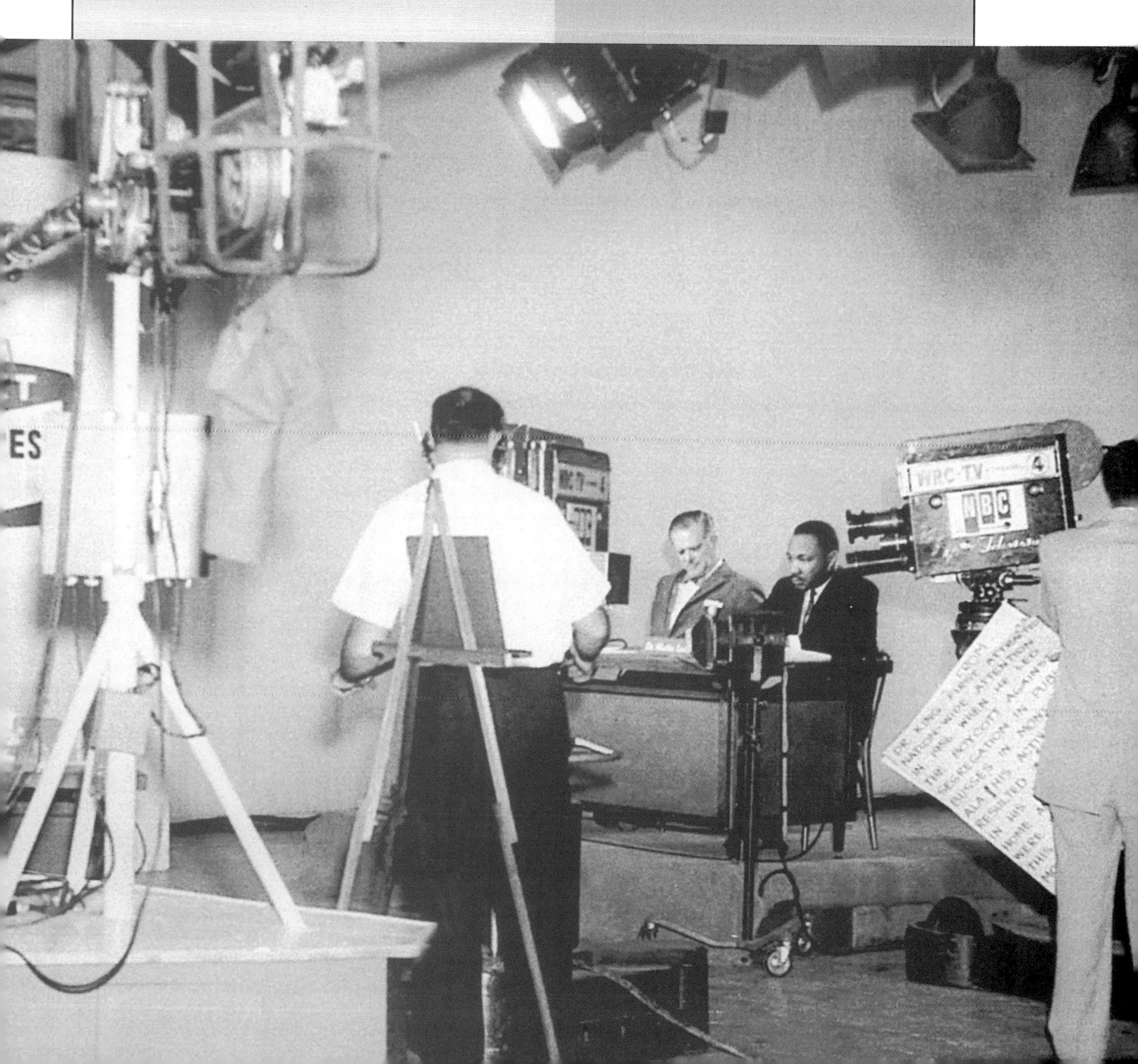

May 15, 1960

The cold war continues in the 1960s, with each side deeply suspicious of the other's intentions. Relations between the United States and the Soviet Union are particularly strained as *Meet the Press* goes overseas for the third time, to film an interview with West Berlin Mayor Willy Brandt on the front line of the cold war. Lawrence Spivak and moderator Ned Brooks flew to Berlin for the interview at the West Berlin studios of Radio Free Berlin. Marquis Childs of the *St. Louis Post-Dispatch* and NBC's German correspondent John Rich completed the panel.

Two days before the filming, American pilot Gary Powers's U-2 spy plane was shot down deep inside the Soviet Union, a major propaganda coup for Moscow and a mortal blow to the Paris Summit Conference. Describing Berlin as "a lie detector for international politics," Brandt warns that the Russians may "transform what is a sector borderline, which goes through the city today, into what we could call a state borderline. This from a human point of view would be a terrible thing." Fifteen months later the Berlin Wall divides Brandt's city.

May 22, 1960

The U-2 incident is still in the headlines as Aleksandr Kaznacheev, a twenty-eight-year-old former Soviet intelligence agent, speaks out about Russia and its spying operations around the world. He suggests that any Soviet citizen abroad is likely to be a spy.

> KAZNACHEEV: The Soviet Embassy in Rangoon, I mean the political section, consists of twenty so-called diplomats. You would be surprised that only three of them are really people who make the diplomatic war. Seventeen are . . . very high-class intelligence officers of different intelligence groups.
>
> . . . [T]here are several factors which constitute the stability and strength of the Communist regime inside the Soviet Union. The first factor is the cold war, the international tension and the armaments race. The second factor is successes of international communism abroad and the success of Soviet foreign policy. And the third factor, and I think primarily and above all, is the ignorance of the entire Soviet people of reality, of life abroad, of the real reasons of the international tension, cold war and the armaments race.

Kaznacheev was a clean-shaven blond when he attended a preshow meeting with *Meet the Press.* On the day of his appearance, apparently fearful of a Russian assassin, he was wearing a rather bad red wig and matching false mustache, and Lawrence Spivak barely recognized him.

July 10, 1960

The televised debates between the rival presidential candidates Senator Kennedy and Vice President Nixon introduce a dramatic new element into the election. *Meet the Press* foreshadows the debates

In 1960 Senators John F. Kennedy (above) and Lyndon B. Johnson (opposite) appear on Meet the Press *as rivals for the Democratic presidential nomination and later as presidential and vice presidential nominees.*

MEET
THE PRESS
NBC

on the eve of the Democratic National Convention in Los Angeles, when the three declared candidates for the presidential nomination—Senators Stuart Symington, John Kennedy, and Lyndon Johnson—make their cases on a *Meet the Press* ninety-minute special from convention headquarters in the Biltmore Hotel. Spivak has an NBC man following each of the three senators around the hotel all day "because I knew they were busy with delegates and would not be watching the time too closely."

Spivak requests extra police assistance from Los Angeles Police Chief William Parker to ensure crowd control and access to the "studio," which was converted from a hotel nightclub. *Meet the Press* gave out about 150 audience tickets, but the combined muscle of security forces and NBC executives is needed to push the studio's iron gates closed against the weight of a ticketless horde trying to enter the show area. Senator Kennedy has to be routed through the basement kitchens and back stairs to reach the studio. The three candidates are seated just in time to be questioned separately by the panel.

Asked about choosing a running mate, Kennedy states his preference for "someone from the Middle West or Far West," and Lyndon Johnson declares himself uninterested in the office of vice president.

> JOHNSON: I'm not interested in the vice presidency. . . . Bearing in mind the vice president has been there seven years now, and I have watched him, I recognize the fact he's only had an opportunity to express himself on seven votes, seven occasions where we've had a tie. I think I voted more than that last week, so I wouldn't want to trade my vote for a gavel. . . . Most vice presidents don't do very much, even at that.

Senator Johnson's forces are using a ballroom adjoining the studio to hold a somewhat raucous reception, which periodically seeps into the *Meet the Press* audio.

SEPTEMBER 25, 1960

***M**eet the Press* **becomes the first news program to be televised on a regular basis in color. The guest is Amb. James J. Wadsworth, new U.S. representative to the United Nations. The live telecast originates in NBC's New York studios. Before this date, color has been used only intermittently.**

After facing the *Meet the Press* panel on October 16, 1960, Sen. John F. Kennedy gives a speech at Montgomery Blair High School, Silver Spring, Maryland, in which he says, "We have been to New Jersey today and Delaware—and to the fifty-first state, as I call *Meet the Press*, and tonight we go to Ohio."

September 11, 1960: Republican presidential candidate Vice President Richard M. Nixon and Lawrence Spivak.

Physicist Dr. Edward Teller worked on the atomic bomb project at Los Alamos in the 1940s. He spoke on *Meet the Press* on August 21, 1960.

MAY 21, 1961

Fears of Communist conspiracy in the United States survive into the 1960s. New groups are occupying the antired spot vacated by Senator McCarthy.

NED BROOKS: In recent weeks the organization known as the John Birch Society has been gaining increasing public attention. Its leaders describe it as a right-wing, patriotic group devoted to stamping out the Communist conspiracy. Its critics condemn it as a witch-hunting organization engaged in irresponsible attacks on public figures. The society was founded two years ago by Mr. Robert Welch, who is our guest today. Mr. Welch is a retired businessman.

Lawrence Spivak questions Welch about his assertion that General Eisenhower is "a dedicated, conscious agent of the Communist conspiracy."

WELCH: I never called him a card-carrying Communist anywhere in writing or in words.

SPIVAK: Do you deny that you did in [your manuscript] "The Politician"?

WELCH: I certainly do. You prove—show me anywhere I called him a card-carrying Communist in "The Politician."

SPIVAK: Not "card-carrying," but "a Communist"?

WELCH: Oh, that's different.

May 28, 1961

Russian cosmonaut Yuri Gagarin's spaceflight has shocked the American public into an unpleasant awareness of the Russians' early lead in the space race. Within three weeks NASA responds by firing Cmdr. Alan B. Shepard, Jr., into space, and two weeks later *Meet the Press* examines the space race.

NED BROOKS: President Kennedy a few days ago laid before Congress his recommendations for a vast forward push in the conquest of outer space. He proposed that the nation embark on an all-out effort for landing the first man on the moon ahead of the Russians. He acknowledged that the price will be high.

Our guests today are the two men chiefly responsible for developing the president's program, Dr. Hugh Dryden, the deputy administrator of NASA, and the administrator, Mr. James E. Webb.

. . .

DRYDEN: The landing of three men on the moon is a symbol of a gigantic enterprise that will involve our whole nation. It will involve all of science and technology; it will certainly stimulate the education of people in new directions; it will leave us at the end of this period with a technology and science whose influence will be felt throughout our whole country. . . . If you like, it is insurance against winding up at the end of this decade with a science and technology inferior to that of another nation which has pushed forward along the frontiers. . . .

JOHN FINNEY (*New York Times*): Were we wise in choosing this race since the Soviets have such an advantage now in rocket power?

WEBB: I think we were wise in choosing this particular objective. There are certain intermediate objectives in which the Russians might have more of an advantage. In this one we believe that

Lawrence Spivak (standing) made no exception to his no smoking rule for heavy smoker Edward R. Murrow (holding unlit cigarette). Ned Brooks (left) acted as moderator.

we have the capacity, the know-how, the industrial plant in this country that can do the work, the scientists.

July 9, 1961

Many believed that the abuse of trade union power could endanger America's industrial progress. Teamster president James R. Hoffa's name was often heard on *Meet the Press* when questions involved trade union corruption, but this is his first personal appearance. It was postponed several times because the interview had to be fitted in between Hoffa's string of indictments.

Hoffa remains cool and charismatic as he shrugs off questions of impropriety.

> LAWRENCE SPIVAK: Would you say you have or have not at any time associated with thugs and gangsters? This is not illegal, but the question is, Have you done this and is it right?
>
> HOFFA: I say, Mr. Spivak, no more so than any one of the reporters sitting at this table have I associated with any thugs or gangsters, but in the course of negotiations, in the course of organizing, I must necessarily meet with those who management hires.

Spivak asks him if his insistence on dealing only in cash and keeping very few records gives an appearance of impropriety.

> HOFFA: I deal in cash or in money orders whenever I believe it is necessary, and if you will check the record of General Motors, check the record of every state government in the United States, check the city governments, you will find there is nothing unusual about the question of cash being used as a medium of exchange in the United States or in the world markets. What is so peculiar about a labor leader?

After the show, Spivak bumped into Hoffa and two of his aides on Madison Avenue. Spivak describes the scene: "He began by saying that he had a long dossier on me, going back to my days at Harvard, and that it was obvious that I lived most of my life in a hotel suite far away from reality, with little knowledge of what was actually going on in the world. He interrupted himself at one point to ask me who I thought was the most powerful man in the country. When I said, 'President John Kennedy,' he said, 'That's how much you know. The most powerful man in America today is Bobby Kennedy.'

"He was furious because of the way the *Meet the Press* interview had gone, indignant that I had

asked him why he conducted most of his transactions in cash, why he kept few records, and why he associated with thugs and gangsters. He kept emphasizing over and over again that despite many investigations, nobody had been able to convict him—clear proof that he was innocent of the charges against him.

"It was obvious from everything he said that he had accepted our invitation to be interviewed to make the point that he had done nothing illegal, and he was clearly nettled because we had indicated in our questioning that a leader of a great union had to be concerned with ethics and morality as much as legality."

BROTHERS ON
Meet the Press

William and Robert BENNETT

James and William BUCKLEY

John Foster and Allen W. DULLES

John, Robert, and Edward KENNEDY

David, Winthrop, and Nelson A. ROCKEFELLER

James and Franklin D. ROOSEVELT, Jr.

Morris and Stuart UDALL

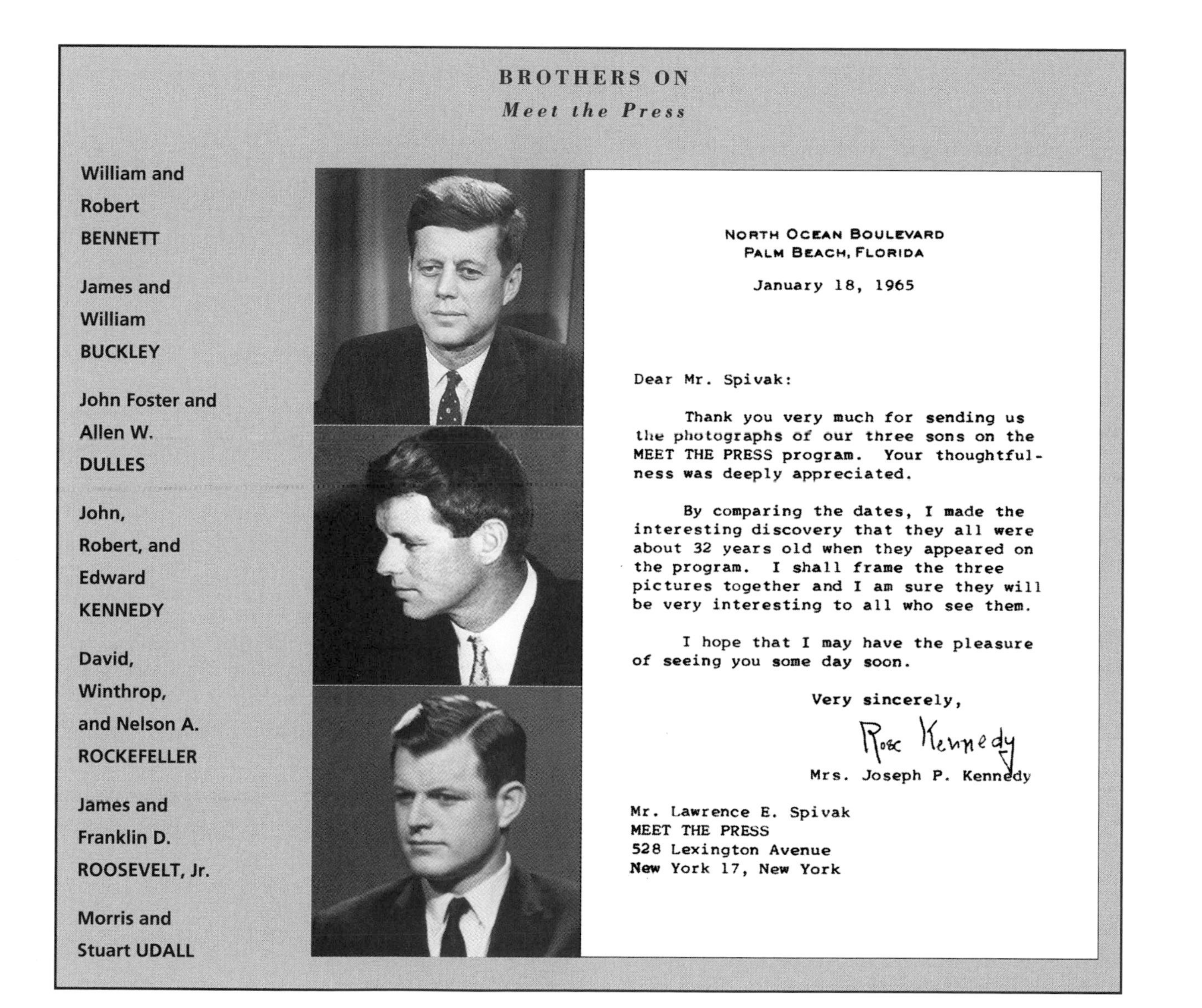

NORTH OCEAN BOULEVARD
PALM BEACH, FLORIDA

January 18, 1965

Dear Mr. Spivak:

Thank you very much for sending us the photographs of our three sons on the MEET THE PRESS program. Your thoughtfulness was deeply appreciated.

By comparing the dates, I made the interesting discovery that they all were about 32 years old when they appeared on the program. I shall frame the three pictures together and I am sure they will be very interesting to all who see them.

I hope that I may have the pleasure of seeing you some day soon.

Very sincerely,

Rose Kennedy

Mrs. Joseph P. Kennedy

Mr. Lawrence E. Spivak
MEET THE PRESS
528 Lexington Avenue
New York 17, New York

August 20, 1961

Willy Brandt, mayor of West Berlin, warned the world about Soviet intentions in the city on *Meet the Press*. On March 12, 1961, he said: "I am inclined to believe that we will not have a new Berlin crisis within the next few months, but . . . new pressure might come sometime later this year." Five months later, on August 13, the Soviet Union closes the border with West Berlin. A wall will divide the city for almost forty years. Secretary of State Dean Rusk explains the administration's position.

> RUSK: This issue is a problem of the great worldwide confrontation between the Sino-Soviet bloc and the free world, and it is of great importance that we make our commitments clear.
>
> PAULINE FREDERICK (NBC News): Mr. Secretary, we have been trying for some weeks to impress upon Mr. Khrushchev the fact that there is a point beyond which we will not go without fighting. Would you please make it clear to us about what we will fight?
>
> RUSK: This is a problem which involves vital interests of the United States and of the West, and one of the problems of diplomacy, one of the functions of diplomacy, is to protect these vital interests without a war. But those vital interests are the presence of the West in West Berlin, the freedom and security of that city, its ability to live, its physical access to the rest of the world. . . . [W]e will not be pushed out of West Berlin.

Secretary Rusk points out the real purpose of the wall.

> RUSK: These fences are not put up to keep people from coming into East Germany and East Berlin. They are put up to keep people from coming out. The immediate cause, I think, for the blockade was the increasing rush of refugees, demonstrating the election of people in East Germany and East Berlin between the two patterns of life.

September 24, 1961

Attorney General Robert Kennedy—"the most powerful man in the country," in Jimmy Hoffa's opinion—makes worldwide headlines at the height of the confrontation with the Soviet Union over the newly erected Berlin Wall. He warns that President Kennedy will "stand up" on Berlin even if it means using nuclear weapons.

> KENNEDY: If it comes to that, he will use nuclear weapons. . . . I think as the president said continuously, again, if we do not stand up on Berlin, when can we ever be expected to stand up? And he is going to stand up.

Cuba is another nuclear flashpoint, and the Bay of Pigs fiasco is on the panel's mind. Kennedy says that the president "takes full responsibility for the failure of that operation and feels that it is within the national interest not to try to find any other scapegoats. . . . I think I will just let it rest at that."

Kennedy also outlines the administration's stance on the balance of powers between the executive and legislative branches of government.

> KENNEDY: I don't say that there might not be an instance where executive privilege might have to be used, but I think it is terribly important with the executive branch of government as powerful and strong as it is that there be some check and balance on it. And in the last analysis the group that can best check and insure that it is handling its affairs properly is the Congress of the United States. So we will lean over backwards to make sure that they get the information they request.

October 22, 1961

Nuclear confrontation with Moscow seems frighteningly close, and activity on the home front increases. Thirty million copies of the pamphlet *The Family Fallout Shelter* have been distributed, and President Kennedy's chief civil defense adviser, Frank B. Ellis, comes to *Meet the Press* to explain the massive shelter program, which involves locating and marking fallout shelters for fifty million Americans and encouraging individuals to construct their own.

LAWRENCE SPIVAK: Mr. Ellis, if we had a nuclear attack today or in the weeks ahead, do you think there are many Americans who would know what to do?

ELLIS: I think that the number would be very limited. . . .

SPIVAK: Do you seriously believe that this country will ever have a decent shelter program unless the federal government or unless the state governments do it?

ELLIS: I am convinced that the federal government is going into—the program they are now going into is a decent program. As a matter of fact, I think it is outstanding. And I think when you are able to mark fifty million shelters, or if you develop the ventilation system as the DOD [Department of Defense] is working on today, that that number might be materially increased. I think really that that federal example is going to set in motion a chain of circumstances that will bring about group shelters by people all over America and individual family shelters in large numbers.

SPIVAK: Mr. Ellis, do you believe that our survival as a nation may depend upon our shelter program?

ELLIS: I would say, sir, in a nuclear attack, without a protected population, that while we might retaliate to destroy the Soviet Union, this nation would suffer irreparable injury.

November 5, 1961

Jawaharlal Nehru, prime minister of India, is interviewed in New York a few hours after landing in the

United States on November 5, 1961. The next day he attends a White House reception where President Kennedy expresses his regrets that "I can't match the warm welcome you got from Lawrence Spivak."

March 11, 1962

A third Kennedy brother is beginning his political career and making his first national television appearance on *Meet the Press*. Edward M. Kennedy is expected to announce his candidacy for the Democratic nomination as U.S. senator from Massachusetts soon after his *Meet the Press* interview.

LAWRENCE SPIVAK: People say there are two Kennedys in important political offices now and that a third would be one too many. What is your answer to that?

KENNEDY: Mr. Spivak, I am not—if I do announce for the Senate, I will not be running as the Kennedy candidate but, I would hope, as the Democratic candidate.

March 11, 1962: President John F. Kennedy coached his younger brother Edward M. Kennedy (right) before his national television debut on Meet the Press.

. . .

RICHARD CLURMAN (*Time*): I wonder if you can tell us how you feel about the presence of a family, such as yours, occupying that number of key positions in American life?

KENNEDY: Mr. Clurman, if you are talking about too many Kennedys, you should have talked to my mother and father at the time they were getting started.

President Kennedy was against his brother's going on *Meet the Press,* telling him he had much to lose and nothing to gain, but Teddy insisted. Lawrence Spivak recalled the president turning to one of his aides and complaining, "How much power do I have if I can't keep my little brother off television?" Presidential aide Theodore Sorensen and President Kennedy prepared Teddy for his *Meet the Press* debut by seating him in the president's Oval Office chair and peppering him with questions. President Kennedy delayed his departure from Palm Beach in order to watch the show, and he later told Teddy that he was almost too nervous to watch. When it was over, he called Spivak to say how pleased he was with his brother's performance. "How do you think he did on that church-state issue?" Kennedy asked. "Frankly I haven't the slightest idea what Teddy was talking about," Spivak admitted. "Yes," enthused the president, "wasn't that good!"

July 29, 1962

President Kennedy and Attorney General Robert Kennedy are under pressure from the civil rights movement to honor a campaign pledge to introduce civil rights legislation. Dr. Martin Luther King, Jr., is scheduled to discuss the issue on *Meet the Press* on July 26, but he is jailed in Albany, Georgia, two days before the interview. He informs Lawrence Spivak that he will not, on principle, put up bond, so his place is taken by his associate Dr. William G. Anderson, president of the Albany, Georgia, movement, who accepts release from prison in order to face the panel on *Meet the Press.*

LAWRENCE SPIVAK: Dr. Anderson, a thousand of your followers in Albany, Georgia, have been arrested, and more than a hundred, including Reverend King, are now in jail. . . . Have you accomplished anything at all, in your judgment?

ANDERSON: I certainly think we have accomplished a good deal. Not so much materially, but we have accomplished a good deal as far as the individual Negro is concerned. He has a new sense of dignity and respect that heretofore has not been demonstrated or made manifest, and this I believe will be the ultimate salvation of the Negro in the South.

. . .

EDWIN NEWMAN (NBC News): Is there any inclination in Albany among Negroes to join the Black Muslim movement?

ANDERSON: Absolutely not, and as long as Dr. Martin Luther King and the other advocates of nonviolent resistance do stay in the city of Albany, there will be no tendency or leaning toward the Black Muslim movement.

The guest on *Meet the Press*'s fifteenth anniversary show is James Farley, who was interviewed on the program's television debut in 1947. He is asked if television has had an impact on American politics.

FARLEY: I have watched men and women on programs where they are being interviewed, and it is obvious the way they dodge the questions they are not telling the truth, and for that reason I think the viewers of the program know whether the truth is being told, and for that reason I think great strides have been made in television. I don't think demagogues can do as well on television as they could on radio. Am I clear in what I am saying to you?

JOHN CHANCELLOR (NBC News): Yes, sir. You are saying that television is a good lie detector.

FARLEY: There is no doubt about it.

April 21, 1963

President Kennedy's plan to put a man on the moon before the end of the decade takes a giant leap forward when Col. John H. Glenn, Jr., becomes the first American to orbit the earth. He declares himself absolutely confident that the Apollo project will reach the moon.

LAWRENCE SPIVAK: What makes you so sure?

GLENN: We need no big, new scientific breakthroughs to complete this. . . . Most of the technical details are known. It is now a lot of very hard and long engineering spade work.

QUESTION: And would it not make more sense to put instruments on the moon rather than men?

GLENN: We could design instruments for the knowns. For the unknowns, which I think will be most productive in the space age or space race, man has to be there to make these observations.

BONNIE ANGELO (*Newsday*): If something unforeseen happens, wouldn't this be a terrible setback to the nation's prestige?

GLENN: . . . As in flying airplanes, sometime we are going to have a fatality, . . . but we hope that this doesn't cause everyone to lose support for the program. . . .

At the end of the interview Peter Hackes of NBC News raises an interesting possibility for Colonel Glenn: political office. "That is a new thought," says the astronaut, who later has a distinguished career as a U.S. senator.

Astronaut John H. Glenn, Jr., was invited to speak on Meet the Press *as the first American to orbit the Earth. In 1983 he returned as Sen. John Glenn (D-OH), candidate for the Democratic presidential nomination.*

May 26, 1963

Events in the South are forcing presidential action on the country's racial problems. A month before President Kennedy makes good on his campaign promise to send a civil rights bill to Congress, James H. Meredith is introduced on *Meet the Press* as "the first Negro student ever knowingly admit-

Attempts to desegregate the University of Mississippi at Oxford led to violent riots and harassment of James H. Meredith, the first African American student at Ole Miss. Above left: Chief U.S. Marshal James J. P. McShane (left) and John Doar, deputy director of the Department of Justice's civil rights division (right), escort Meredith to his class. Above center: On May 26, 1963 Meredith appears on Meet the Press *with moderator Ned Brooks. Three months later (above right) he receives his bachelor of arts degree in political science.*

ted to a white university in Mississippi. His enrollment precipitated one of the nation's most serious domestic crises since the Civil War."

LAWRENCE SPIVAK: Would you have enrolled if you had known in advance how much difficulty you were going to have?

MEREDITH: Certainly. The point is not the difficulty. The most important point is that I feel that all citizens should be entitled to education that is offered by their states, and certainly this was the objective.

Spivak asks him if he is concerned about sparking a white backlash.

MEREDITH: I still have great faith that this idea of white supremacy is going to lose its effect in this country, and I certainly hope that anything I have done hasn't helped it.

. . .

HERBERT KAPLOW (NBC News): Mr. Meredith, what effect do you think your experience had on the overall desegregation issue?

MEREDITH: It has proven one thing, that the 1954 Supreme Court decision was not completely adequate. It has to be reinforced.

The following week, the segregationist governor of Alabama, George C. Wallace, faces the press.

June 2, 1963

There are threats to Gov. George Wallace's life if he dares appear at the NBC studio, and the show—from New York—is surrounded by what Spivak called "the largest contingent of police protection that New York had up to that time given anybody, including Khrushchev when he visited the UN." Bomb squads search all buildings with RCA links before the broadcast. Wallace arrives safely at 30 Rockefeller Plaza and is introduced by Ned Brooks.

BROOKS: Our guest today is Governor George C. Wallace of Alabama. His state is the only one in the country today whose schools are completely segregated. Next week the issue heads for a climax when two Negro students will seek to enroll at the University of Alabama.

Governor Wallace has been quoted as saying that he will personally bar their entrance despite a federal court order and a threat of federal troops. . . .

LAWRENCE SPIVAK: Governor, . . . can these students be enrolled at the University of Alabama without the use of troops?

WALLACE: That remains to be seen. We do not want troops at the University of Alabama, nor in the state, because domestic tranquillity will prevail, and there will be no need for troops.

In a response that foreshadows the tracts of antigovernment extremists thirty years later, Wallace says he is making a stand against central power.

> WALLACE: I think it is a dramatic way to impress on the American people this omnipotent march of centralized government that is going to destroy the rights and freedom and liberty of the people of this country if it continues, and we in Alabama intend to resist this centralized control, where they now tell us whom you can eat with and whom you can sit down with and swim with, and whom you can sell your house to. This is the great constitutional principle upon which we stand in Alabama.

June 23, 1963

Two weeks after the shooting of Medgar Evers, President Kennedy sends a civil rights bill to Congress, and Attorney General Robert Kennedy is questioned about it on his seventh appearance on *Meet the Press*.

> LAWRENCE SPIVAK: Do you think . . . if the president's civil rights proposals are not enacted that we are headed for a real racial explosion?
>
> KENNEDY: . . . I think that the legislation that the president has suggested will be extremely helpful in alleviating some of these problems. . . . I think we will still have troubles because of unem-

June 2, 1963: Gov. George Wallace meets the press. Nine days later he blocked the entrance to the University of Alabama in Tuscaloosa in an attempt to stop the integration of the university.

ployment among Negroes, lack of education, lack of skill, and a great deal needs to be done in this field as well as in the field and category of civil rights.

SPIVAK: Negro leaders are planning a march on Washington with possibly a hundred thousand demonstrators. Do you think such a march is going to help get civil rights legislation through, or do you think it is going to hurt?

KENNEDY: I think that perhaps the announcement of such a march is premature. I think there is a right to petition, and there is a right of Negroes as well as others to make their views known. . . . I certainly think that at the present time the Congress should have the right to debate and discuss this legislation without this kind of pressure. . . .

SPIVAK: Do you think that the Negro is entitled to special treatment because of past discrimination against him?

KENNEDY: What I think is that he is entitled to special attention to try to remedy the sins of the past. . . . I don't think that an individual should be hired just because he is a Negro, but on the other hand I think Negroes are not qualified for certain positions of skill because they have been discriminated against in the past, so I think we should make an extra effort to make sure that that problem has been remedied, that we do more for vocational training, that we do more for education, that we see that they then are entitled to the same privileges that the white person is entitled to.

August 25, 1963

Washington is nervously awaiting the arrival of a hundred thousand civil rights marchers demonstrating in support of civil rights legislation before Congress. Roy Wilkins of the NAACP reassures the *Meet the Press* audience that riots are neither planned nor expected.

August 25, 1963: Dr. Martin Luther King, Jr., (far right) and NAACP Executive Secretary Roy Wilkins are the guests on Meet the Press *three days before a huge civil rights demonstration in Washington, D.C. (opposite).*

Eighty-two women had appeared as guests on *Meet the Press* as the program entered its fiftieth year. Seventeen appeared in the program's first fifteen years on network television.

ELIZABETH BENTLEY, former Communist: September 12, 1948, and December 6, 1953

VIVIEN KELLEMS, crusader against income tax: September 26, 1948

INDIA EDWARDS, Democratic National Committee: December 10, 1949

REP. EDNA K. KELLY (D-NY): December 17, 1949

MRS. J. WATIES WARING, critic of racial bigotry, wife of North Carolina federal judge: February 11, 1950

SISTER ELIZABETH KENNY, developer of new polio treatment: October 1, 1950

VIJAYA LAKSHMI PANDIT, Indian ambassador to the United States: December 31, 1950

LADY ASTOR, first woman elected to Britain's House of Commons: April 15, 1951

FRIEDA B. HENNOCK, commissioner of the Federal Communications Commission: July 10, 1951

ANNA ROSENBERG, assistant secretary of defense: December 14, 1952

OVETA CULP HOBBY, secretary of health, education, and welfare: October 23, 1954

GOLDA MEIR, foreign minister of Israel: December 2, 1956

AMBASSADOR CLARE BOOTHE LUCE: December 30, 1956

MADAME CHIANG KAI-SHEK, wife of the president of Nationalist China: September 21, 1958

ELEANOR ROOSEVELT: April 11, 1954 (first of six appearances)

BARBARA WARD, economist: May 3, 1959

DR. TERESA CASUSO, defector from Castro's Cuba: October 30, 1960

Clare Boothe Luce (above) and Dr. Teresa Casuso (left).

LAWRENCE SPIVAK: Mr. Wilkins, what gains do you think you could make as a result of this march that will outweigh the risks you take? . . .

WILKINS: We don't regard the risks as being that great, and we think the gains are immeasurable, because we will bring to the capital of the nation, to its proper place, and to the Congress of the United States, the deep concern of millions of Americans over this question. . . . We think it is time they should pass a lot of laws.

On the same program, Dr. Martin Luther King, Jr., is asked if the civil rights movement is demanding too much too fast.

KING: We have waited for well-nigh three hundred and forty-five years for our basic constitutional and God-given rights, and we still confront the fact that we are at the bottom of the economic ladder. We confront the fact that the gap between the medium income of Negroes and whites is widening every day. We confront the fact that the Negro is still the victim of glaring and notorious conditions of segregation and discrimination. I think instead of slowing up, we must push at this point, and we must continue to move on, and I am convinced that our moving on will not only help the Negro cause, so to speak, but the cause of the whole of America, because the shape of the world today just doesn't permit our nation the luxury of an anemic democracy.

On October 13, 1963, Madame Ngo Dinh Nhu (center), sister-in-law of South Vietnam's President Diem, uses her daughter, Mlle. Le Thuy (right), as translator. She expresses confidence that Vietnam is winning the war of minds against the Communists but concern about America's commitment to the anti-Communist cause. "I can assure you that the American government in the Vietnamese eyes looks much less anti-Communist than the Vietnamese government, that is sure."

On November 24, 1963, *Meet the Press* is preempted because of the assassination of President Kennedy. Lawrence Spivak on President John F. Kennedy: "I found the late President John F. Kennedy one of the most stimulating and fascinating men in Washington. He was always a pleasure to interview, because he reacted so quickly, his answers were usually responsive to the questions, were briefly stated and invariably informative. He seemed to enjoy tough and challenging questions, and more than anything else in one way or another, he always generated excitement."

November 24, 1963: A nation mourns an assassinated president.

On January 5, 1964, Sen. Barry Goldwater (R-AZ) appears on *Meet the Press* two days after announcing his decision to run for the presidency in 1964. Some believe he has timed his announcement with his *Meet the Press* date in mind. His plan backfires. Although his opinions reach a national audience and make headlines in Monday's newspapers, he is suffering from a painful foot ailment and gives a performance described by Robert Novak in his book *The Agony of the GOP* as "an absolute disaster. Never before had a political appearance on a television question and answer show hurt so badly." According to Novak, "Many party leaders, gathered in Washington, watched with unbelieving eyes." Eighteen months later Senator Goldwater returns to *Meet the Press* in better health and gives a widely praised interview.

After she was elected prime minister of India in 1966, Indira Gandhi grew more concerned about her television image and contacted *Meet the Press* to request a replica of all the makeup used for her recent *Meet the Press* interview. The *Meet the Press* makeup artist checked her notes and sent Mrs. Gandhi a supply of the dozen or so items of makeup, complete with sponges and instructions for application.

Indira Gandhi appeared seven times on *Meet the Press* before her assassination at the hands of Sikh bodyguards in October 1984. *Meet the Press* has interviewed five members of the distinguished Nehru family to which she belonged: her father, who preceded her as prime minister of India; her aunt, who was India's ambassador to the United States; her son, also prime minister; and a cousin, who was also India's ambassador to the United States.

April 26, 1964

India boasts of being the world's largest democracy, and the Nehru family's status in India is comparable to that of the Kennedys in the United States. Indira Gandhi has been called the most important woman in India. She is the daughter and confidante of Prime Minister Nehru, and like her father and

April 19, 1964: Lawrence Spivak and Hussein I, king of Jordan, who was in Washington on a state visit to President Johnson.

grandfather before her, she has served as president of the Congress Party, the ruling political party in India.

LAWRENCE SPIVAK: Would you like to be prime minister of India?

GANDHI: I would not.

. . .

MARGUERITE HIGGINS (*Newsday*): If the will of the people of India were such that you were clearly the wish of the majority, would you serve as prime minister?

GANDHI: I find that very difficult to believe that there will be such an overwhelming demand or whatever you like to call it.

In 1966, Indira Gandhi was elected prime minister of India.

On June 28, 1964, Maurice Couve de Murville, French foreign minister, is interviewed by satellite from Paris by panelists in Washington. The Telstar satellite was available only in certain positions, and the program had to be taped and played back within the available hour. The satellite became available twenty-five minutes before airtime. The show was therefore taped in two parts, and the first half was broadcast while the second half of the show was still being taped. It was a risky procedure, but it worked perfectly.

The First Ten *Meet the Press* Interviews via Satellite

1. Guest Maurice Couve de Murville and one newsman in Paris, others in Washington: June 28, 1964
2. Guest Harold Wilson in London, panel in Washington, for the first live satellite broadcast of *Meet the Press:* September 19, 1965
3. Guest Dean Rusk in Washington, interviewed live by Lawrence Spivak in Washington and newsmen in London, Paris, Bonn, and Rome. The first hour-long satellite broadcast of *Meet the Press:* January 23, 1966
4. Guest George W. Ball in Paris, interviewed by European newsmen in London and Lawrence Spivak in Washington. The first live color *Meet the Press* interview by satellite: April 2, 1967
5. Seven participants in the Pacem in Terris Conference answer questions from a moderator and two reporters in Geneva and two reporters in Washington: May 28, 1967
6. Six American governors interviewed live from the annual Governors' Conference, meeting in San Juan, Puerto Rico: September 12, 1971
7. Guest Salvador Allende interviewed from Santiago, Chile, by one NBC correspondent with him in the studio and three reporters and a moderator in Washington. The first *Meet the Press* program to use simultaneous translation: October 30, 1971
8. Ferdinand Marcos interviewed live from his palace in Manila by an NBC correspondent at the palace and panel members with the moderator in Washington: October 8, 1972
9. King Hussein of Jordan interviewed by a panel in Amman: December 4, 1977
10. Sadegh Ghotbzadeh interviewed by one NBC correspondent in the Teheran studio with him and a panel in Washington: December 9, 1979

July 26, 1964

With Vice President Lyndon Johnson taking over the presidency on the death of President Kennedy, Sen. Eugene McCarthy (D-MN) is spoken of as a possible Democratic vice presidential nominee. He encourages the notion on *Meet the Press*.

ROBERT GORALSKI (NBC News): What is your concept of the vice presidency?

McCARTHY: It is a rather difficult—most everyone who has held the office recently has been reported as giving new meaning to the office, which would probably indicate that no one has a very clear view of it.

August 23, 1964: Sen. Hubert H. Humphrey (left) and Sen. Eugene McCarthy at the Democratic National Convention in Atlantic City.

President Johnson did not like going on *Meet the Press* according to Lawrence Spivak. "He appeared on the show only because he felt he had to." But Johnson was a keen watcher of the program. He called McGeorge Bundy (special assistant to the president) simply to tell him that his hair looked odd. The tradition of presidential calls to *Meet the Press* was begun by President Truman, who phoned the Mutual Broadcasting studio on August 15, 1947, to express his pleasure at the performance of Sen. Claude Pepper (D-FL).

***Meet the Press* guests telephoned by President Lyndon Johnson immediately after the broadcast:**

- **Sargent Shriver, director of the Peace Corps: December 15, 1963**
- **Sen. Hubert H. Humphrey (D-MN): March 8, 1964**
- **Dr. Milton S. Eisenhower, chairman of the Critical Issues Council: April 5, 1964**
- **Sen. Hubert H. Humphrey (D-MN) and Sen. Eugene J. McCarthy (D-MN): August 23, 1964**
- **Secretary of State Dean Rusk: August 30, 1964**
- **Sen. Russell Long (D-LA): February 28, 1965**
- **McGeorge Bundy, special assistant to the president: April 4, 1965**
- **Thanat Khoman, foreign minister of Thailand: May 9, 1965**
- **Henry Cabot Lodge: May 23, 1965**
- **John Connor, secretary of commerce: July 18, 1965**
- **Gen. Maxwell Taylor: August 8, 1965**

August 30, 1964

In 1967 Lyndon Johnson's former press secretary Bill Moyers told *Meet the Press* that the president saw his inability to find a peaceful solution in Vietnam as the great failure of his presidency. The key moment in his escalation of military involvement occurs with the Gulf of Tonkin incident. One month after two reports of attacks on American vessels in the Gulf of Tonkin, and the subsequent congressional approval to expand United States involvement in Vietnam, Secretary of State Dean Rusk explains American policy.

RUSK: In the first place, the policy of the United States in South Vietnam is utterly simple and well known both here and throughout the world. For the past ten years we have been engaged in giving assistance, and large assistance, to the government of South Vietnam and to its people to enable them to defend themselves against the aggression from the North represented by these guerrillas called the Vietcong. That has been a consistent effort for at least a decade. That is our purpose. When that country becomes safe and independent, secure, so that the people can work out their own future for themselves, American military presence will not be required, and South Vietnam can be independent.

. . .

JOHN HIGHTOWER (Associated Press): Under present circumstances, do you see any possibility at all in the predictable future of making a negotiated settlement?

RUSK: We had a negotiated settlement in 1954; we had another one in Laos in 1962. It is hard for me at the moment to envisage just what a negotiation would be about—what speeches the delegates would make when they first sit down at the table, because if the North is prepared to leave their neighbors in the South alone, then there is no problem.

Juana Castro, sister of Cuban Premier Fidel Castro, gives Meet the Press *her first interview after fleeing Cuba. Although she supported her brother in the struggle to overthrow Batista, she now devotes herself to his overthrow. The November 22, 1964, broadcast attracts the largest ever number of requests for* Meet the Press *transcripts.*

INTERVIEWS PRODUCING MOST TRANSCRIPT REQUESTS

1. November 22, 1964: Juana Castro
2. February 24, 1960: Adm. Hyman G. Rickover
3. February 12, 1967: William Manchester

Transcripts of *Meet the Press* were originally produced by the NBC News Press Department in New York for the benefit of the wire services and major news organizations. Later a court reporter took down every word off the air, and within approximately three hours a typed transcript was ready to be photocopied and distributed by messenger around Washington. When the public started writing in for transcripts, the job was handed over to a printer. For a while transcript requests were handled by the National Publishing Company, but soon the program ended with the famous invitation "For a printed transcript of today's interview, send ten cents in coin and a stamped self-addressed envelope to Merkle Press, 809 Channing Street North East, Washington 18, D.C." The address became so well known that Johnny Carson used it as a running joke on *The Tonight Show*.

In 1975 the price rose to twenty-five cents, and two years later the Kelly Press of Washington, D.C., took over the printing of transcripts. Prices doubled in the 1980s from fifty cents to one dollar, a price held until printing moved to Burrelle's Information Services in Livingston, New Jersey, at the end of 1992.

States sending most letters to *Meet the Press:* California, Florida, Ohio, and New York. A Wisconsin farmer wrote to say he planned his milking times around *Meet the Press*.

Newly elected Sen. Joseph Tydings (D-MD) faces questions on campaign finance (December 20, 1964):

RAY SCHERER (NBC News): Mr. Tydings, . . . how much did you have to spend to win your senatorship?

TYDINGS: In the general election it was approximately two hundred and fifty thousand dollars, and in the primary a little less than that.

SCHERER: Isn't that an awful lot of money for a state like Maryland?

TYDINGS: This is an awful lot of money, Mr. Scherer. It is too much.

The issue of campaign finance remains unresolved in the 1990s, when Senator Tydings's $250,000 would not go very far. In 1996 the average expenditure for a Senate campaign was $3.6 million.

March 28, 1965

A sequence of assassinations changes the political landscape in the 1960s. A month after the murder of Malcolm X, Dr. Martin Luther King, Jr., is interviewed in San Francisco. He recently led a civil rights march from Selma to Montgomery, Alabama, after which a Detroit woman drawn into the march through her religious convictions was murdered. Former President Truman has dismissed the march as "silly."

> KING: I would say that the march was not silly at all. . . . I think it was the most powerful and dramatic civil rights protest that has ever taken place in the South.

Lawrence Spivak asks Dr. King if it is time for a respite in Alabama.

March 28, 1965: A month after the assassination of Malcolm X, Dr. Martin Luther King, Jr., is in San Francisco to deliver a sermon at Grace Cathedral. He is interviewed by a Meet the Press *panel in Washington, D.C.*

KING: This is a state that continues to deal with human life as if it is nothing. This is a state that continues to make murder a sort of nice pastime and gives respectability to resistance and defiance of the law.

Dr. King then proposes an escalation of the campaign against Alabama, and his statement becomes a major news story.

KING: I think that it is necessary for the nation to rise up and engage in a massive economic withdrawal program on the state of Alabama. To put it another way, I think the time has come for all people of goodwill to join in an economic boycott of Alabama products.

I believe that the presidency seeks the man and that if the man is not destined at a particular time and place to lead the country, he will not be elected.

—Richard Nixon, September 12, 1965

On September 19, 1965, British Prime Minister Harold Wilson appears on the first live interview via satellite (from London), provoking an international press reaction.

The *Age*, of Melbourne, Australia, reports: "The British Prime Minister was able to put his country's case in America yesterday with a force and persuasion never before available to the great British Prime Ministers of the past.

"The first live trans-Atlantic 'Meet the Press' television programme introduced a new element in Anglo-American relations. . . .

"Here was the British Prime Minister speaking to an American coast-to-coast audience . . . with candor, persuasion and dignity on distasteful as well as favored American topics. . . ."

December 12, 1965

In the summer of the deadly Watts riots, Daniel Patrick Moynihan's paper on *The Negro Family* had a high—and controversial profile. Lawrence Spivak asks him why he wrote that "the United States is approaching a new crisis in race relations."

MOYNIHAN: I felt that the great crises having to do with the protection of the liberties of Negro Americans in the South were probably coming to an end. . . . It seemed to me that we would now turn to the problems of the northern ghettos.

His concern in writing *The Negro Family* was to humanize "the cycle of no jobs and bad education and bad housing [that] just reproduces itself. . . . The point about the family is that it is a good place to see the results of unemployment, the results of discrimination, the results of bad housing and education. And you can't do anything about a family life if men don't have jobs, if schoolchildren don't have good schools, if people live in ghettos. . . .

"[A]t any given moment two-thirds of the Negro families are husband and wife families, but over their lifetime only a little more than a third of Negro children come of eighteen having lived all their lives in such a family. That hurts people, that deprives them of opportunities, not to have a father, not to have a mother. You have lost something that helps you in life, and so this process feeds back into the cycle. So we can't act as if the family were just a result; it is also an effect. And strong families produce strong peoples. Look at Martin Luther King. Where would he be without the Reverend King? . . . Think of great men anywhere, how often they have strong parents who give them education, a sense of moral urgency to problems and the courage to face up to them."

Moynihan's warnings about the plight of African American families went largely unheeded for three decades, but his comments on strong parents are echoed movingly on *Meet the Press* in February 1997 by basketball star Charles Barkley.

January 9, 1966

Screen and television actor Ronald Reagan has announced he will seek the Republican nomination for governor of California. Why, Lawrence Spivak wonders, does he think he would be a good governor?

REAGAN: Maybe because I have so much faith that government should be of the people and my

belief that we have had too much government, particularly in the state of California, by administrative edict and rule. I happen to believe that the people of California can do a pretty good job of running their own affairs.

Spivak asks the candidate how he will counter accusations that his campaign is, in the words of the *Washington Post,* "an attempt to turn an actor into a believable candidate for Governor and to make voters forget [his] right-wing views."

REAGAN: I think by simply telling the truth. . . . I think the people, if they will listen to me, will find out the false image doesn't stand up.

DAVID KRASLOW (*Los Angeles Times*): Have your views changed substantially in any regard since the 1964 campaigns?

REAGAN: No. As a matter of fact, my views haven't changed an awful lot since I was a Democrat. I believed then that anything, whether it came from labor, management, or government, that imposed unfairly on the individual or the freedom of the individual was tyranny and should be opposed. I still feel that way.

The first one-hour satellite news interview program in the history of television takes place on January 23, 1966, when Secretary of State Dean Rusk is interviewed in Washington by leading foreign journalists based in London, Paris, Bonn, and Rome. And on April 2, 1967, Meet the Press *provides the first live color interview via satellite, as Undersecretary of State George W. Ball, in Paris, is interviewed by journalists in London (above).*

March 13, 1966: Vice President Hubert H. Humphrey makes headlines with his statement that the United States favors "containment without necessarily isolation" of Communist China. It is the first public acknowledgment by a top official of what many news reports hail as a significant shift in U.S. policy. Interviewed by eight leading newspaper editors and publishers, the vice president says the administration's plan to allow scholars, journalists, and doctors to visit China "could be the beginning of a much better relationship." But he predicts only slow improvement. "I am afraid that we are going to have to wait until the men of the Long March, of the Mao generation, are out of positions of leadership. But in the meantime we ought to maintain as best we can a spirit of friendship towards the Chinese people, but recognizing what the regime is."

Youth is a matter of which side you look at it from. I mean, if you ask a twenty-year-old, forty-seven, forty-eight seems quite old. Of course, if you ask someone who is eighty years old, he will think it is young. I think in experience I am quite old by now.

—Indira Gandhi, April 3, 1966

Auto safety crusader Ralph Nader's appearance on May 29, 1966, generates a huge mailbag for both *Meet the Press* and Nader. The post office finally calls *Meet the Press* and offers to deliver Nader's mail directly to him.

Guests on shows receiving the most letters from viewers: Dr. Linus Pauling, Anastas Mikoyan (deputy premier of the Soviet Union), Fidel Castro, Robert Welch (founder, John Birch Society), Fred C. Schwarz (director, Christian Anti-Communism Crusade), Gov. George C. Wallace, Dr. Martin Luther King, Jr., and Ralph Nader (right).

June 26, 1966

As the number of American troops in Vietnam rises, the war overshadows all other events. The administration remains publicly optimistic about progress. George W. Ball, undersecretary of state, considers himself among the optimists.

JOSEPH C. HARSCH (NBC News): We have been bombing for over a year and a half. Is there any evidence at all that that bombing has had the effect of pushing the enemy towards peace, or hasn't it actually worked the other way, of stiffening their will to war?

BALL: I think that has achieved a number of results. It has greatly increased the cost of infiltrating men and material into the South. I think that it has had a very real effect on the morale of the fighting forces of the Vietcong in the South.

. . .

CHALMERS ROBERTS (*Washington Post*): Are you any more hopeful now than you were some months back, or is it more or less the same thing we have been saying for months?

BALL: I think anyone who has watched the war carefully must be gratified and pleased and more encouraged by what has occurred on the military side.

August 21, 1966: Guests (above) and audience (below opposite) for the Meet the Press *civil rights special. The program attracted extensive press comment.*

August 21, 1966

On a *Meet the Press* special about race, the guests are: Dr. Martin Luther King, Jr., president, Southern Christian Leadership Conference; Roy Wilkins, executive director, NAACP; Whitney M. Young, Jr., executive director, National Urban League; Floyd B. McKissick, national director, Congress of Racial Equality; Stokely Carmichael, chairman, Student Nonviolent Coordinating Committee; James H. Meredith, leader of a recent march through Mississippi.

The *New York Times* prints a full page of excerpts from the special, and it is reported overseas. Writing in the *Manchester*, England, *Guardian*, Alistair Cooke says the six guests "were questioned, and sometimes challenged, by four newsmen and prodded at all times by the programme's chairman, Lawrence Spivak, whose waspishness has the great virtue of expressing what the viewer thinks he would say and what the reporters in attendance would like to say but don't."

LAWRENCE SPIVAK: Dr. King, I am sure you either heard or read President Johnson's speech yesterday when he warned that violence and discord would destroy Negroes' hopes for racial progress. Isn't it time to stop demonstrations that create violence and discord?

KING: . . . I think demonstrations must con-

[T]wo little bitty words in the English language. One, "black"—everybody who has gone through the sixth grade knows what "black" means. "Power"—everybody who has gone through the sixth grade knows what that means, and I get a letter from a professor at Harvard saying, "Explain black power."

—Floyd B. McKissick, national director of the Congress of Racial Equality (CORE), August 21, 1966

tinue, but I think riots must end, because I think they are socially disruptive. I think they are self-defeating, and I think they can destroy the many creative steps that we have made in a forward sense over the last few years.

JAMES J. KILPATRICK (*Richmond,* Virginia, *News Leader*): Dr. King, you have been quoted as saying that you have encountered more hatred among white opponents in Chicago than you have encountered in the Deep South. How do you account for this?

KING: I think for years the hatred existed beneath the surface in northern communities, and as I said earlier, it is coming out now. I think also we have to see that this is something of a dislike for the unlike.

. . .

Lawrence Spivak asks Stokely Carmichael what he means by saying Negroes who fight in Vietnam are black mercenaries.

CARMICHAEL: A mer- cenary is a hired killer, and I think that when this country says to black youths in the ghetto and to black youths in the rural South that their only chance for a decent living is to join the army—and then they throw in all sorts of rationalizations about, you can get skills and there is a chance for them to advance, et cetera, et cetera—they are saying to that black man that his only chance for a decent life is to become a hired killer because that is the sole function of an army.

James Meredith has spent most of his adult life in the military, and his attitude contrasts starkly with Carmichael's. He sees the Vietnam War as a great opportunity for black men and asserts "that these soldiers are not going to come back over here and accept white supremacy any more."

February 12, 1967

Before the publication of his controversial book *Death of a President,* author William Manchester gives his side of the feud with the Kennedy family, who claim he broke an agreement with Robert Kennedy that the book would not be published "unless and until approved by Jacqueline Kennedy and Robert Kennedy." Manchester claims Robert Kennedy sent him a telegram stating that "members of the Kennedy family will place no obstacle in the way of publication of the book." The one-hour special program attracts one of *Meet the Press*'s largest audiences ever.

February 26, 1967

A special edition of *Meet the Press* examines the Central Intelligence Agency. Guests are Sen. Joseph S. Clark (D-PA), Foreign Relations Committee; Sen. Henry M. Jackson (D-WA), Armed Services Committee; Robert Amory, Jr., former deputy director for intelligence, CIA; Sam Brown, chairman, National Supervisory Board, National Student Association; Dennis Shaul, former president, National Student Association.

Recent disclosures of CIA subsidies to the National Student Association have again focused attention on the agency. Serious questions are being raised about the CIA's undercover activities and about the need for greater control over it.

THOMAS B. ROSS (*Chicago Sun-Times*): The agency has been involved in various enterprises overseas, such as attempts and sometimes successful attempts to overthrow foreign governments. By what right and with what justification has the agency involved themselves in these various operations?

AMORY: The agency . . . is an operational agency that does what it is told by the constitutional authorities of the United States. It may be the president himself in a specific, important issue, and if you are talking about major things like Guatemala, which is now a part of history, that was a presidential decision taken with the full knowledge of the senior members of the Senate and House. . . .

ROSS: Senator Jackson, you were a member of Congress in 1947 when the National Security Act was passed, establishing the CIA. Were you aware at that time that the CIA was being authorized to conduct extensive operations, both at home and abroad?

JACKSON: I would have been disappointed if they were not to undertake that. I have been abroad enough to know that there are a lot of things that we needed to do abroad at that time. It was a period of great ferment. . . . There was a great threat to the

In May 1967 a survey was carried out to measure *Meet the Press* viewing habits among government officials, with a view to selling *Meet the Press* as an advertising vehicle to companies wishing to reach government officials. The conclusion was that "*Meet the Press* has exceptional cumulative reach among high-level government officials. Over 76% watch *Meet the Press* at least now and then, a considerably larger audience among this influential group than for other programs of this type. . . . 77% sometimes watch *Meet the Press,* compared to 63% for *Bonanza,* 69% for Jackie Gleason and 56% for The *Man from U.N.C.L.E.*"

free labor movement and to the youth groups, and that problem is even greater today than it was twenty years ago.

. . .

ROSS (to Senator Clark): To liberals of your persuasion, does not this turn the argument towards the president himself? Must not your misgivings about the CIA really be directed to the president and to whether or not the United States government, as policy, should engage itself in these types of activities?

CLARK: No, because I think the answer begs the question. The fact of the matter is, from the very beginning—let's take the Bay of Pigs as an example. That was CIA-inspired; it was CIA-promoted; it was sold to President Eisenhower by intelligence people who had a conflict of interest. It was then sold to President Kennedy. He didn't know how to get at it, and to pretend that this starts with the president and works back to that willing agent, the CIA, I think is most disingenuous. . . .

EDWIN NEWMAN (NBC News) (to Amory): You shook your head when Senator Clark said it originated with the CIA.

AMORY: It didn't. It originated with the genuine worry of the whole United States government: What were we going to do when we had a Communist state ninety miles off the coast of Florida?

March 5, 1967

David Ben-Gurion, the first prime minister of Israel, headed his government for thirteen years. He is visiting the United States on the occasion of his eightieth birthday when he appears on *Meet the Press*.

Before the show begins, Ben-Gurion's wife and his aides engage in a prolonged battle over the interviewee's hair. The aides fluff up the tufts that sprout densely on each side of Ben-Gurion's largely hairless head, and Mrs. Ben-Gurion promptly flattens them down. The aides resume fluffing and Mrs. Ben-Gurion flattening in consequence. Eventually the aides—having finally fluffed—stand in front of Ben-Gurion, blocking his wife's view of his head until the moment before the program starts.

Mrs. Ben-Gurion is more successful in her assertion that her husband must have orange juice, a reasonable request since the interview is taking place in Florida, but one that proves surprisingly hard to satisfy. After much searching, fresh juice is found. Perhaps preoccupied by this hair and orange juice epic, Mrs. Ben-Gurion walks off with a book about Israel that Lawrence Spivak has asked her husband to autograph.

The show begins, live and unrehearsed, on time, and Spivak poses his typically direct questions.

March 5, 1967: Israel's first prime minister, David Ben-Gurion, is interviewed in Florida.

SPIVAK: Could you tell us why any American Jews should leave this rich, prosperous country to come to the Negev?

BEN-GURION: I put this question to Einstein in 1951 and again in 1960 to Robert Oppenheimer, when he came to Israel. I asked Einstein whether Jewish scientists would come to Israel. He said, "Oh, yes."

I said, "Why?"

He said, "They are not trusted here."

In 1960 Robert Oppenheimer came to visit Israel. I told him about the discussion with Einstein. But I said, "Things have changed since then. McCarthy is gone, and the Jew is not now discriminated against. Will they come?"

He said, "Yes."

I said, "Why?"

He said, "I will tell you. There are two types of human beings. One—this is the majority—wants to take, to get. There is another type—a minority—who has a great need to give, to create.

"This is the meaning of life. There is no meaning of life in America, in England, in France. . . ."

SPIVAK: If your fondest dreams were realized, what percentage of the Jews of the world do you think could live—

BEN-GURION: This is difficult to say. If you had asked me sixty years ago, the year when I went to Israel, I would tell you I am sure that six million Jews from Europe will come. I knew there were six million who needed Israel, wanted Israel, and were capable of creating Israel. They are destroyed. They don't exist anymore.

May 21, 1967

President Kennedy's deadline for a moon landing is approaching, and memories of January's Apollo disaster are fresh, as NASA astronauts Walter M. Schirra, Frank Borman, and Thomas P. Stafford discuss the Apollo program and the race to beat the 1970 deadline.

STAFFORD: To me, we would certainly like to make the lunar mission by the end of 1969, prior to 1970, but I am certain that if it is a tight fit on the schedule at the end, if there is any safety involved, we will let the date go right past. It will be a safe mission for the lunar surface and return, regardless of when it takes place.

QUESTION: Why is a manned mission necessary?

SCHIRRA: We are getting information now from unmanned vehicles which are exploring the moon, and it is only natural that man must go out there and look for himself.

June 25, 1967

Two weeks after Israel's stunning victory over Egypt, Jordan, and Syria in the Six-Day War, Minister for Foreign Affairs of Israel Abba Eban is in the United States for a United Nations debate on the Middle East.

PAULINE FREDERICK (NBC News): The United States resolution in the General Assembly calls for discussions that encompass withdrawal of armed services, among other things. Do you agree with that?

EBAN: . . . If the United Nations were simply to ask for a withdrawal of troops, then in the words of the prime minister of Italy, . . . "it would share the blame for a return to a situation which has caused two wars in two decades."

. . .

DONALD GRANT (*St. Louis Post-Dispatch*): Do you feel that any Arab government now in power can survive politically at home if it engages in direct negotiations with Israel?

EBAN: I frankly have enough trouble looking

> after our own political situation without worrying about the stability or instability of Arab governments and politicians. I really think that Arab public opinion might applaud the courage and the statesmanship of a leader who, after so many years of failure, undertook a new and dramatic direction. . . .

Lawrence Spivak asks Mr. Eban whether Israel plans to annex Jerusalem.

> EBAN: I think the only matter that is now open in Jerusalem is how to satisfy the international religious interests which revolve around the holy places and religious institutions. The unity of Jerusalem, the peace of Jerusalem, and access to the holy places have been assured, and therefore the problem remaining for negotiation is how to see that the international universal religious interests in the holy places are expressed.
>
> SPIVAK: That means that she plans to annex the other section of Jerusalem, is that correct?
>
> EBAN: Mr. Spivak, I have my own vocabulary, and I prefer to rest upon it.

July 30, 1967

Race riots rip through urban neighborhoods in the summer of '67. Twenty-six people are left dead by July rioting in Newark, New Jersey, with over a thousand injured. A week after an uneasy calm settles over Newark, Detroit is devastated by what *Meet the Press* moderator Edwin Newman calls "the worst racial violence in modern history." Thousands are made homeless as black neighborhoods burn, and over forty lives are lost in the rioting. On *Meet the Press* Detroit Mayor Jerome P. Cavanagh makes a plea for greater government concern, involvement, and money for the big cities. Admitting, "I don't know of any government in America, local government, state government, or national government, or any institution for that matter, that is communicating in any way or carrying on any kind of a dialogue with the so-called have-nots," Cavanagh asks, "what will it profit this country if we, say, put our man on the moon by 1970 and at the same time you can't walk down Woodward Avenue in this city without some fear of violence?" He blames Congress for the neglect of the inner cities.

> CAVANAGH: They laugh and holler and rail when they vote down a minor rat-control bill for the cities and yet pay two or three or four times that amount of money just for the storage of cotton in any one year. . . . There is a madness in this country, and the Congress reacts by being indifferent, sometimes not just indifferent, just by being completely negative about it.

August 6, 1967

A week after Mayor Cavanagh's tirade, Sen. Robert F. Kennedy (D-NY) makes a plea for a change in the nation's priorities.

KENNEDY: [I]f we can spend twenty-four billion dollars for the freedom and the liberty of the people of Vietnam, certainly we can spend a small percentage of that for the liberty and the freedom and the future of our own people in the United States.

DOUGLAS KIKER (NBC News): The program that you have suggested as a cure for the rioting and urban ills that plague us today would cost an awful lot of money. Would you support a tax increase for a massive increase in this sort of federal aid?

KENNEDY: . . . I don't think it's just the federal government coming into the ghetto and spending large sums of money. I think we should make it attractive through credits, depreciation, in various tax ways, for the private enterprise system to make investments in the ghetto, to make investments in housing, to make investments in the construction of businesses which will employ people.

Dr. Martin Luther King, Jr., dedicates a book for Lawrence Spivak.

August 13, 1967

The civil rights movement is blamed in some quarters for the summer of riots. Dr. Martin Luther King, Jr., denies responsibility.

> KING: I have never advocated anarchy, I have never advocated lawlessness, I have never advocated violence, I have never advocated arson, I have never advocated sniping or looting. . . . There is no doubt that some Negroes are disenchanted with nonviolence. They feel that we haven't made enough progress in general and through nonviolence, and as a result of this, they have started talking more in terms of violence.
>
> I still believe, however, that the vast majority of Negroes feel that nonviolence is the best strategy.

Dr. King suggests that the continuing war in Vietnam will provoke a spread of civil disobedience.

> KING: Many young men have already made it crystal clear that they are opposed to the war, and it may be necessary for these young men, if this war continues, to engage in a massive campaign of conscientious objection. Also, it may be necessary for clergymen to go on record denying their draft-exemption status and file as conscientious objectors, so that it will be made clear that this war is destroying so much of what we hold dear in this nation.

September 10, 1967

Protest against the Vietnam War is rising, and it takes many forms. Some protesters burn their draft cards; others turn to flower power and the hippies' summer of love in San Francisco. A large antiwar demonstration is organized at the Pentagon. Meanwhile, America's troop strength in South Vietnam grows by 90,000 in 1967, bringing the total to

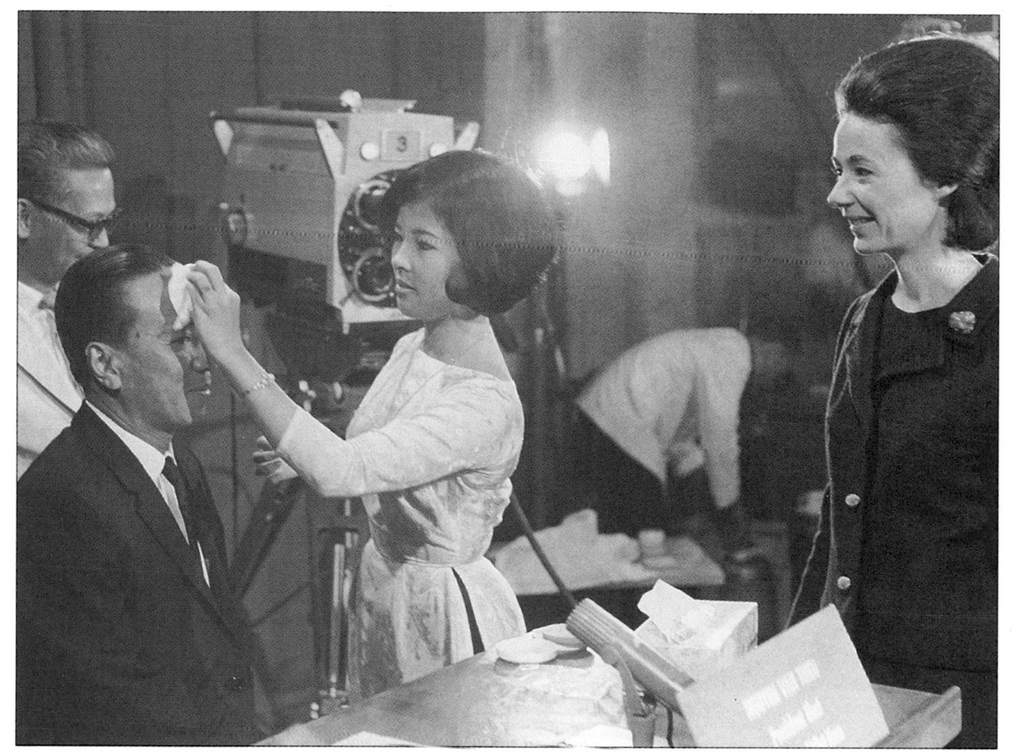

Vietnam's President-elect Nguyen Van Thieu (far left) is made up for his Meet the Press *interview in Saigon, watched by Associate Producer Betty Cole Dukert. The interview ended in drama when Vice President Ky's aides tried to seize the tapes.*

475,000. The Communist Tet offensive attack on Saigon is five months in the future when *Meet the Press* travels to Vietnam to interview President-elect Nguyen Van Thieu.

It was not possible to transmit a live program by satellite from Saigon, so *Meet the Press* arranged to videotape the interview on Thursday and fly it back to the United States in time for Sunday presentation. Hours before the scheduled interview, the president-elect sent word that he wanted a week's postponement. Associate Producer Betty Cole Dukert decided the situation called for a face-to-face meeting with Thieu. To reach him, she had to penetrate the television studio where he was about to record a speech. She strode past the armed guards blocking the route—"I guess they didn't think I looked dangerous"—and entered the studio.

"After listening to [Thieu's] speech twice—he wanted to hear a playback—I had a chance to say hello and make my plea. His reason for postponing the interview was to await the official election returns. I suggested that since American news reports had already proclaimed him the winner, a postponement of the publicized *Meet the Press* interview might cast doubt on the certainty of victory. He agreed to do the program the following morning."

Thieu remained adamant on one point: He refused to allow Vice President Ky to appear on the program with him as planned. "The tensions between Army General Thieu and Air Force General Ky were such that we weren't sure who controlled just what, and the day of the taping there were air force personnel guarding the studio. Our director, Max Schindler, decided it was prudent to grab the show tapes from the tape room as soon as the interview ended and quickly put blank tapes on the machines." The precaution was wise: Ky's men burst in and confiscated the tapes on the machines—the wrong tapes. The right tapes were rushed to the airport just in time to catch the last commercial flight that would get tapes and production team home in time to air the program. "As we reached the Los Angeles airport, we saw headlines: THIEU THROWS KY OFF TV PROGRAM. And the world had its first intimation of the hostility between Thieu and Ky."

Meet the Press promised to reschedule the Ky interview, which eventually took place on November 29, 1970, when Vice President Ky was visiting the United States. A live Sunday interview was planned, but on Tuesday a bomb threat was received preceding a Ky speech at the National Press Club in Washington, and the room had to be evacuated temporarily. The producers therefore decided it would be prudent to tape the interview with Ky an hour prior to air time, without announcing the switch. Ky readily agreed, although his entourage seemed unconcerned, and the program went off without a problem.

On the Saturday afternoon before the planned interview with Prime Minister Lee Kuan Yew of Singapore on October 21, 1967, *Meet the Press* producer Betty Cole Dukert arrived at her New York hotel to find a message asking her to call a State Department protocol officer assigned to Lee's visit. The message was marked "urgent." Fearfully she dialed the number, "trying quickly to think of newsworthy replacements at the same time."

"The prime minister has several requests," the protocol officer began. "He would like tea available in the studio, without cream. He prefers the temperature to be sixty-eight degrees, and he would like to know who will be meeting him at the door."

November 19, 1967

The election of Thieu does not soothe a growing antiwar movement at home. A month after a huge protest outside the Pentagon, Ellsworth Bunker, ambassador to Vietnam, and Gen. William Westmoreland, commander of the U.S. forces in Vietnam, insist that the war is going well, that "the will of the South Vietnamese people to continue the war effort is firm" [Bunker] and that now is "the time to reinforce this success with troop augmentations. . . . We are winning a war of attrition" [Westmoreland].

February 4, 1968

Forecasts of victory in Vietnam are jarred when the North Vietnamese and Vietcong mount a massive offensive in South Vietnam. Secretary of State Dean Rusk and Secretary of Defense Robert McNamara make a rare joint appearance on a one-hour *Meet the Press* special at the time of the Tet offensive. McNamara has previously refused to appear on a television interview show. "No one believed they would accept except at the direct urging of President Johnson," Spivak said.

The panel expresses Americans' shock that such a large incursion was possible, but McNamara insists that the "North Vietnamese and the Vietcong have not accomplished either one of their major objectives, either to ignite a general uprising or to force a diversion of the troops which the South Vietnamese and the United States have moved into the northern areas of South Vietnam."

McNamara also offers *Meet the Press* viewers an intriguing insight into the failed Bay of Pigs operation in Cuba: "I have never said publicly, and I want to say today, that when President Kennedy assumed full responsibility for that action, he didn't say what he might have said, that every one of his advisers, me included, recommended it. So I was responsible for that."

February 11, 1968

Sen. Eugene McCarthy (D-MN) is a critic of the Johnson administration's Vietnam policy, and he has presidential ambitions.

McCARTHY: My objective is to bring about a change of national policy, both with reference to the war and also with reference to national priorities. As I see it, in order to accomplish that, as things are going, it would be necessary to take the nomination for the Democratic party from President Johnson, so that that is my objective.

February 18, 1968

There are fears that antiwar demonstrators may disrupt the summer Democratic National Convention in Chicago. Attorney General Ramsey Clark expresses ultimately misplaced confidence in the ability of the Chicago police to keep order.

CARL STERN (NBC News): Mr. Clark, the sheriff of Cook County, Illinois, wants an armed posse of one thousand volunteers to guard against disorders at the Democratic National Convention in Chicago this summer. Do you think that would be useful?

CLARK: . . . I think the notion of a posse is an unfortunate way to put it. We need professional law enforcement men, ready for any contingency.

April 7, 1968

Attorney General Ramsey Clark returns to *Meet the Press* two months later to discuss a tragic development: the assassination of Dr. Martin Luther King, Jr., in Memphis.

In 1968 Lawrence Spivak gave the Library of Congress almost five hundred sixteen-inch acetate discs of early *Meet the Press* broadcasts, followed by some two hundred kinescope prints of *Meet the Press* in 1969. The library now has copies of all extant *Meet the Press* video recordings. The collection is updated at the end of each year.

President Nixon told Spivak that "your incisive questioning is precisely the kind of national service that the Fathers meant to guarantee when they wrote 'freedom of the press' into the First Amendment."

HAYNES JOHNSON (*Washington Evening Star*): Mr. Clark, Martin Luther King preached a philosophy of nonviolence, and yet today I think many Americans are concerned that we are headed toward a violent future. How do you see the future of this country?

CLARK: . . . Perhaps the cruelest tragedy of the murder of Dr. King, who believed in this country, who preached and practiced throughout this land nonviolence, would be for the violence that brought his death to undermine his philosophy. . . . These are turbulent times. We are a disturbed nation, and the risks are great, and violence more than anything else risks further division. . . .

ROSCOE DRUMMOND (Publishers-Hall Syndicate): What should be done about the statement of Stokely Carmichael that Negroes should get guns and retaliate in the streets?

CLARK: That is absolutely impossible. It is impossible for the Negroes of America. It would be suicidal. . . . And the Negro people are committed to its not happening. We may have random violence, we may have random physical assault, but we are a mighty nation of two hundred million people, and we have to expect some of this.

May 12, 1968

With an election approaching, what issues have the polls identified? Louis Harris and Richard M. Scammon are questioned on the polls and the state of the art of polling.

HARRIS: We found up until very recently that Vietnam was the number one issue, that perhaps more volatile and more emotional yet is the division over race. And a third which is there as well is the whole division over nonconformity—call it the generation gap or what you please—but these are tearing our electorate up in a fashion which I would say is well-nigh unrecognizable.

. . .

HARRIS: I think that any leader who makes public policy on the basis of polls is doing a disservice to the country. I think that issues that face the nation must be made on the merits of the issues involved and certainly not on the basis of any polls.

LAWRENCE SPIVAK: Don't leaders very often use the polls to change their image and change their position on issues, and isn't this harmful in a democracy?

SCAMMON: I don't think it is particularly harmful. I think there is a certain value obtained by the leadership of a democracy, knowing what the people want. I would not think it is wise that the leadership not know what the people want.

May 26, 1968: Moderator Edwin Newman (left) and Lawrence Spivak watch guest Gov. Ronald Reagan of California on a studio monitor.

June 9, 1968

Within weeks of the assassination of Martin Luther King, another killing rocks America. In another Kennedy family tragedy Robert F. Kennedy is shot dead by a Palestinian gunman at the Ambassador Hotel in Los Angeles. On the Sunday following the murder, and in the week President Johnson calls on Congress to give the country the gun control law it needs, Sen. Joseph Tydings (D-MD) tells the *Meet the Press* audience to make its views on gun control known to Congress.

In his call for gun control on *Meet the Press,* Senator Tydings says: "Nothing is going to move the Congress, nothing is going to move the state legislatures across the country except a most tremendous outpouring of demands from the citizens of this country. It is only the people who are going to do it. The Congress is not going to change; we are not going to get a bill through the Senate unless the people themselves get on the telephone and get hold of their Senators and say, 'We demand action.'"

The senator is highly critical of the National Rifle Association.

> TYDINGS: Ostensibly they [the NRA] represent the sportsmen, but actually they are the voice of the munitions makers and the gun sellers in the United States. They have a tremendous amount of power in the Congress, unfortunately, in state legislatures. They have always opposed any type of responsible, effective gun legislation.

Public response is instant and huge. "Letters began pouring into my office at the rate of 1,200 a day," Tydings wrote in *Playboy* in March 1969. "It was the greatest volume of mail on any Senate issue since the McCarthy censure fight."

Clashes between antiwar demonstrators and police brought mayhem to the Democratic National Convention in Chicago. Meet the Press*'s eve-of-convention guest Sen. Edmund S. Muskie returned to the program a week later as the vice presidential candidate.*

August 25, 1968

Violence is in the air on the eve of the ill-fated Democratic National Convention in Chicago. Sen. Edmund S. Muskie (D-ME) is asked about the divisive contest between the "hawkish" vice president, Hubert Humphrey, and "dove" Sen. Eugene McCarthy.

> MUSKIE: The nominee of this convention is going to face difficulties, depending upon whether or not the divisiveness of the preconvention period is carried over into the election campaign . . . I think those who disagree on Vietnam, especially on Vietnam, . . . [ought to] consider whether party unity and victory in November is worth the effort to compose differences here.

The event degenerates into mayhem, with police officers losing control of the crowd and themselves. To chants of "The whole world's watching," the police club and drag demonstrators, and the world sees the Democratic party lose its claim to be a party of order.

Betty Cole Dukert, at the time associate producer of *Meet the Press,* recalls watching the violent scenes on television in her Chicago hotel room and suddenly realizing that the noise was coming not from the television but from the street outside.

September 8, 1968

Some hold government responsible for the growing divisions in society. Richard Nixon's vice presidential running mate, Gov. Spiro T. Agnew (R-MD), pinpoints another cause of the trouble: the demonstrators themselves.

> AGNEW: The yippies and the hippies, I am frank to confess, I will have no truck with. . . . I haven't seen many people who align themselves with these undertakings who don't burn the American flag, who don't fly the flag of the Vietcong, who don't swear allegiance to Ho Chi Minh and Mao Tse-tung and do things that are generally calculated to disrupt the dignity and stature of the United States, and I don't agree with that kind of conduct. . . .
>
> Right now, if three hundred people walked into this studio and stood in front of your cameras and disrupted this program, they would be completely nonviolent, but nonetheless they would be interfering with the rights of others, your sponsors, and you. . . .
>
> JOHN CHANCELLOR (NBC News): Governor, there are people who have been watching both campaigns and they say [Richard Nixon] is going to be the statesman and you are going to be the one who talks out on the hard issues. Is that true?
>
> AGNEW: Do you mean to say that you believe that someone who talks out on hard issues is not a statesman? I thought that was the definition of a statesman.

September 8, 1968: In a typically forthright performance, Republican vice presidential candidate Gov. Spiro T. Agnew of Maryland attacks the "yippies and the hippies" and "the permissiveness that pervades society today."

October 20, 1968

A third party is involved in the 1968 presidential election. George Wallace, the controversial former governor of Alabama, leads the American Independent party into the elections as the first significant third party since 1948. But could he govern the nation?

> WALLACE: I might say that our country hasn't been governed too well in the last number of years. We have a balance of payments problem, we are about to go broke, we have anarchy in the streets of our country, we have a complete destruction of the right of local people to determine local policies, we are bogged down in a no-win war in Asia. We have our friends trading with the enemies of our country. So I don't know that we have been governed too well in the last decade or so.

October 27, 1968

Democratic presidential candidate Hubert H. Humphrey is trailing Richard Nixon in a close race. He accuses the Republican candidate of economic irresponsibility.

> HUMPHREY: He talks about cutting the costs of government, and yet his own proposals on security would cost an extra fifty billion dollars, it is estimated.

Where are you going to get that fifty billion dollars and still have a balanced budget or still cut the federal budget?

Charles W. Bailey of the *Minneapolis Tribune* questions Vice President Humphrey on measures to improve the racial climate.

HUMPHREY: The first thing we must do is to get people to understand that when you help someone who may be deprived or who may be in despair or unemployed, you not only help that person, you help everybody. . . . I believe that when people work together, they tend to learn how to live together. I believe that when you have recessions that divide people from those that are employed and those that are unemployed, it exacerbates the racial tensions.

And what, Jack Perkins (NBC News) asks, if he should lose the election?

HUMPHREY: I have a field of activities that I would engage in, but may I just concentrate for the moment on winning this election, because I really believe I would be a better president of the United States than I would be a professor of political science, because I am a practical man. I have dreams for this country; I have hopes for America. I think that we are going to live during the most exciting period of our history in these next few years, and I want to be a part of it. In fact, I want to be able to lead it.

Lawrence Spivak considered Hubert Humphrey to have one of the most powerful intellects ever to be interviewed on *Meet the Press*. "He doesn't talk off the top of his head. He knows," Spivak told a reporter. "One of his troubles in the 1968 presidential campaign was that a lot of people wouldn't believe that one man could know so much."

November 3, 1968

Richard M. Nixon appears on *Meet the Press* two days before his election as president. He has said that the election is about restoring the people's respect for their government. Vermont Royster (*Wall Street Journal*) asks Richard Nixon why he is the right man for this task.

NIXON: First, I think, Mr. Royster, because Mr. Humphrey is a man of the past and a man who obviously is imprisoned by the record of the past—a record in which the respect for the United States has sunk to its lowest point that we have had in our history, or at least in any recent history. I think he would have great difficulty in restoring that respect.

. . . I think it is the division in the United States, the fact that Mr. Johnson doesn't seem to have control of things, that has destroyed respect.

November 10, 1968

Six months before the moon landing and just after their eleven-day, four-and-a-half-million-mile journey orbiting the earth 163 times, *Apollo 7* astronauts Wally Schirra, Donn F. Eisele, and Walter Cunningham meet the press. There are unconfirmed reports that NASA is about to send astronauts around the moon. Colonel Eisele believes the rumor could soon be reality.

EISELE: I would say that from what I have seen of the spacecraft and the Apollo design in flight that there is no reason from that point of view that you could not embark on such a mission.

Lawrence Spivak asks Walter Cunningham whether the undeclared race to reach the moon before the Russians really matters.

CUNNINGHAM: The term "race" has a certain trite sound to it. I would rather say that two people are after the same goal, and if the Russians are indicating they are any less concerned now about that goal than they were in the past, it is because of their looking at the handwriting on the wall, and it is looking like they are not running number one. I feel very strongly that we have got every chance in the world to keep them running number two.

October 26, 1969: Meet the Press *has an exclusive interview with the shah of Iran during his visit to the United States. A crowd of NBC personnel and other guests gather in the studio after the interview. The shah seems to make a point of shaking hands with only one person, a military-looking young man in a handsome uniform. He is an NBC page, who accepts the greeting graciously and delightedly.*

During a visit to the United States, Bernadette Devlin, twenty-two-year-old Irish Catholic militant elected to the British Parliament, discusses the troubles in Northern Ireland, where she was recently manning the barricades in Derry. Her August 24, 1969 Meet the Press *interview is her first appearance on national TV during the trip.*

September 21, 1969: Russian dictator Joseph Stalin's daughter Svetlana Alliluyeva speaks out.

November 9, 1969

The *Meet the Press* interview with Prince Philip, duke of Edinburgh, causes a storm of controversy in England and leads directly to an improvement in the royal finances. Prince Philip announces that the royal family will go into the red next year because Parliament has not given them a raise for eighteen years. He laments that "we had a small yacht, which we have had to sell, and I shall probably have to give up polo fairly soon." Although the prince's remarks are delivered lightheartedly, they are taken literally in London, where the *Daily Express* is appalled. National honor is at stake. Prime Minister Harold Wilson makes a statement on the floor of the House of Commons, and Parliament soon approves a big increase in the royal family's allowances.

July 13, 1969: Prelaunch coverage of the historic Apollo 11 *moon landing (opposite) mission features the commanders of the three previous Apollo missions: Frank Borman, James A. McDivitt, and Thomas P. Stafford. The interview, from NBC space headquarters at the launch site, takes place just after Borman's return from a tour of the Soviet Union and the* Luna 15 *Soviet moon mission.*

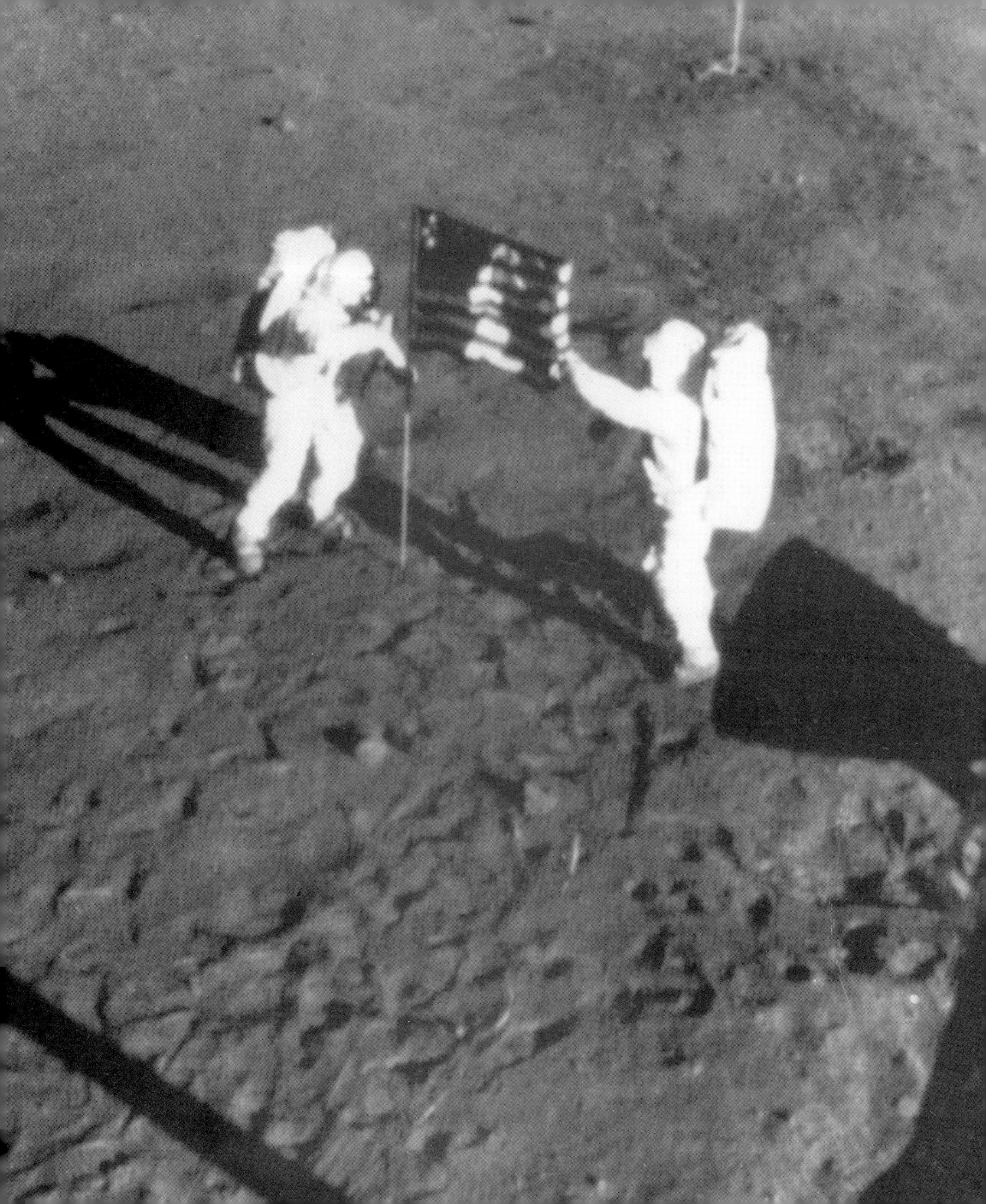

IN THE NEWS

1970

- The Ohio National Guard kills four students at the Kent State campus. Ten days later two more students are shot dead by the National Guard and police at Jackson State College, Mississippi. No one is indicted.
- President Nixon appoints the Scranton Commission to investigate causes of campus unrest. Its report declares the attacks at Kent State and Jackson State unjustified.
- Marxist Salvador Allende is elected president of Chile.

1971

- Cigarette advertising on television is banned.
- A constitutional amendment lowers the voting age to eighteen.
- Publication of the secret *Pentagon Papers* begins in the *New York Times*. The U.S. Supreme Court upholds the press's right to publish under the First Amendment.
- The Chilean government seizes American-owned copper mines.
- Prisoners take over Attica Prison. State troopers and police invade the prison, killing thirty-nine.

1972

- President Nixon meets Mao Tse-tung and Chou En-lai in Peking. They sign an agreement calling for the normalization of relations.
- Nixon and Brezhnev reach a significant agreement on the limitation of strategic nuclear arms.
- Gov. George Wallace of Alabama, running for the Democratic presidential nomination, is shot in Maryland and paralyzed from the waist down.
- Arrests are made following a burglary of Democratic campaign headquarters in the Watergate Hotel.
- At the Olympic Games in Munich, Arab Black September terrorists assault a building housing the Israeli Olympic team, killing two and taking nine hostage. The terrorists' helicopter is attacked on the ground by German sharpshooters. Five terrorists are killed, but not before they murder all nine hostages.
- Richard Nixon wins the presidential election by a landslide over challenger George McGovern.

1973

- The Buffalo Bills' O. J. Simpson reaches two thousand yards rushing.
- The "Watergate 7" go on trial. The burglars' links to the Committee to Reelect the President (CREEP) emerge.
- Jeb Magruder, deputy director of CREEP, confesses, saying Attorney General John Mitchell approved the break-in. Magruder also names President Nixon's counsel John Dean. It emerges that Acting FBI Director L. Patrick Gray has destroyed evidence.
- The Supreme Court rules that a state cannot stop a woman from having an abortion in the first six months of pregnancy (*Roe v. Wade*).
- Cease-fire comes to Vietnam, as Secretary of State William P. Rogers signs the Agreement on Ending the War and Restoring Peace in Vietnam.
- Demands for the return of prisoners of war and information on Americans missing in action are not satisfied. The POW-MIA controversy grows.
- The last American troops leave Vietnam, but the bombing of Cambodia goes on.
- President Nixon announces on television that he has accepted the resignations of his closest aides, Bob Haldeman, John Ehrlichman, and John Dean.
- In televised hearings of the Senate Watergate Committee, evidence of a cover-up mounts.
- Alexander Butterfield reveals that there are tape recordings of all the president's conversations.
- Mitchell, Dean, Ehrlichman, and Haldeman are sentenced to prison.

THE 1970s

- Special Watergate Prosecutor Archibald Cox demands the tapes, but Nixon refuses and orders Attorney General Elliot Richardson to fire Cox. Richardson resigns. Nixon then orders Deputy Attorney General William Ruckelshaus to fire Cox; he also refuses and resigns. Nixon orders Solicitor General Robert H. Bork to fire Cox; he does. The press labels the affair the "Saturday Night Massacre."
- The House votes to cut off funds for the Cambodia bombing.
- The Allende government in Chile is overthrown.
- Yom Kippur: Syria and Egypt carry out a surprise attack on Israel. The Israelis quickly push the Syrians back and are poised to crush Egypt when a cease-fire is negotiated.
- Arab oil exporters put a total ban on oil exports to the United States. The ban is lifted in 1974.
- Vice President Spiro Agnew resigns following charges of income tax evasion. Gerald Ford replaces him.
- A huge rise in the price of oil leads to recession.

1974

- The U.S. Supreme Court rules that President Nixon must hand over the Watergate tapes. Within a week the House Judiciary Committee votes three articles of impeachment against him.
- President Nixon announces his resignation on television. Gerald Ford becomes president.

1975

- President Duong Van Minh of South Vietnam surrenders to the Communists.
- The Rockefeller Commission report on illegal CIA activities is released.
- Newspaper heiress Patricia Hearst is arrested after an armed robbery in Los Angeles.

1976

- The death of Mao Tse-tung is followed by the arrest of the "Gang of Four."
- On July 4, the United States celebrates the two hundredth anniversary of the Declaration of Independence.
- In a raid on Entebbe Airport in Uganda, Israeli commandos rescue 104 hostages held by pro-Palestinian terrorists.
- Jimmy Carter is elected president, promising to "sweep the house of government clean."
- Inflation rises, and the deficit grows.

1977

- Oil shortages mount.
- President Carter pardons Vietnam War draft evaders.
- Elvis Presley dies, at age forty-two.

1978

- The exiled Khomeini calls a general strike in Iran.
- In a mass suicide at Jonestown, Guyana, 909 followers of cult leader Jim Jones die.

1979

- Congress ratifies a treaty giving Panama control of the Panama Canal in twenty years.
- The shah flees Iran and goes to the United States. An Islamic revolution brings Ayatollah Khomeini to power.
- The Camp David Accords are signed by President Sadat of Egypt and Prime Minister Begin of Israel.
- A safety system failure at the Three Mile Island nuclear plant in Pennsylvania causes fears of nuclear disaster.
- President Anastasio Somoza of Nicaragua flees to Miami, and the Sandinistas take over.
- Students seize the U.S. Embassy in Teheran, taking sixty-two Americans hostage.
- Soviet forces invade Afghanistan.

On July 4, 1976, the United States celebrates the Bicentennial, a moment of national unity in a turbulent decade.

Confrontations between government and dissenters explode violently in 1970. During antiwar protests at Kent State University, Ohio, the National Guard kills four students and stuns the nation. Within days the scene is repeated in Mississippi, where police and National Guard gunfire kills two students at Jackson State College.

Congress clashes with presidential power over the Vietnam War, and President Nixon is criticized for the bombing of Cambodia. But the last American troops leave Vietnam in 1973, and the long war ends.

Presidential abuses are uncovered in the Watergate affair. The scandal begins before the 1972 presidential election, with a burglary at the Democratic party headquarters in Washington's Watergate Hotel. It leads to the resignation of President Nixon in 1974 and threatens America's faith in the probity of its government. Georgia Gov. Jimmy Carter is elected president in 1976 on a promise of simple honesty. On his first day in office he tries to heal old wounds by pardoning Vietnam draft evaders.

Détente makes real progress. In a sea change in world politics President Nixon visits Chinese leaders Mao Tse-tung and Chou En-lai. In Moscow the president negotiates a major agreement on strategic arms limitation with Soviet Premier Leonid Brezhnev. And in 1979 Presi-

dent Carter brokers a peace agreement between Israel and Egypt. But new threats to peace appear as the decade ends. With internal strife rumbling through the Kremlin, Soviet troops enter Afghanistan in 1979. This unwinnable war will leave Russian morale bleeding for years.

The invasion of Afghanistan comes after the overthrow of the shah of Iran by followers of the exiled Islamic scholar Ayatollah Khomeini. The Iranian Revolution brings an unfamiliar but ancient threat to the West: Islamic fundamentalism. Militant Iranian students seize the American Embassy in Teheran, taking sixty-two hostages. Worldwide television audiences see the hostages forced to walk through hostile streets humiliated. The hostage crisis overshadows the final year of the Carter administration.

The Middle East casts a shadow over the decade. Arab terrorism makes a shocking entry on the world stage when Black September terrorists slaughter Israeli athletes before the 1972 Munich Olympic Games. America is soon forced into awareness of its dependence on fickle Middle Eastern oil supplies. The decade sees a huge rise in the price of oil, and a briefly alarming ban on Middle Eastern oil exports to the United States leads to recession. Long lines form at gas stations, and tempers fray, as America contemplates the prospect of gas rationing. This awareness—and a near disaster at the Three Mile Island nuclear plant—boosts the environmental movement and stimulates a search for alternative energy supplies.

The 1970s see high levels of unemployment and a spate of strikes. In 1979 inflation reaches 18 percent. America is ready to change.

A third-rate burglary at the Watergate Hotel in Washington, D.C., leads to the resignation of a disgraced president. Faith in politicians suffers, but investigative journalism receives a boost.

Bill Monroe became moderator and executive producer of *Meet the Press* on Lawrence Spivak's retirement in 1975. He had previously acted as occasional moderator and panel member.

Monroe came to NBC as Washington bureau chief in 1961 after six years as news director of WDSU-TV in his native New Orleans. He was at one time the only full-time radio news reporter in New Orleans, and his broadcasts were sponsored by a Bourbon Street nightclub. A Phi Beta Kappa graduate of Tulane University, Monroe entered journalism with United Press International. During his tenure as associate editor at the *New Orleans Item* he edited a letters page, and he introduced a viewers' letters segment to *Meet the Press*, seeing this dialogue with viewers as part of the democratic process. He also experimented with the use of two guests airing opposing views on the same program.

His most visible innovation at *Meet the Press* was to sit with the panel. Previous moderators sat alongside the guest, opposite four reporters. Monroe changed the formation by joining three reporters facing the guest, which created a more dramatic confrontation.

Monroe left *Meet the Press* in September 1984 after nine years in the moderator's chair. Before coming to *Meet the Press*, he had been Washington editor and interviewer for the *Today* show for seven years, and in 1984 he introduced a regular letters to the editor segment on the *Today* show.

The letters segment on *Meet the Press* ended with Monroe's departure, partly because it reduced the time available for questioning and partly because the producers realized that much of the letter writing was organized by campaigns and lobbies.

January 18, 1970

The United States is confronting some of the most serious problems in its history as Congress begins its first session of the 1970s. Lawrence Spivak asks the two Republican leaders of Congress—Senate Minority Leader Hugh Scott of Pennsylvania, and Gerald R. Ford of Michigan, House minority leader—to outline their priorities.

> SCOTT: I think the first priority on the domestic scene is a lawful, ordered society, and therefore the entire package of proposed crime legislation should be given the earliest possible priority. I think that backed up with that are, of course, all of the measures needed to improve the quality of our environment.
>
> FORD: I would say we need to change welfare to workfare, the president's recommendation to overhaul our welfare program. . . . Too many of those in the past under existing programs who wanted to extricate themselves from the welfare cycle have been penalized when they got a job.

Ford also expresses optimism about further troop reductions in Vietnam. "The president has a program, as you well know, for the orderly and constructive withdrawal of American combat military

personnel from Vietnam. The program was announced early in 1969. It is proceeding actually ahead of schedule, because of the Vietnamization program."

April 26, 1970

Unrest on the nation's campuses is a major obstacle to Senator Scott's "lawful, ordered society." On April 26, 1970, the report of the Special Committee on Campus Tensions is published, and three committee members—chairman Sol M. Linowitz, Robben W. Fleming of the University of Michigan, and Stanford University student body president Patrick Shea—come to *Meet the Press* to explain their findings.

Shea warns that the worst is yet to come.

SHEA: At Stanford the other day people proudly announced that we had moved out of the sixties, when nonviolent sit-ins were the way of confronting the university and that we now had to move into violent mobile tactics. . . .

JERROLD K. FOOTLICK (*Newsweek*): It is also said that a very small group of radicals, "by finding an issue," can mobilize the great sort of uncommitted mass in the center. How is it that students in the center who might not agree with the radicals' first issue can be mobilized so quickly?

SHEA: It is because of the basic tone of alienation that underlies almost every student's participation in the university and the polarizing comments that come from what I consider to be very ill-informed and oftentimes ignorant politicians, be it on the local level, the state level, or the federal level.

John D. Rockefeller IV, secretary of state of West Virginia, becomes the fourth Rockefeller to "meet the press," on March 29, 1970. The Democrat follows three Republican uncles: Gov. Nelson A. Rockefeller of New York, Gov. Winthrop Rockefeller of Arkansas, and David Rockefeller of the Chase Manhattan Bank.

April 26, 1970: Student leader Patrick Shea (near left) warns that student unrest could lead to violence. Eight days later, four students are killed at Kent State University in Ohio (opposite).

Committee Chairman Sol Linowitz is equally pessimistic:

LINOWITZ: We do say in the report, and say it I think forcefully, that so long as young men are obliged to fight a war in Vietnam with which they disagree and which they regard as unjust, as long as we continue to demean the quality of our environment, as long as racial discrimination flourishes, there is going to be trouble on the campus. . . .

EDWIN NEWMAN (NBC News): Suppose the United States becomes more deeply involved in Cambodia; what do you think the effect will be on the campus?

LINOWITZ: I think quite clearly it will exacerbate the situation.

On April 30, President Nixon sends thirty thousand troops into Cambodia. Four days later the Ohio National Guard kills four students on the campus at Kent State University.

May 3, 1970

On the eve of the Kent State massacre, a ray of hope. Christiaan Barnard, the South African surgeon who performed the world's first successful transplant of a human heart, talks about his breakthrough.

> BARNARD: We have learned that one can take a patient who is dying from an incurable heart disease with a very low heart output, that we can take the heart from a corpse, from a cadaver, that we can transplant this heart into the patient and immediately within a few minutes, increase his cardiac output by threefold, that these patients will lose all the symptoms and signs of terminal heart failure and that they will survive for some months and some even a year and more after such a transplant. . . . There is no doubt that once we solve the problem of rejection, then this will be the operation for most of the heart diseases we treat today in a quite different way.

Dr. Barnard also expresses himself on an issue destined to remain a more divisive and durable force in American life than campus tensions: abortion.

> BARNARD: I am absolutely opposed to abortion unless it is in cases where there is a great belief that the child will have gross congenital anomalies and where it is believed the mother's health will

suffer as a result of the pregnancy. I feel that as doctors our duty is to save lives and preserve lives, and therefore, I cannot agree with abortions just because the female is pregnant.

Two weeks later on *Meet the Press* (May 17, 1970), Robert Packwood (R-OR), youngest member of the Senate, disagrees with Dr. Barnard's view. He recently introduced a bill to eliminate all restrictions against abortion and another to limit to two the number of children who can be declared as personal income tax exemptions.

PACKWOOD: I think it is a matter of private conscience and personal choice. Most of the people in this country do not regard abortion as murder. Most of the people, unless I misjudge their feelings, think that it ought to be a matter of personal conviction for any woman. Those who believe it is murder, those who don't want to do it certainly are not compelled to.

On September 7, 1995, Packwood resigned from the Senate following charges of extensive sexual harassment.

September 27, 1970

Law enforcement officers kill four students on the Kent State, Ohio, campus and two students at the Jackson State, Mississippi, campus during protests. Grand juries indict no one. President Nixon appoints the Scranton Commission to investigate the causes of campus unrest, and on the weekend their report appears, chairman William W. Scranton (former governor of Pennsylvania) comes to *Meet the Press* with commission members James Ahern (chief of police of New Haven, Connecticut) and Joseph Rhodes, Jr., of Harvard University.

RHODES: One of the hard things we have to get across in the country is that people are really being

April 18, 1971: Al Hubbard (left) and John Kerry (right) of Vietnam Veterans Against the War defend their position. In May 1988 Kerry appeared on Meet the Press *as chairman of the Senate Foreign Relations Subcommittee on Terrorism, Narcotics, and International Communications.*

killed. I mean, when you talk about punishing criminal students, you are sometimes talking about killing somebody's children, and we have to remind the American people that that is the consequence and the cost of bringing down repression on the student movement.

We found people in law enforcement in Jackson who demonstrated a remarkable incredible lack of concern for the human life of black people. . . . We found that in both cases the use of the deadly force was completely unjustified.

AHERN: I think that there are some fundamental problems in our society and in this country, and police have been put in the role of being the cutting edge of government.

Meet *the Press* celebrates its twenty-third television birthday on November 6, 1970. "Only one big issue today did not appear in the early years of *Meet the Press*—campus unrest," observes Lawrence Spivak.

In the early 1970s the war in Vietnam was a continuing cause of division at home.

May 30, 1971: The consumer movement was a growing force in the 1970s, with Ralph Nader its charismatic crusader. On his second *Meet the Press* appearance, Nader says that "the entire economy in this country depends on responsible corporate power," but that the corporations are not taking responsibility for the pollution they cause. "They all respond to the same syndromes. That is, if a company is not going to be subjected to greater costs for polluting than not polluting, its internal economical calculus is to continue polluting because it doesn't pay the cost. The public pays the cost. . . . What we simply need to do is to make an inventory of all the impacts that the corporations have on society and ask: Why are the costs not integrated into the costs of doing business? Once they are, then the motivation becomes quite appropriately channeled in the direction of the public interest."

September 19, 1971

The continuing Vietnam War is a major cause of confrontation within the United States, but in a foreign policy development of major significance, America's relations with Red China are improving. President Nixon has been invited to visit China, and a key United Nations vote on the admission of Communist China to the UN is imminent. The United States—reversing a long-held position—has drafted resolutions calling for the admission of Peking in both the Assembly and the Security Council, and it is widely assumed the UN will vote to admit China. Before the vote, Taiwan's foreign minister, S. K. Chow, says "we would have to protest" China's admission, which could "spell the end of the UN itself." He considers China's groundbreaking invitation to President Nixon to be no more than a stage in Peking's long-term plan to destroy Nationalist China. Could the improvement in America's relations with Peking force Taiwan to seek help from Moscow? the panel wondered.

CHOW: Well, Churchill once said that if the devil could save England, he would conclude an alliance with the devil. In the first place, our position is not desperate. In the second place, no devil is in sight.

LAWRENCE SPIVAK: Are you investigating the possibility of an alliance?

CHOW: We will see when the devil appears.

October 31, 1971

Links with Asian Communist regimes may be forming, but the United States remains determined to stop Castro's Cuba from infecting South America with communism. In 1971 the focus is on Chile and its Marxist president, Dr. Salvador Allende. *Meet the Press* Associate Producer Betty Cole Dukert travels to Santiago with a technical expert to set up an interview with Dr. Allende, the first freely elected Marxist head of state in the Western Hemisphere. A month before, Allende's government nationalized American-owned copper mines. The president justifies this act, arguing that "the interests of the two private enterprises cannot prevail over the interests of a people," and that "copper means eighty-three percent of the foreign exchange earned by my country." After explaining his brand of socialism, Allende positions himself.

ALLENDE: I am not only an admirer of Fidel Castro's, I am also an admirer, and deeply so, of those who fought and gave freedom to the United States. I am an admirer of Lincoln, for example, when he said that a country cannot survive half slave and half free. And I apply these standards. I don't have the gall to be an autocrat. I am an authentic democrat, but I believe that democracy is not the formal democracy that has existed in developing countries basically.

JEREMIAH O'LEARY (*Washington Star*): I would say the only similarity between Castro and Lincoln is that they both have beards.

The interview was by satellite, with three questioners and the moderator in Washington, Allende and NBC Latin American correspondent Tom Streithorst in a government-controlled television station in Santiago. Betty Cole Dukert remembers a confrontation with the station manager, who appeared

Chile's Marxist President Salvador Allende was interviewed via satellite from a government-controlled television station in Santiago (right).

to be a key press aide to the president as well. "He tried hard to get me to change the introduction to the program, which our moderator in Washington was to read. The manager was disputing our introduction of President Allende as the first freely elected Marxist head of state in Latin America. He insisted to me that Fidel Castro was the first. I held my ground that Fidel Castro had not been freely elected, and he eventually dropped his opposition."

President Allende spoke in Spanish, not a new problem to Betty Cole Dukert. "For interpreted programs, we insist upon UN or State Department-quality interpreters, but always ones the guests approve of as well. Otherwise, if they didn't like the way the questioning went, they could blame the interpreters." Dukert agreed in advance with the Chilean Embassy upon two interpreters who were to provide simultaneous interpretation from the studio in Washington. All ran smoothly. "After the program I found out that the station manager had positioned a third interpreter in a control room at the Santiago station, ready to override the Washington interpreter for the president if the manager thought it necessary. That would have caused technical, if not diplomatic, chaos on the air undoubtedly. Fortunately, the Chilean 'censor' didn't find it necessary to interfere."

Two years after the interview Allende's government was overthrown in a coup that put General Pinochet in power.

December 5, 1971

Instability in the Middle East remains a foreign policy concern. Since swift victory in the Six-Day War, Israel has occupied Egypt as far west as the Suez Canal. Golda Meir, prime minister of Israel, is asked if Israel might withdraw from its position east of Suez, as Egypt demands.

> MEIR: What kind of arrangement is this that we step back from our fortifications and they immediately come over?

However, her assessment of the risk of renewed Suez hostilities is optimistic.

> MEIR: [President Sadat] said the decision has been taken: We will meet in the Sinai. Well, it is better than what the late President Nasser said in '67: We will meet in Tel Aviv. . . . We hope that President Sadat will think once more and will be prepared to come to the negotiating table, direct or indirect, with no preconditions, and in that way the problems can be solved.

Bill Monroe (NBC News) and Golda Meir.

At the decade's end Egypt and Israel will reach a peace agreement at Camp David.

May 7, 1972

President Nixon's triumph in Peking is not matched by success at home. Increasingly, the Nixon administration has been expressing concern about media hostility, and White House aide Pat Buchanan recently has called for antitrust proceedings against the media giants because of perceived anticonservative bias. John Ehrlichman,

I think the President was as good a poker player as he was because of his emotional makeup. He is not an individual who reacts emotionally to what someone else does. He is coolest when he is under fire, and I think, using the poker analogy from my own observation, he is a man who very seldom is called when he doesn't have the cards in his hand. He doesn't run a bluff.

—John Ehrlichman on Richard Nixon, May 7, 1972

assistant to the president for domestic affairs, reassures the panel that in spite of appearances, no such proceedings are planned. "I don't think that the media's problem is one of antitrust, it is really one of public trust," he says.

Ehrlichman is concerned by the growth of "advocacy journalism and the dedication of young journalists today to salting away in their reporting on facts their own personal points of view on what should or should not be done." The phenomenon to which he refers was widely known as the New Journalism, in which a new breed of journalists was making an impact as personalities. But the real threat to the Nixon administration would come from old-fashioned investigative reporting in the Watergate affair.

July 16, 1972

Four months before the presidential election Watergate makes its appearance on *Meet the Press,* as Sen. Robert Dole, chairman of the Republican National Committee, faces Robert Novak of the *Chicago Sun-Times.*

NOVAK: Senator Dole, while everybody's attention was focused on the Democrats in Miami Beach, there was a development in the U.S. District Court in Washington in connection with the million-dollar damage suit that the Democratic National Committee has brought against the Committee to Reelect President Nixon, in connection with the break-in and bugging at the Democratic national headquarters, and the lawyers for the Republican committee asked for a postponement until after the election on the grounds that the hearings would "cause grave damage to the president's campaign and perhaps force disclosure of confidential information." Senator, just what is it you have to hide in this case?

DOLE: I don't have anything to hide. . . . The Republican National Committee hasn't been sued.

July 16, 1972: Meet the Press *Producer Lawrence Spivak is the moderator as Bob Dole makes one of his record fifty-six appearances.*

. . . But in any event the suit was filed, knowing the federal discovery rules would allow all kinds of witch hunts, and that is what they want.

. . .

NOVAK: Senator, you repeatedly differentiate between the Republican party and the Committee to Reelect President Nixon. On July 1, you said "the Republican party" certainly had nothing to do with the Watergate caper. Are you suggesting maybe the Committee to Reelect President Nixon did have something to do with it?

DOLE: No, I am not suggesting that at all. John Mitchell has spoken out on that many times, as has Clark MacGregor, as has Chuck Colson in the White House, but my responsibility as chairman is with the Republican National Committee, and I made that statement on behalf of the committee.

September 10, 1972

The Supreme Court's *Roe v. Wade* ruling was to come in January 1973, and abortion is a contentious issue in the approaching presidential election. Representatives of the National Women's Political Caucus—founded in 1971 to win a bigger role for women on the political stage—attend both party conventions. Two members of the Policy Council appear together on *Meet the Press*—Gloria Steinem and Jill Ruckelshaus. Both express disappointment that the Republican and Democratic parties appear to be ducking the abortion issue.

RUCKELSHAUS: I think the public is way out in front of the politicians on this issue. The politicians have listened, I think, probably to the intensity of the argument rather than to the diversity of the argument. . . .

SHANA ALEXANDER (*Newsweek*): Ms. Steinem, I think we would all agree with you that the women's movement has made greater progress in

the last year or two than in the fifty years since women got the vote, but since it is a militant movement, I would like to ask you, as you see it, who is the enemy now?

STEINEM: I wouldn't call it a militant movement, because "militant" connotes violence, and to me, I would more likely call the Pentagon a militant movement. . . . [T]he adversary, which is the word that I prefer to "enemy," are those individuals who have usurped control of our lives, and who in general turn out to be that three percent of the population which is white, male, over thirty, and college-educated.

. . .

RUCKELSHAUS: I think what this movement is about is the full expression of a woman's potential, and that includes for many women a husband and a family. But that is not the full expression. The husband and family cannot be the full expression. I think many women stop short of their own evolution when they think they have reached their capacity, when they are married and raising a family.

. . .

STEINEM: What kind of choice is it, after all, to be able to go out and earn half as much as a man for doing exactly the same work? Could she support her family? Could she support her children? Should she tell her daughter that she could? I think not.

October 1, 1972

With only a month to go before the presidential election, Democratic challenger Sen. George McGovern is lagging dismally behind President Nixon in every poll. How, *Meet the Press* asks his wife, Eleanor McGovern, can he persuade the American people to be angry and come over to his side?

MCGOVERN: I fervently believe that this is the most corrupt regime that we have had in recent American history, and I think people, when they know the full story, won't like that.

I think that this is a regime where we have lost freedoms, and we are not aware of it. It is some insidious thing that comes upon us very slowly.

I think that is the lesson of Watergate. If one administration can feel free to bug the private office of another major party, then there will be no refraining from bugging the offices here, or your office, or our homes.

October 8, 1972: President Marcos of the Philippines is grilled by the *Meet the Press* panel about his imposition of martial law on September 21. And the peculiar result is a rise in his popularity in the Philippines, where the show is seen by a huge television audience in spite of a 1:00 A.M. showing. Filipino viewers find themselves supporting their beleaguered president as he fends off aggressive questions.

The interview had to take place in the palace as it was not safe for Marcos to go outside. A Marcos aide proposed the roof, but the noise of nearby river traffic was too loud. The aide suggested simply stopping the boats but before that became necessary, Marcos agreed to be interviewed in his office. The president turned the occasion into a party, inviting the entire Cabinet and Imelda to a reception and dinner before the interview.

October 22, 1972

With his latest poll showing President Nixon with a commanding twenty-five-point lead over George McGovern, Louis Harris is the guest on *Meet the Press*. He tells NBC's Paul Duke that "the Watergate issue is beginning to take some hold, and we do find it making some dents in Mr. Nixon now." Nevertheless, it is Nixon—not McGovern—the electorate says, who "represented the kind of change that they hoped would take place in America in the next four years," thanks in great part to his bold and successful visits to Peking and Moscow.

May 30, 1972: Democratic presidential candidates Hubert Humphrey and George McGovern (back to camera) are the guests in a one-hour Meet the Press *special.*

> **E**valuating *Meet the Press* both as a viewer and one who has appeared on the program, I feel that *Meet the Press* has made a tremendous contribution to the people's right to know and has been of inestimable value in keeping the public informed.
>
> —Gerald R. Ford, commenting on the program's twenty-fifth anniversary

November 5, 1972

Meet the Press celebrates its twenty-fifth anniversary with a one-hour special. The guests are Secretary of State William Rogers and George Shultz, the secretary of the treasury.

The secretary of state is asked to justify Henry Kissinger's dramatic preelection claim that "peace is at hand" in Vietnam.

> ROGERS: We do have a deal that we have worked out with North Vietnam that I am confident can be completed in the near future.

November 26, 1972

Gov. George Wallace withdrew from the Democratic presidential primaries in May after being wounded in an assassination attempt in Maryland. In November he appears on *Meet the Press*.

He was in very poor physical condition following the attempt on his life, and the *Meet the Press* staff was concerned that he might not have the stamina to complete the show. As a precautionary measure the program was recorded a day in advance, and an arrangement was made for him to press a button to alert the producers if he felt he could not go on. But when the interview began, he rose to the challenge.

> PETER LISAGOR (*Chicago Daily News*): Governor Wallace, a great many Americans are interested in your disability. Can you tell us how great it is and whether you can remain active?
>
> WALLACE: Mr. Lisagor, I can remain active. In fact I have been active. As you know, I attended the Democratic convention itself, only a few weeks after I was shot in Maryland.
>
> I am not able to jump over some of the fences at the airports where I land, like I used to be able to do, but my condition is coming along all right, other than the fact that I am paralyzed and I recognize the fact that there is not much chance that I will ever walk again.

October 14, 1973: Former Teamsters Union President James R. Hoffa returns to Meet the Press.

January 7, 1973

President Nixon was reelected in November, but suspicions are mounting about the Watergate burglary. The day before the trial of the alleged Watergate burglars, John Ehrlichman and Herbert G. Klein, director of communications for the executive branch, answer questions. Watergate is on everyone's mind.

> EHRLICHMAN: There was an investigation conducted with regard to the question of whether or not anyone in the administration was involved in the Watergate case, and that investigation disclosed . . . that there was no involvement by anyone in the administration in that particular set of circumstances.

April 22, 1973

Sen. Edward W. Brooke (R-MA) expresses doubts about the White House Watergate story.

> BROOKE: It is difficult to understand how persons working with the president would not have made known to him an enterprise of this magnitude, involving hundreds of thousands of dollars and involving such potential risk as the Watergate incident involved. It is inconceivable to me that they would not have told the president about this matter, in fact that they wouldn't have asked for his approval or disapproval.

May 20, 1973

Watergate is not the only revelation to rock the public's faith in government in the early 1970s. In 1971 a former State Department and Defense Department worker, Dr. Daniel Ellsberg, gives the *New York Times* the sensational *Pentagon Papers*, a secret study on U.S. decision making in Vietnam. A Supreme Court decision upholding the newspaper's right to publish does not clear Ellsberg, who is tried for espionage, theft, and conspiracy. He goes free when his trial comes to a sudden end after eighty-nine days. On *Meet the Press* Dr. Ellsberg denies that his actions compromised any secret negotiations and tries to distinguish between his behavior and the Watergate burglars'.

> ELLSBERG: I have not met a lawyer in this country who could say clearly that the acts I admitted doing—copying the *Pentagon Papers*, of which

May 20, 1973: Dr. Daniel Ellsberg justifies his behavior in releasing the secret Pentagon Papers *to the press. "I still think it was the right thing to do," he says.*

I had authorized possession, and giving those copies to the Senate Foreign Relations Committee, ultimately to the press—violated any law.

LAWRENCE SPIVAK: Because of our involvement in Vietnam and because of what has happened with the *Pentagon Papers* and the Watergate case, a great many of our youth have lost faith in our institutions. Have you? You have thirty seconds.

ELLSBERG: I never did, and I am glad to say right now I have never had more hope, not based on faith but on evidence of what I see these days, that our government is functioning. Our government is not the president; the government is not the executive branch. These other branches of government are functioning to protect us from abuses by the executive branch, and they have never functioned better in our history.

REPORTERS WITH THE MOST *Meet the Press* APPEARANCES*

David S. Broder (*Washington Post*): 306
May Craig (*Portland*, Maine, *Press Herald*): 243
Robert Novak (*Chicago Sun-Times*): 210
Richard Wilson (*Cowles Publications*): 175
Marquis Childs (*St. Louis Post-Dispatch*): 163
Elizabeth Drew (*New Yorker*): 132

*Through June 30, 1997.

October 21, 1973: (left to right) David S. Broder, George Will, Robert Novak, and Tom Brokaw.

June 10, 1973

The Watergate hearings are a month old when George Bush, now chairman of the Republican National Committee, discusses the issue on *Meet the Press*.

> BUSH: I have made the point ever since I came here and before I came here, publicly, openly, that we want to see this thing fully resolved. To my knowledge, the Republican party National Committee is not involved. I have said if I found anybody there that was involved, they would be fired. We are going to keep this party clean, and the sooner the matter—the sooner the system works, the better off we are.
>
> . . .
>
> One thing we can do with this Watergate deal is to prove that we have a good system. We have to purge ourselves on the highest levels.

Bush's aggressive response does not augur well for the president.

July 29, 1973

Mohammed Reza Pahlavi, the shah of Iran, heads the world's oldest monarchy and the second-largest oil producer in the Middle East. On *Meet the Press*

The *Meet the Press* unit produced a one-hour prime-time special entitled "June 30, 1971, A Day for History: The Supreme Court and the Pentagon Papers," which won NBC an Emmy Award in 1972 for Outstanding Achievement in Coverage of Special Events. Lawrence Spivak was executive producer of the program, which was moderated by Edwin Newman (NBC News). Guests were Benjamin Bradlee (executive editor, the *Washington Post*), Max Frankel (Washington bureau chief, the *New York Times*), Sen. Henry M. Jackson, and Deputy Undersecretary of State William McComber.

he has a warning for the West: "[I]f you started to form a coalition against the price of oil, then tomorrow we will form a coalition against the price of tin cans. This cannot go on."

> ROBERT KEATLEY (*Wall Street Journal*): Your Majesty, what is the possibility that Arab oil producers, including Saudi Arabia, may attempt to use oil as a political weapon in the Arab-Israeli problem?
>
> SHAH: This is always a possibility.

December 9, 1973: Saudi Arabia's Minister of Petroleum Sheik Ahmed Zaki al-Yamani is the guest as oil price rises force Western nations to regret their dependence on foreign supplies.

September 9, 1973

The revelation that the Nixon administration secretly recorded White House conversations—including discussions of Watergate—leads to demands for the tapes from the Senate select committee investigating the Watergate affair. After the White House wins a court delay in responding to the committee's suit, committee member Sen. Daniel Inouye (D-HI) tells *Meet the Press* the committee can proceed without the tapes.

> INOUYE: If this were a criminal matter, I would say that the tapes are absolutely necessary, essential, but in our case I think we can proceed and file an adequate report without the tapes.

This statement by Senator Inouye made *Meet the Press* part of the Watergate story. On October 4, at a hearing to determine whether the Senate Watergate Committee was entitled to the Watergate tapes, U.S. District Judge John Sirica read out a transcript of Inouye's remarks on *Meet the Press*. Chief committee counsel Samuel Dash was forced to admit that the committee could do without the tapes.

When the public saw transcripts of the White House Watergate tapes, they saw *Meet the Press* mentioned again. The White House, it emerged, had been looking for ways of getting out its message, and President Nixon considered the options. "Rather than going to a hearing," he told his inner circle, "do *Meet the Press*, and that will force the hearing to call [Sullivan]." Former FBI official Sullivan was believed to have information on President Johnson's alleged bugging of Spiro T. Agnew's campaign plane. President Nixon was well aware of the program's power. In 1972 he had written to Lawrence Spivak, "For twenty-five years you have provided a fair and vital forum from which men and women in the public eye have been able to meet the press."

In December 1973 a rise in the price of oil brings on recession in the United States.

October 21, 1973

Tom Brokaw makes his first appearance on the *Meet the Press* panel, the day after the "Saturday Night Massacre," during which Watergate Special Prosecutor Archibald Cox was dismissed on the orders of the president. Brokaw has reason to remember the experience. "It seemed like it was going to be a routine week. Melvin Laird, who was the White House counsel at the time, was the guest. And then the Saturday Night Massacre happened the night before I was to appear.

"I arrived at the studios early, and Larry Spivak met me at the front door, all four foot nine inches of him or whatever he is—one hundred four pounds—and I felt as if I were going up against Woody Hayes.

"He grabbed ahold of me and dragged me into a room and he said, 'Listen, this is going to be the most important program all year, and tradition has it that the NBC correspondent gets to ask the first question, so it better damn well be a good question. You've got to get to the heart of the news right away, because the whole program will depend on it.'

"And I am quavering at this point. . . . So I said my opening question to Mel Laird. 'Mr. Laird, given the events of last night in Washington, D.C., is there any reason whatsoever that the House of Representatives shouldn't begin immediate impeachment proceedings against the President of the United States?'

"And with that Lawrence E. Spivak leaned back and smiled, and we began a lifelong friendship."

January 6, 1974

The Nixon administration is under siege, and the American people can see the story unfold on television. In October 1973 Vice President Spiro Agnew resigns after charges of income tax evasion. Gerald Ford takes over as vice president, the first vice president in history to be nominated by a president and confirmed by Congress. When Ford appears on *Meet the Press,* Watergate questions dominate, and he declares himself certain of the president's innocence.

> FORD: I am sure he turned to those running the reelection campaign and said, "I have these major matters that involve the national security and the well-being of the American people, and you run the campaign."
>
> Unfortunately, those that ran, some of them apparently ran it badly, but I am convinced that the

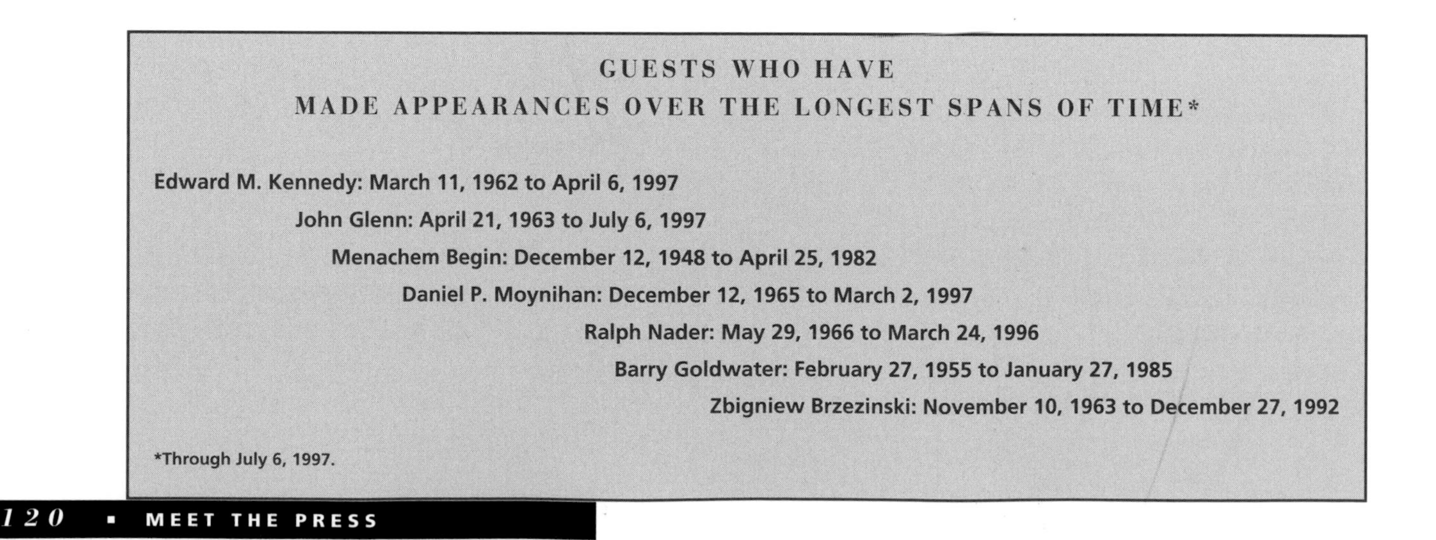

GUESTS WHO HAVE
MADE APPEARANCES OVER THE LONGEST SPANS OF TIME*

Edward M. Kennedy: March 11, 1962 to April 6, 1997

John Glenn: April 21, 1963 to July 6, 1997

Menachem Begin: December 12, 1948 to April 25, 1982

Daniel P. Moynihan: December 12, 1965 to March 2, 1997

Ralph Nader: May 29, 1966 to March 24, 1996

Barry Goldwater: February 27, 1955 to January 27, 1985

Zbigniew Brzezinski: November 10, 1963 to December 27, 1992

*Through July 6, 1997.

president was preoccupied with these very important matters, and therefore am convinced he had nothing whatsoever to do with Watergate.

January 20, 1974

Gov. Ronald Reagan of California is being mentioned for the 1976 Republican presidential nomination.

LAWRENCE SPIVAK: There are many political observers who are convinced no conservative can be elected president of the United States. Obviously you don't think so. Do you mind telling us why you think a conservative can be elected president?

REAGAN: We get into those definitions again of what is a conservative and what is a liberal. Some people, when you say that word "conservative," automatically think you are talking about a monster who eats his young.

April 28, 1974

Elliot Richardson resigned as attorney general in October 1973 rather than obey President Nixon's order to dismiss Watergate Special Prosecutor Archibald Cox. It was Solicitor General Robert H. Bork, acting as attorney general, who agreed to fire Cox (see *Meet the Press,* October 4, 1987). On *Meet the Press* Richardson reflects on the use and abuse of presidential power.

PETER LISAGOR (*Chicago Daily News*): Do you think the president has become too powerful, so that he has reached beyond the point of being checked and balanced out by the other branches?

RICHARDSON: I do think there has been an excessive concentration of power in the hands of the presidency, and I think part of the answer to this is the assertion of more aggressive oversight by the Congress of executive branch functions.

May 5, 1974

James D. St. Clair, special counsel to the president, was appointed by President Nixon in January 1974 to take charge of legal affairs associated with Watergate. He rarely spoke to reporters, but after the damaging release of transcripts of White House tape recordings, he appears on *Meet the Press* to put the case for an increasingly beleaguered White House. "I think the president feels he has given them everything that he thinks they need," he says, "and I hope they come to the conclusion that this is, in fact, as the president says, the full story of Watergate."

GEORGE F. WILL (*National Review*): Mr. St. Clair, on March 21, Mr. Nixon said to Mr. Dean that a one-hundred-and-twenty-thousand-dollar hush money payment to Howard Hunt was—and I quote—"the thing that you better get done." . . . Do you think it is important to Mr. Nixon's defense that it be shown that there was not a payment that night?

ST. CLAIR: No, I don't think it is. Mr. Nixon's defense is not dependent upon whether or not such a payment was made. His defense is dependent upon whether he authorized it or even knew of its payment, and the tapes, in my judgment, make it clear that he neither authorized it nor knew that it had been paid.

June 2, 1974

Six governors, including Jimmy Carter of Georgia, are asked if the best interests of the country would be served by the president's leaving office through resignation. All six (four Democrats and two Republicans) reply that he should resign or be impeached, and they are equally unanimous about his obligation to hand over the subpoenaed tapes to the Judiciary Committee.

CARTER: One of the most devastating consequences this year of the impeachment preoccupation by the president and his administration is that there has been a breakdown in the normal federalist system of cooperation between the state and federal governments. In the field of revenue sharing, for instance, there was no revenue to spare. . . . [There] has been in the last two years an almost complete inability for state governments to deal in a predictable way with the federal government.

June 30, 1974

President Nixon briefly leaves domestic pressures behind. Henry Kissinger and he are in Moscow, negotiating a strategic arms pact with Soviet Premier Leonid Brezhnev, when Adm. Elmo R. Zumwalt, chief of naval operations, appears on *Meet the Press* on the eve of his retirement after thirty-five years in the navy. The admiral makes it clear that he has been ordered to say nothing about strategic weapons.

JOHN W. FINNEY (*New York Times*): Admiral, this muffled Zumwalt is most uncharacteristic. I wonder, where did the orders come from that you were not to discuss strategic matters today?

ZUMWALT: Let me say, first, that I have always meticulously carried out my orders. This is just another order. This particular order emanates from the secretary of defense.

June 30, 1974: Adm. Elmo R. Zumwalt (seated next to Lawrence Spivak) brings his family to the studio.

In 1976 Zumwalt was campaigning for a Senate nomination when he named Secretary of State Henry Kissinger—not Secretary of Defense James Schlesinger, who relayed the message from Moscow—as "the driving force" behind the ban. He further claimed that President Nixon had threatened him with a court-martial if he discussed strategic weapons on *Meet the Press*. A Kissinger spokesman was reported as calling Zumwalt's charge "characteristically irresponsible."

July 28, 1974

Prof. Charles L. Black, Jr., of Yale Law School, is the author of *Impeachment: A Handbook*. The impeachment of President Nixon is under way as the professor explains the process on *Meet the Press*. Three weeks later President Nixon resigns.

October 20, 1974

Within a month of President Nixon's resignation, President Ford has granted the disgraced former president a full pardon. Is it fair, the *Meet the Press* panel asks Watergate Special Prosecutor Leon Jaworski, that Mr. Nixon's former subordinates should be prosecuted when their boss has been pardoned, even though the tapes show he ordered at least parts of the cover-up?

> JAWORSKI: I think the pardoning power is one that ought to be exercised individually and on a basis of individual facts. I do not believe in any across-the-board pardoning power.

Robert Woodward of the *Washington Post* is on the panel. The *Post*'s Watergate coverage by Woodward and his colleague Carl Bernstein played a crucial role in revealing the Watergate scandal to the public. Many of their major revelations were inspired by a mysterious informer known as Deep Throat.

> WOODWARD: In the cover-up trial it was stated by some of your assistants that John Mitchell approved the Watergate break-in. How come there has not been an indictment of Mr. Mitchell for that alleged involvement?
>
> JAWORSKI: Bob, I am sorry. Mr. Mitchell is on trial, and I just simply cannot answer that question. I am not going to ask you, either, who Deep Throat is.

December 15, 1974

The guest is Gov. Jimmy Carter (D-GA), who this week announced his candidacy for the 1976 Democratic presidential nomination. He explains where he stands.

> CARTER: I think on civil rights, on environmental questions that I would be considered to be very moderate or perhaps liberal, liberal by Georgia standards, moderate by standards of most of the rest of the nation.
>
> On businesslike management of a government mechanism, on fiscal restraint, on refusing to waste the taxpayers' money, I think I would be considered to be quite conservative. It is hard for me to say. I am not as hawkish as Senator Jackson on some aspects of foreign policy. I am certainly not as liberal on many elements of importance to the American people as was George McGovern.

And how will his campaign be financed?

> CARTER: I will comply completely with the new campaign finance law from the very initiation of my campaign, which began the first couple of weeks in November. I think the American people are very eager to see political candidates be very modest in their acceptance of large campaign contributions.

Saigon falls to the Communists in 1975. In early May frightened Vietnamese scale the fourteen-foot wall of the U.S. Embassy in Saigon in a desperate attempt to reach the helicopter pickup zone.

June 15, 1975

A nation already suspicious of its leaders in the wake of the Watergate cover-up is rocked by further revelations when Vice President Nelson A. Rockefeller's commission investigating CIA activities in the United States releases its report. Rockefeller reveals on *Meet the Press* that the gathering of information was hindered by "a real problem of amnesia of many who were still around who might have had more detailed information." Clifton Daniel of the *New York Times* picks him up on an intriguing answer.

DANIEL: Did you say some of the American leaders who might have been involved in possible assassination plots had themselves been assassinated?

ROCKEFELLER: I did.

DANIEL: Would you be willing to name those particular leaders?

NOBEL PRIZE WINNERS ON *Meet the Press*

Dr. Harold C. Urey	1934	Chemistry
Sir Bertrand Russell	1950	Literature
Dr. Glenn T. Seaborg	1951	Chemistry
Dr. Linus C. Pauling	1954	Chemistry
Lester B. Pearson	1957	Peace
Philip J. Noel-Baker	1959	Peace
Dag Hammarskjöld	1961	Peace
Dr. Linus C. Pauling	1962	Peace
Dr. Martin Luther King, Jr.	1964	Peace
Prof. Paul A. Samuelson	1970	Economic Science
Aleksandr Solzhenitsyn	1970	Literature
Willy Brandt	1971	Peace
Dr. Henry Kissinger	1973	Peace
Dr. Friedrich von Hayek	1974	Economic Science
Dr. Milton Friedman	1976	Economic Science
James Tobin	1981	Economic Science
Bishop Desmond Tutu	1984	Peace
Oscar Arias Sánchez	1987	Peace
Dr. Norman Ramsey	1989	Physics
Mikhail Gorbachev	1990	Peace
Yasir Arafat	1994	Peace
Yitzhak Rabin/Shimon Peres	1994	Peace

The 1970 Nobel Prize winner for Literature, Aleksandr Solzhenitsyn (left), was exiled from his Russian homeland in February 1974 after publication in the West of his novel The Gulag Archipelago, *which describes the Soviet Union's brutal security and prison systems. The writer became a symbol of resistance to political oppression, and he was welcomed in the West as a hero. He was in the United States as a guest of the AFL-CIO, when he was interviewed on* Meet the Press *on July 15, 1975.*

ROCKEFELLER: As I said, we have no conclusive proof, but the president of the United States and the attorney general of the United States were both assassinated tragically in this country. . . . I think it is fair to say that no major undertakings by the CIA were done without either knowledge and/or approval of the White House.

GEORGE F. WILL (*National Review*): Mr. Vice President, why do so many conservative Republicans dislike you so much?

ROCKEFELLER: It is sort of visceral.

November 9, 1975

On the twenty-eighth anniversary of *Meet the Press,* Gerald Ford, president of the United States, is the guest on a one-hour special. This is the first time a sitting American president has appeared on the program. President Ford accepted the invitation to be interviewed as a tribute to *Meet the Press* founder Lawrence Spivak, who was making his farewell appearance as host of the program.

Asked about the achievements of his fifteen-month-old administration, the president says, "I have restored public confidence in their government at the federal level. . . . I believe also that we are slowly but surely making headway toward a resolution of our dependence on foreign oil. We are getting, hopefully, a bit of progress and necessary action in the area of energy independence. . . . We have had a very successful result in the Middle East with the Sinai agreement, and we are continuing to work with both the Soviet Union and the People's Republic of China."

. . .

The *Congressional Record-Senate*, November 19, 1975, has the following entry, under the heading "LAWRENCE SPIVAK RETIRES":

GOLDWATER: Mr. President, just 2 weeks ago Mr. Lawrence Spivak retired after nearly 30 years of leading the Nation's most provocative talk show, "Meet the Press." I can remember well my first appearance on that show. I was, as I guess everyone else has been, apprehensive about what would confront me. I was pleasantly and happily surprised to learn that this was not a brutal experience, but a very pleasant one under the guidance of Mr. Spivak. I also learned that he and his team of reporters were exceedingly well versed on the subjects they had chosen for interrogation and that the person sitting in the hot seat need never worry if he just told the truth. The only people I have ever seen squirm on Mr. Spivak's show were those who tried to lie on the question. Mr. Spivak brought to radio and television reporting a kind of technique, expertise and honesty that is sorely missing from so much of our reportorial efforts today. We all owe him a vote of thanks for this and we all hope that "Meet the Press" in the future will carry the same high standards that he always demanded.

Spivak is the best such interrogator in the business. In contrast with others, he knows his subjects and he asks and presses the right questions.
—John Kenneth Galbraith

Meet the Press **was started as a promotion for** ***The American Mercury*** **magazine, which I was editing. I never expected that it would take hold the way it did. I certainly didn't expect that we would interview so many times so many men who later became president—and finally interview the president himself. —Lawrence Spivak, October 17, 1975**

Lawrence E. Spivak died from congestive heart failure, on March 10, 1994, age ninety-three.

LAWRENCE SPIVAK: Before I retire, I want to thank those of you in our audience who have supported the program over the years with both criticism and encouragement. I want also to thank our staff and technical crew who contributed so much and whose credits you will soon see.

NBC has placed *Meet the Press* in capable hands. Bill Monroe will be executive producer and a regular member of the panel. He is a first-rate journalist with a well-earned reputation for fairness and responsibility.

Betty Cole Dukert will be the producer. She has been my associate for eighteen years and has contributed much to the success of *Meet the Press*. I commend them both to you. I may be back for an occasional guest appearance. Until then, this is Lawrence Spivak saying thank you and good-bye for myself, for President Ford, and *Meet the Press*.

Twenty-four years later, as *Meet the Press* prepared to celebrate its fiftieth anniversary on NBC television, Betty Cole Dukert was still contributing to the success of the program, as executive producer.

On Lawrence Spivak's retirement, *Meet the Press* led a nomadic life for a while. The production office was moved in 1975 to a Quonset-type hut behind the NBC building in Washington. It then found temporary shelter in a nearby commercial office building while construction was completed on the large addition to the NBC building on Nebraska Avenue, which became the program's permanent home.

February 1, 1976

The coming Carter administration was to make a real breakthrough in Middle East peace negotiations, but the Palestinian problem remained unsolved. Yitzhak Rabin, prime minister of Israel, states his position on *Meet the Press*.

RABIN: The declared goal of the PLO is the destruction of Israel, the expulsion of two million Jews back to the countries where they came from and to build on the ruins of Israel their country. . . .

In 1947, when the partition plan of former Palestine to a Jewish state and an Arab state was proposed, we accepted it. The other side rejected, went to war against the plan, against the very existence of the Jewish state, and now they claim that they have suffered from the war that they initiated. Had they accepted the partition plan, there would have been a Jewish state and a Palestinian state, and not one Palestinian would have been in the status of a refugee.

February 8, 1976

One week after Prime Minister Rabin's appearance on *Meet the Press*, the guest is Yasir Arafat, chairman of the Palestine Liberation Organization, leader of the Palestinian people, and—in Israeli eyes—terrorist. For more than twenty years Arafat has been fighting to establish a homeland for three and a half million Palestinians scattered across the Arab world.

NBC had only a small office in Beirut at the time of the *Meet the Press* interview, so the program sent crews and production staff from Washington. Arrangements were made through the PLO office at the UN in New York. Security was intense for Arafat, and exact details of where and when the program would be recorded could not be determined before arrival in Beirut. The producers had been promised, however, that they would not have to spend more than three days in Beirut—in contrast with long waits then being experienced by various press representatives trying for interviews with the Palestinian leader. There was also assurance that the program would have a choice of at least two locations for the actual program.

After arrival, producers Bill Monroe and Betty Cole Dukert were told that only two persons would be taken to scout the location choices on the evening before the recording. They designated the two top technical members of their group to make the selection. They found the first place offered, a residential apartment, quite satisfactory.

The next morning the crew was picked up by PLO cars and taken to the location to begin setting up the equipment. Monroe and Dukert were picked up a few hours later by another PLO driver, who spoke no English. He drove them through packed downtown traffic until advancing became impossible. He then proceeded to back down a hill, amid deafening horn blasts, to take a different approach.

Stopping in front of the apartment building, he held up five fingers and motioned the pair inside. On the fifth floor they followed a trail of cables leading to an attractive private apartment, where a mother and young son welcomed them with cookies and orange juice. A couple of hours later Arafat appeared with a retinue of attendants and guards. His heavy attire suggested he had come from the mountains. All windows were shuttered throughout his time in the apartment.

> ARAFAT: My aim and the aim of my organization and the aim of my people is to establish our democratic Palestinian state, where Jews, Christians, and Muslims can live in equality and friendship.

Bill Monroe points out that many Americans consider the PLO primarily a terrorist organization and asks, "In view of the record of the Jordanian prime minister being assassinated, eleven Israeli athletes being assassinated in Munich, the American ambassador and two others killed in Khartoum, eighteen dead in the Savoy Hotel raid in Tel Aviv less than a year ago, is that not justified, at least to an extent?"

ARAFAT: George Washington had been named once upon a time by the British emperor: He is a terrorist. The Vietnamese—recently you used to call them terrorists too, the Algerians, but all the freedom fighters used to have this name before their independence. So we don't look too much about the names of the Zionist propaganda.

MONROE: What about the Savoy Hotel, Mr. Arafat?

ARAFAT: It is a military operation done by our volunteers, which are going to their homeland to resist the occupied forces called the Israeli forces.

February 22, 1976

The new director of Central Intelligence—George Bush—acknowledges on *Meet the Press* that there were abuses of CIA power in the past, but as "soon as the Rockefeller Commission report came out, the former director very promptly put out regulations addressing himself to specifics." In spite of the revelations of abuses, the director is upbeat. "I have the comforting feeling that the American people support the concept of a strong CIA and a strong intelligence community."

ANTHONY LEWIS (*New York Times*): September 15, 1970, President Nixon instructed one of your predecessors to encourage a military coup against the democratic system of another country, Chile. If someone said that to you now, ordered you to do that, would you do it? . . .

BUSH: I wouldn't do it. . . . And the assassination thing has been ruled out by law.

April 18, 1976

The Watergate affair is a central issue in the coming presidential election. The *Washington Post*'s chief Watergate reporters Bob Woodward and Carl Bernstein answer questions from their colleagues on the publication of their book *The Final Days*, a follow-up to *All the President's Men*.

BILL MONROE: Would President Nixon have resigned, Bob, had it not been for you and Carl?

WOODWARD: No, that gets into what is called "if" history. Suppose we had not written those stories; we have thought about it, and we realize it is futile, because you can't answer it. If "x" happened, and it caused "y," would something else have caused "y"? Very often it would have.

May 16, 1976

Jimmy Carter's pledge of honesty makes him a strong candidate in the post-Watergate atmosphere. Would he face Gerald Ford or the conservative Republican Ronald Reagan? On the question of Reagan's ability to beat Jimmy Carter in the November presidential election, Sen. Paul Laxalt (R-NV), chairman of Citizens for Reagan, says, "I don't think there is any question about it. I think that we are finding here—and it is not a matter of just semantics—we are finding in this country a reemergence of a new majority. We are finding that conservatives throughout this country are going to marshal together and present, I think, a formidable political challenge."

May 30, 1976

A rising star in the Democratic party appears on a one-hour *Meet the Press* special featuring five influential black leaders.

The Rev. Jesse Jackson, national president of Operation PUSH, is interviewed along with Barbara Jordan (D-TX), scheduled keynote speaker at the Democratic National Convention in July; Lt. Gov. Mervyn Dymally of California; Vernon Jordan, executive director of the National Urban League;

May 30, 1976: Jesse Jackson sits between Vernon Jordan (top row, left) and A. Jay Cooper for the hourlong Meet the Press *special. In the front row are Barbara Jordan and Mervyn Dymally.*

Mayor A. Jay Cooper of Pritchard, Alabama, president of the Southern Conference of Black Mayors.

Jesse Jackson defines the issues in the coming election.

JACKSON: I think the issues are very specific. For example, the code word for racism in this campaign has been the bus. It is not the bus, it is us. . . .

CAROLE SIMPSON (NBC News): Do you think the country is ready yet for a woman, for a black woman on the national ticket?

JORDAN: The country is not ready, but it is getting ready, and I will try to help it. . . .

SIMPSON: With the recent revelation that the Senate Intelligence Committee uncovered about surveillance of black leaders, would you say that the FBI destroyed the civil rights movement in this country?

JACKSON: No. I think the civil rights movement changed its phases. I think it would be fair to say that the memos from the FBI indicating that it played an active role to disrupt, discredit, or destroy the black movement, that part of its job was to neutralize black leadership, to stop the rise of the black messiah, in that case perhaps Dr. King, meaning it was perhaps involved in his assassination, and that needs to be put in clear perspective. That study doesn't need to stop until we get an independent investigator who can lend credence to a very serious investigation.

On the other hand, the roots that were sown in the South in 1966 have borne certain national fruit that we must see in perspective. I think about 1966: We had three black congressmen; today we have seventeen black congresspersons. At that time we had no black mayors; today we have nearly one hundred and twenty. We had two million registered black voters; today we have seven point five million. . . . [H]ands that picked cotton in '66 will pick presidents in '76.

June 6, 1976

President Ford's prospects of election victory are believed to have been harmed by the full pardon he granted to his disgraced predecessor, Richard Nixon. Top Nixon aide John Ehrlichman is still embroiled in Watergate problems.

BILL MONROE: Our guest today on *Meet the Press* is John Ehrlichman, former chief domestic adviser to President Nixon. Mr. Ehrlichman quit his White House job three years ago in the aftermath of Watergate. He has been convicted of authorizing a break-in into a psychiatrist's office, participation in the Watergate cover-up, and perjury. If his legal appeals fail, he could go to prison for eight years.

CARL STERN (NBC News): Do you have any hope that President Ford might give you a pardon as he gave Richard Nixon a pardon?

EHRLICHMAN: None whatever.

STERN: You may have noticed the other day the CIA informed leaders on Capitol Hill that pursuant to their statutory authority, they were planning to destroy records and papers and so on of the Watergate era. Does that scare you?

EHRLICHMAN: It certainly gives me concern. I suspect that the really important stuff has already gone. I have no reason to say that except—

STERN: Gone how?

EHRLICHMAN: Gone. Been destroyed. That is just a hunch I have, that the really—

STERN: Destroyed by whom?

EHRLICHMAN: By the CIA.

July 11, 1976

Jimmy Carter's triumph in the 1976 primary elections in effect won him the presidential nomination weeks before the Democratic National Convention in New York City. On the eve of the convention he speaks on *Meet the Press*.

CARTER: I think I am sensitive, I am tough. I think I am a good planner, and I am still searching for answers to complicated questions. I have always avoided trying to give simplistic answers just for political expediency. I have had another very unique opportunity, almost unique, in not having to respond to the pressures of special interest groups.

September 6, 1976: Rosalynn Carter is the guest.

. . .

The one single issue that comes to mind with which I have had the most difficulty has been the amnesty question. I struggled with this a number of months before I finally arrived at a decision that suits me. It is the one that is expressed now in the Democratic party platform, which I favor. That is, to pardon those who have defected from our nation during the Vietnamese War in violation of the draft laws, but to deal with deserters on an individual case basis. This decision is not acceptable to a lot of American people, but it is what I intend to do.

I think those sharp differences that used to exist between the liberal and conservative elements of our society have pretty well been removed.

—Jimmy Carter, July 11, 1976

August 29, 1976

America's faith in its institutions has been sorely tested by revelations about the abuse of government power. Support for the American system comes from an unlikely source on *Meet the Press*, former Black Panther leader Eldridge Cleaver. Cleaver fled the country not to escape the draft but to avoid trial on charges of attempted murder. The author of *Soul on Ice* spent seven years in Cuba, Algeria, and France before returning voluntarily to the United States. He was a fierce critic of American society. What has changed?

> CLEAVER: I left here because the California Adult Authority was trying to imprison me illegally . . . but in my travels around the world I took note of the fact that there are a lot of shortcomings in the form of governments that I have seen.

Ford Rowan (NBC News) asks him about revelations of FBI agents provocateurs disrupting the Black Panthers.

> ROWAN: The Senate Intelligence Committee said the FBI used "lawless tactics.". . . Is that what you like about America? . . .
>
> CLEAVER: It is not what I like about America. What I do like about America is the fact that the Senate was willing to probe that area and to air that in public and to come up with that information to the American people, because in a similar situation in other countries it would never meet the light of day.

May 1, 1977

Ronald Reagan, former governor of California and the man who challenged President Ford for the 1976 Republican presidential nomination, is already considered a contender for 1980. He is

critical of President Carter's approach to the energy crisis.

REAGAN: I have felt for a long time that the government is not the answer to the energy problem. Government is the problem. We are not troubled so much by a shortage of energy as we are by a surplus of government. The great problems in the energy field came about with the government's involvement in the marketplace, regulation, price-fixing, and so forth, and I think that today the answer lies in the marketplace.

July 10, 1977

As oil shortages grow, President Carter's energy adviser, James R. Schlesinger, tells *Meet the Press* that the administration is considering rationing at the pumps to reduce gas consumption.

July 24, 1977

President Carter's concern with the Middle East is focused not only on oil supplies but also on peace. One of the triumphs of his presidency is the Camp David agreement between Israel and Egypt. Menachem Begin appears on *Meet the Press* as prime minister of Israel, two months after the election victory of the conservative Likud party and after meetings with President Carter. Begin was interviewed on *Meet the Press* in 1948 as leader of a new opposition group in forthcoming elections and former commander in chief of the Irgun underground, which led the resistance to the British before establishment of the state of Israel.

BEGIN: Under no circumstances shall we return to the lines of the fourth of June 1967, because such a return may mean the beginning of the end of the Jewish state, and we care that the Jewish state exists forever.

The prime minister is adamant that "not a man of the so-called PLO" will be allowed to participate in any talks. Bill Monroe points out that his predecessor, former Prime Minister Rabin, was willing to talk about possible PLO participation and asks him, "Are you willing to do that?"

BEGIN: No. I don't think so, and this is one of the reasons why I am now the prime minister and not Mr. Rabin.

August 14, 1977

Ambassador Ellsworth Bunker warns of trouble if the Senate rejects the new Panama Canal Treaty, which grants Panama control over the canal and the Canal Zone by the year 2000 but gives the United States the indefinite right to defend the waterway. "I think it will certainly produce unrest in Panama," he says. He believes a refusal to have negotiated the treaty "would have been looked on by other countries in Latin America as though we had not given up our imperialist notions."

August 21, 1977

Conservative Republican Senators Strom Thurmond of South Carolina and Jesse Helms of North Carolina are leading the opposition to the Panama Canal treaty. Asked about the possibility of a Senate filibuster, Senator Helms declares, "You can count on that."

> THURMOND: I think the world is going to have more respect for us if we stand up for property that belongs to us. . . . I don't see how we can afford to let American property go down the drain, or the rights of Americans, simply under threats of coercion or blackmail from a dictator as we have in Panama.

Thurmond is concerned that loss of the canal could threaten survival of the United States because "the naval vessels of our enemies could encircle the United States."

November 6, 1977

Vice President Walter Mondale defends President Carter's position on the Panama Canal. He points out that "we have the right to bring in U.S. troops if necessary to see that the Panama Canal is protected—not the country of Panama itself, but the Canal."

The vice president also discusses President Carter's courage in the Middle East, saying, "He is totally committed to the security of Israel and of the other states, but it takes a great deal of courage to step in the way he has to try to bring peace there."

> **We strongly support the concept that this nation, through its president and through its foreign policy, must speak to the human rights needs around the world. We think those values are so basic to American lives that to have a foreign policy that does not pursue those values is one that will not deserve the respect and the trust of the American people and will not be credible.**
>
> **—Vice President Walter Mondale, November 6, 1977**

December 4, 1977

The *Meet the Press* interview with King Hussein I of Jordan is relayed to the United States by satellite from Amman, the Jordanian capital only forty miles northeast of Jerusalem. Hussein is concerned about a split in Arab unity at a delicate time in the negotiations with Israel. A rift has developed between Syria and Egypt over Egyptian President Sadat's visit to Israel, and King Hussein announces that "the possibility is I'll be going both to Damascus and Cairo to see what we can do to bring an Arab cohesion at this very vital moment." He believes the consequences of a split in the Arab world are potentially dire.

> HUSSEIN: I see the possibilities of war. Maybe with Israel's superiority she could be provoked into one. On the military side, I can see disillusionment. I can see a drift toward extremism, chaos in the entire area, this affecting not only the area and all the people here but the world as well.

February 12, 1978

Israeli Foreign Minister Moshe Dayan, visiting the United States, accuses the Carter administration of favoring Egypt on the question of Jewish settlements in the Sinai. He says that Secretary of State Cyrus Vance "is taking sides, which won't make his job as a mediator any easier for us."

March 26, 1978

The Panama Canal treaty focuses attention on the issue of drug trafficking. Sen. Bob Dole of Kansas has raised the question in the Senate.

STANLEY W. CLOUD (*Time*): Senator, at your insistence about a month ago the Senate spent a couple of days discussing whether or not General Torrijos of Panama was involved in or knew about some drug traffic that allegedly went on down there. What relevance did that have to the Panama Canal debate?

DOLE: . . . It was relevant from the standpoint of the man's integrity and whether we are going to prop up some government with American dollars for the next twenty-two years or more that engaged in drug traffic.

May 21, 1978

The struggle for racial equality continues. The Rev. Jesse Jackson, president of Operation PUSH, addresses the contentious issue of quotas in affirmative action programs.

BILL MONROE: Can't you have affirmative action without quotas and without preference?

JACKSON: At first we went from a quota of zero, where there was absolute denial, to equal opportu-

February 12, 1978: The guest is Israel's Foreign Minister Moshe Dayan.

nity, where the argument was "We tried to find them, but they were not available," to now affirmative action, where we, by number, begin to challenge people by law to go out of their way to overcome the historical barrier based on race.

Let us not forget that black America was not set back based upon character or lack of it or lack of intelligence. We were set back by race.

. . .

In Washington, if one goes to Lorton Penitentiary for four years, it will cost slightly more than sixty-four thousand dollars. If one goes to Howard University for four years, it will cost less than twenty thousand dollars. It will cost more to keep blacks ignorant and incarcerated than educated and employed.

. . .

I think the trade union movement has been most resistant to training young blacks, young browns, to opening up for us. I mean, we need to be trained to lay bricks, so that in our training we can lay them rather than in our lack of training end up in desperation having to throw them.

May 28, 1978

Relations with the Soviet Union and Cuba take a turn for the worse with accusations of a Soviet arms buildup in Europe and Cuban involvement in the invasion of Zaire's Shaba Province. On *Meet the Press* President Carter's security adviser, Zbigniew Brzezinski, says that recent Soviet actions are incompatible "with what was once called the code of détente."

BRZEZINSKI: It seems to me essential for everyone to understand that in this day and age the intrusion of foreign military power to determine the outcome of specific and particular African conflicts is intolerable to world peace and is an insult to the Africans themselves.

May 7, 1978: Thirty years after his first Meet the Press *interview, Menachem Begin returns as prime minister of Israel.*

In Moscow, the Soviet Communist party newspaper *Pravda* responds angrily to Brzezinski's allegations on *Meet the Press,* calling him "an enemy of détente" and "an enemy of international cooperation."

November 19, 1978

The need to crush Communist influence in African affairs is a justification for the South African government's hostility to SWAPO, the South West Africa People's Organization. In an interview recorded in Pretoria, South Africa's new prime minister, Pieter W. Botha, talks about his government's policy.

BILL MONROE: If South Africa is seen to undermine the plan for UN-supervised elections and to insist upon a government in Namibia favorable to itself, could that not lead to a future of growing guerrilla warfare and possibly UN sanctions?

BOTHA: No, it is not a question of undermining. The United Nations decided to proclaim SWAPO as the sole representative of the peoples of South West Africa. We say we can only determine who the leaders of the peoples of South West Africa are if you have a proper election. SWAPO was invited to take part in that election. They preferred not to take part, because they are not interested in elections. They are interested in foisting their own ideas at the point of a gun on the majority of the people of South West Africa . . . and SWAPO's boss is in Moscow.

The policy of apartheid, the separation of races, is at the core of conflict in South Africa.

BOTHA: Let me first of all remove a misunderstanding about the word "apartheid." "Apartheid" is an Afrikaans word which means "separate, to be separate." It is a description of the position of the nations in Europe. Although they have bridges uniting them in common interests, they also have separateness in different countries. "Apartheid" is not a word which means that you want to deny others the same rights that you enjoy.

Secondly, I have grown up on a farm in South Africa. I have played with small black boys. I have swum with them in the rivers. . . .

February 4, 1979

It is over fifteen years since the assassination of President Kennedy, but many Americans believe the conspiratorial truth about the killing has never been told. David Belin tries to persuade the unconvinced.

JIM HARTZ (NBC News): Our guest today on *Meet the Press* is David Belin. Mr. Belin, as a staff counsel to the Warren Commission, concentrated on the question of identifying President Kennedy's assassin or assassins. His work contributed to the commission's conclusion that there was but a single gunman who fired three bullets, a conclusion now challenged by the House Assassinations Committee. [The committee concluded that there probably was a conspiracy.]

BOB KUR (NBC News): As Jim suggested, you worked on the Warren Commission, which concluded that Lee Harvey Oswald acted alone. Has the recent House committee investigation changed your mind?

BELIN: It has not. The House committee is plain wrong when a majority says there was a second gunman firing at the president from the grassy knoll.

Jeremiah O'Leary (*Washington Star*) asks Belin why he urged Congress in 1975 to reopen the JFK investigation.

BELIN: The major reason I changed my mind was that when I had undertaken an investigation of the CIA, I had discovered for the first time that the CIA had been involved in assassination plots directed against Fidel Castro and that that information had been withheld from the Warren Commission.

April 15, 1979

In 1979 the shah of Iran is deposed by followers of the exiled Islamic fundamentalist leader Ayatollah Khomeini. As a student at Yale University Shahriar Rouhani has for years been among the masked Iranian students demonstrating in support of the ayatollah. Now he is chief spokesman for the revolutionary committee running the Iranian Embassy in Washington. The first question to him, from moderator Bill Monroe, is about people "being executed by anonymous judges in closed courtrooms, apparently without any legal rights to adequate defense."

ROUHANI: It is undoubtedly the case that the form of the trials which are being held is not in exact accordance with Islamic law, but it must be understood that this is a revolutionary process.

Asked what kind of society the revolution is creating, Rouhani is optimistic: "It is going to create a society which has the spirituality of Islam and the East, and the dynamism of Islam, and it has got the technology of the West. It is going to [have] the freedom and the full participatory democracy that every nation in the world must have."

May 6, 1979

George Bush, a declared candidate for the Republican presidential nomination next year, is critical of the administration's Iran policy.

BUSH: Now what has happened? Our human rights people, pressing for change. Now, you see these revolutionary tribunals jerking people off the street and assassinating them; you see people cutting hands off of people; you see no human rights at all.

We are in an imperfect world. What we have got to do is spell out our interest in human rights, but not go in there and slap our friends around and be silent in the face of those adversary countries where we know we can't do anything about it.

August 12, 1979

Former Secretary of State Henry Kissinger agrees with Bush's assessment that the overthrow of the shah of Iran is no cause for rejoicing in the free world: "We have seen the replacement of an authoritarian pro-American regime by a more oppressive anti-American regime, and I cannot consider that an asset."

He also has strong reservations about the overthrow of the dictatorial Somoza regime in Nicaragua.

KISSINGER: I believe that the practical consequence of the overthrow of Somoza is to replace an admittedly unattractive regime with another government whose domestic practices may not turn out to be much more attractive, but whose foreign policy implications against the United States are bound to be very serious. All of the propaganda one hears out of Nicaragua is extremely anti-American; it is likely to have an impact on surrounding countries like Salvador, Guatemala, and, in time, even on countries like Mexico.

> I want to reawaken a sense of pride by putting stars in the eyes of the kids in this country. I believe a man can make a difference, you see. I am not cynical; I am not frustrated.
>
> —George Bush, May 6, 1979

Joyful Iranians celebrated the shah's flight from Iran in January 1979, but the world soon learned to fear the Islamic fundamentalist regime that replaced him.

GUESTS THE PROGRAM FAILED TO BOOK

Winston Churchill
Dwight D. Eisenhower (Ike, upset by something in Lawrence Spivak's *The American Mercury* magazine, refused to go on the show.)
Charles de Gaulle
Nikita Khrushchev
J. Edgar Hoover

Kissinger insists that increased defense spending will be needed in the 1980s, in spite of the SALT II agreement. The Russians will remain the global enemy.

> KISSINGER: I would say now we have to count on the fact that the Soviet Union is likely to push to the very limits of the agreement and to do things that we cannot now foresee that would be technically legal but are now unforeseeable. I do not question that.

September 9, 1979

Meet the Press comes from the Israeli city of Haifa, where Israeli Prime Minister Menachem Begin has been meeting today's guest, President Anwar el-Sadat of Egypt. Although expressing optimism about the prospects of agreement, President Sadat is reluctant to give details of his discussions with Prime Minister Begin, saying "If we didn't stick in Camp David to the new order of President Carter that let us refrain from saying anything, we would not have succeeded, so I advise the same thing now."

He does say that a Palestinian presence was not necessary at the talks but thinks the United States should start a dialogue with the PLO: "I urged this during Nixon's administration, in Ford's administration. I asked also President Carter to do this. I think it is very useful."

September 23, 1979

Jane Fonda and Tom Hayden are the first husband-and-wife couple to appear together on *Meet the Press*. They are beginning a tour of key presidential

primary states under the sponsorship of the Campaign for Economic Democracy, which Hayden heads. The controversial political activists are identified with opposition to the Vietnam War, and Fonda's visit to Hanoi during the war still makes her a hateful figure to many Americans. She explains her action.

> FONDA: I believe that my going to Hanoi . . . was needed to help end the war. Everything that I did during the war was to try to bring it to a close.

December 9, 1979

On November 4, 1979, a mob of militant Iranian students attacks the U.S. Embassy in Teheran and takes sixty-two American hostages, demanding the return to Iran of the exiled shah, who is receiving treatment for cancer in the United States. A month later Sadegh Ghotbzadeh, a close associate of the Ayatollah Khomeini's and the newly appointed foreign minister of Iran, is interviewed live by satellite on the hostage crisis.

Bill Monroe puts the question on all Americans' minds: "Will some be released? Will some or all be put on trial?"

> GHOTBZADEH: The fact is, some of these hostages here are spies . . . and we intend, to begin with, to create an international grand jury, not for the trial of these hostages as a basic but to investigate the American intervention and wrongdoing in Iran since the coup d'etat of 1953 against Mossadegh and putting the shah on the throne. . . . Obviously, Imam Khomeini has said over and over, those who are not guilty of spying, they cannot be held forever. But the rest will depend on when the shah will be returned to Iran.

The shah was never returned to Iran. And the hostages were still held in Teheran at the end of the decade.

The December 1979 interview with Sadegh Ghotbzadeh was set up by an Iranian-American contact of Bill Monroe's. This Washington businessman hoped to ease tension between the Iranian and American governments. Inadvertently he raised tension between two American television networks. Monroe was convinced that *Meet the Press* had been offered an exclusive interview and was shocked when ABC announced an *Issues and Answers* interview with Ghotbzadeh on the same day. A call to his contact—Rashad—solved the mystery. "As good a fan of *Meet the Press* as Rashad was," Monroe remembers, "he had not paid much attention to what network it was on. The distinction between ABC and NBC had never come clear to him, and his confusion had spread to Ghotbzadeh and Ghotbzadeh's staff in Teheran. When they got calls from ABC correspondents and from NBC correspondents in Teheran about an upcoming program, they were saying yes to both groups, thinking they were both speaking for *Meet the Press*." It was not until Friday that Rashad resolved the problem, and ABC withdrew.

"The *Meet the Press* interview with Ghotbzadeh made big black headlines in every Monday-morning American newspaper," Monroe recalls. "For weeks there had been no news of what was happening to the American hostages. No outsider was permitted contact with them. *Meet the Press* had obtained the first authoritative word on their condition. Ghotbzadeh gave assurances they were being well treated, and he made one specific announcement—that they were soon to be moved out of the American Embassy to another location. The hostages in fact were never moved. And some months later Ghotbzadeh himself fell out of favor with the Khomeini regime. He was arrested, held for a brief period, and executed."

IN THE NEWS

1980

- Protesting the Soviet invasion of Afghanistan, the United States boycotts the 1980 Moscow Olympic Games. Sixty nations join the boycott.
- The Solidarity trade union is founded in Poland.
- An American military raid to free the Iranian hostages fails.
- The shah of Iran dies in Egypt.
- The Equal Rights Amendment falls three states short of ratification.
- Saddam Hussein's Iraq attacks Iran, beginning the eight-year Iran-Iraq War.
- Ronald Reagan wins a landslide victory against Jimmy Carter, and the Republicans win control of the Senate for the first time since 1952.
- John Lennon is murdered in Manhattan.

1981

- After 444 days, the fifty-two Iranian hostages are released as Ronald Reagan is inaugurated.
- Scientists identify the AIDS virus, HIV.
- President Reagan and his press secretary, James Brady, are shot outside a Washington, D.C., hotel.
- Congress passes Ronald Reagan's tax cut legislation, giving Americans the biggest tax cut in U.S. history.
- President Reagan fires striking air traffic controllers.
- President Anwar el-Sadat of Egypt is assassinated.
- Sandra Day O'Connor becomes the first woman justice on the U.S. Supreme Court.

1982

- Israel invades Lebanon; U.S. Marines join the peacekeeping force.
- President Reagan announces U.S. aid to the contras fighting the Nicaraguan government.

1983

- President Reagan asks Congress for twenty-six billion dollars for "Star Wars," the Strategic Defense Initiative.
- The House of Representatives votes to end aid to the Nicaraguan contras.
- Shiite Muslims bomb the American Embassy in Beirut, killing eighty-seven people.
- A Soviet jet fighter shoots down a South Korean airliner carrying 269 people over Sakhalin Island.
- A terrorist drives a truck loaded with explosives into the U.S. Marine barracks in Beirut, killing 241.
- American troops take over Grenada.

1984

- Soviet bloc countries boycott the Los Angeles Olympics.
- The CIA admits responsibility for mining Nicaraguan ports.
- Indian Premier Indira Gandhi is assassinated by two of her bodyguards.
- Ronald Reagan is elected by a landslide against Walter Mondale, winning every state except Minnesota.

1985

- Mikhail Gorbachev becomes general secretary of the Communist party and leader of the USSR, promising *glasnost* (openness) and *perestroika* (reconstruction).
- Islamic Jihad terrorists hijack TWA Flight 847, taking thirty-nine hostages who are freed when Israel releases thirty-one Shiite prisoners.
- The United States imposes economic sanctions on South Africa.
- Four terrorists seize the cruise ship *Achille Lauro* in the Mediterranean, demanding the release of PLO prisoners in Israel and killing sixty-nine-year-old Leon Klinghoffer, a wheelchair-bound tourist from New York.

1986

- In the War on Drugs, first lady Nancy Reagan's "Just say no" campaign starts.
- Ferdinand and Imelda Marcos flee to the United States.
- The space shuttle *Challenger* explodes in midair, killing six astronauts and schoolteacher Christa McAuliffe.
- U.S. servicemen die in a Berlin nightclub bombing. Holding Libya responsible, the United States bombs terrorist bases in Libya.
- Disaster at the Chernobyl nuclear plant spreads fallout across Europe.
- Nicaragua shoots down an American cargo plane carrying supplies for the contras.
- The Iran-contra link emerges. Congress holds an investigation. White House chief of staff Donald Regan and National Security Council chief John Poindexter resign.

1987

- Confirmation of President Reagan's Supreme Court nominee Robert Bork is blocked by the Senate.
- Gorbachev drops the Soviet demand that the United States abandon the "Star Wars" program.
- The USS *Stark* is hit by an Iraqi missile, and thirty-seven Americans die. Iraq apologizes. When an American ship hits an Iranian mine, the United States responds, hitting six Iranian ships.
- Gorbachev and Reagan meet in Washington, D.C., and sign the Intermediate Nuclear Forces (INF) treaty.

1988

- In Michigan Jesse Jackson becomes the first African American to win a presidential primary election.
- Gorbachev announces withdrawal of Soviet troops from Afghanistan.
- President Reagan visits the Soviet Union.
- The U.S. warship *Vincennes* shoots down an Iran Air passenger jet, killing 290 people.
- A UN cease-fire ends the Iran-Iraq War.
- Speaking to the UN General Assembly in New York, Gorbachev announces Soviet troop reductions in Europe and calls for an end to Communist-capitalist hostility.
- Pan Am Flight 103 explodes over Lockerbie, Scotland.
- George Bush defeats Michael Dukakis in the presidential election after promising "Read my lips. No new taxes" and calling for "a thousand points of light." Democrats control the House and Senate.

1989

- The *Exxon Valdez* runs aground in Prince William Sound, causing a major oil spill.
- In Beijing's Tiananmen Square, more than 1,000 die as the government crushes student demonstrations.
- Hungary opens its border with Austria, creating the first breach in the iron curtain.
- House Speaker Jim Wright resigns after accusations of ethics violations.
- Shiite Muslims hang U.S. hostage Lt. Col. William R. Higgins. The American Embassy in Beirut is closed.
- Nicaraguan Sandinista leader Daniel Ortega signs a treaty with the contra rebels and schedules democratic elections.
- Communism collapses, as East Germany, Czechoslovakia, and Hungary sever ties with Moscow.
- The Berlin Wall is torn down.
- United States troops invade Panama. General Noriega is brought to the United States to stand trial on drug-smuggling charges.
- Tens of thousands die as a Romanian revolution overthrows the Ceauçescu regime.

In January 1981, as Ronald Reagan is sworn in as president of the United States, the American hostages held by Iran are finally freed. The nation shares a sense of release. The Reagan years bring optimism and prosperity, supported by the biggest tax cut in American history and the liberation of enterprise from federal regulations.

Increased personal wealth results in a consumer boom. Sales of personal computers and VCRs soar, as home entertainment options increase. People tend their souls with self-improvement books and cultivate their bodies with diets, gyms, and jogging. Athletic wear and designer labels become significant statements of personal identity.

Not everyone shares in the boom years. The homeless and penniless appear on city streets, many with mental problems, many addicted to a new drug menace—crack. A War on Drugs is declared, with first lady Nancy Reagan leading the "Just say no" campaign. At the decade's end President George Bush sends American troops into Panama to arrest a major drug dealer, Panamanian strongman General Manuel Noriega.

Central America preoccupies the Reagan-Bush administration. A prolonged effort to unseat the Sandinista government in Nicaragua leads the administration into murky waters. Marine Col. Oliver North masterminds a secret plan to use profits from the illegal sale of arms to Iran to finance the contra rebels in Nicaragua. The Iran-contra scandal casts a shadow over Ronald Reagan's presidency,

but the Sandinista government is finally forced to hold free democratic elections.

There are major foreign policy triumphs. Ronald Reagan begins his presidency with a massive increase in military spending and a denunciation of the Soviet Union as the "evil empire." From his position of armed strength, he negotiates unprecedented arms control agreements with the Soviet Union, eliminating short- and medium-range missiles from Europe. President Reagan shares the credit with Soviet leader Mikhail Gorbachev, whose internal policies of *glasnost* (openness) and *perestroika* (reconstruction) at home are matched by calls for an end to cold war confrontation between communism and capitalism.

Before the decade ends, the cold war is over, as communism collapses in Eastern Europe. The iron curtain is first breached when Hungary opens its border to Austria. Soon the Communist regimes in East Germany, Czechoslovakia, and Hungary cut their ties with the Soviet Union. Finally the Berlin Wall, chilling symbol of the cold war, is torn apart by the citizens of Berlin. East and West are united in an embrace. And not a shot was fired.

There is a terrifying new threat loose in the world: the AIDS virus. People die, and controversy rages, as some see the virus as divine judgment on immoral behavior while others look for an elusive cure.

The 1980s have been called the decade of greed, but hunger and pain lived on.

January 20, 1980

One of the most dramatic newsbreaks in the history of *Meet the Press* comes at the start of the new decade. With Soviet armies overrunning Afghanistan, President Carter chooses *Meet the Press* to make a major announcement.

BILL MONROE: Mr. President, assuming the Soviets do not pull out of Afghanistan any time soon, do you favor the U.S. participating in the Moscow Olympics, and if not, what are the alternatives?

CARTER: No. Neither I nor the American people would support the sending of an American team to Moscow with Soviet invasion troops in Afghanistan.

I have sent a message today to the United States Olympic Committee spelling out my own position: that unless the Soviets withdraw their troops within a month from Afghanistan the Olympic Games be moved from Moscow to an alternative site or multiple sites or postponed or canceled. If the Soviets do not withdraw their troops immediately from Afghanistan within a month, I would not support the sending of an American team to the Olympics.

Initial world reaction to President Carter's proposal was cool. The president of the International Olympic Committee said the games could not be moved, and the Soviet Union responded by confirming its participation in the Lake Placid Winter Olympics. Eventually sixty nations joined the boycott.

May 18, 1980

Jimmy Carter's principled stances helped make him president after the scandal surrounding the Nixon administration's final days. Seven years after pleading no contest to a Justice Department accusation of income tax evasion and resigning the vice presidency, Spiro Agnew adds an astonishing footnote to the Nixon years.

BILL MONROE: When you quit as vice president, the Justice Department agreed not to prosecute you on bribery charges, and many people concluded that you took that deal to stay out of jail. Now you say that you were actually fearful that if you did not go along, President Nixon or General Haig—it's not quite clear—might have ordered you assassinated. Could you explain that?

AGNEW: I was concerned, and I think my concern at that time, based on my frame of mind after being seven months in a pressure cooker of attempts to get me to resign office, attempts made by General Haig—five separate occasions—at the same time President Nixon was affirming his belief in me publicly, gave me reason to be concerned.

PRESIDENTIAL APPEARANCES

All post-Eisenhower United States presidents have appeared on *Meet the Press* before, during, or after their presidencies. Three sitting presidents have been interviewed on *Meet the Press*.

PRESIDENT GERALD FORD: November 9, 1975

PRESIDENT JIMMY CARTER: January 20, 1980

PRESIDENT BILL CLINTON: November 7, 1993

May 25, 1980

Richard Nixon owed his election partly to urban mayhem in the Johnson years, when cities burned in nationwide riots. Echoes of that era reappear when serious riots grip Miami. Athalie Range, the first African American to serve as commissioner of the city of Miami, discusses the recent outbreak of rioting. News accounts suggest the violence was triggered by an all-white jury finding four white policemen not guilty of beating a black insurance man to death.

RANGE: The jury acted in very poor faith; the people of Miami responded spontaneously, and as a result of that, we did have the riots.

NAACP Executive Director Benjamin Hooks agrees.

HOOKS: The justice system said to black folk: "Wait on us; give us a chance to prove what we can do," and then the justice system spat on us. When they try the black folk, the system works perfectly. It convicts them without any mercy. Saturday night the man is convicted, Sunday night he's fired from his job without a chance to appeal.

October 12, 1980

The moral well-being of the American family is the concern of television evangelist the Rev. Jerry Falwell. He is president of Moral Majority, which is organizing fundamentalist churchgoers to register and vote according to their religious principles in the 1980 elections. Falwell defines Moral Majority as "a political organization totally of Americans, period, who share the same philosophies on moral issues, such as pro life, pro traditional family, pro American, pro moral, et cetera."

Asked about his endorsement of Ronald Reagan, he says: "I have not endorsed Mr. Reagan. I was asked, when pressed to the wall, 'For whom are you voting?' And I did say, 'Ronald Reagan,' but I made it very clear that I'm not endorsing a candidate."

In Falwell's list of twenty-one moral standards to apply to candidates is the question "Do you favor a reduction in taxes to allow families more spendable income?" Is that, Bill Monroe wonders, dictated by the Bible?

FALWELL: I feel that government is taking away from people, not giving to people. And when they do give to people, they take away from other people to give to people. . . . I do believe that oppression of the poor is very much addressed in the Bible, and I think that too much taxation is oppression of everybody, particularly the poor.

November 2, 1980

Two days before the presidential election former President Gerald Ford answers questions on the influence the continuing Iran hostage situation may have on the vote.

BILL MONROE: Mr. President, do you have the feeling that today's news from Iran, suggesting that the hostages may indeed be released in the next several weeks, will affect the election on Tuesday?

FORD: If the ayatollah on this occasion can have an impact on how people vote in the United States, it's bad, bad precedent for future elections for the president of the United States, because other governments in the future will be able to take some action of one kind or another that might result in extracting from the president certain promises, certain conditions that in a different time would not have been made.

MONROE: Mr. President, you and others have suggested recently that President Carter may have been involved in manipulating the hostage crisis for political gain. . . .

FORD: . . . I think it's a fair assumption that there has been much, much more activity not only in Washington, but elsewhere, in an attempt to achieve some concrete results by November 4.

December 21, 1980

The hostages are not released before the election, which Ronald Reagan wins. Iran demands twenty-four billion dollars to buy the hostages' release, and Secretary of State Edmund Muskie announces the outgoing Carter administration's official reaction on *Meet the Press.*

Part of the "frustrating and at times agonizing effort," he says, "is to make clear to the Iranians, through a third party—which complicates the task—the limits beyond which the president cannot legally go."

January 25, 1981

Ronald Reagan announces the release of the American hostages on inauguration day, exactly a year after President Carter's appearance on *Meet the Press,* and it feels like a new dawn in America.

January 25, 1981: With the Republicans controlling the Senate for the first time since 1952, Sen. Charles Percy (R-IL) becomes chairman of the Senate Foreign Relations Committee. He says Iran must expect "an element of punishment" for the long hostage crisis.

Sen. Charles Percy (R-IL), chairman of the Senate Foreign Relations Committee, is asked about the deal negotiated by President Carter's team.

> PERCY: They refused time after time to accept the terms laid down by Iran. It was Iran that finally accepted the terms that we laid down to them. . . . We're so filled with gratitude that the four hundred and forty days of agony are over.

April 19, 1981

In addition to the hostage crisis, high oil prices deepened the preelection gloom of the Carter administration. In his first major interview on American television for years Saudi Arabia's minister of petroleum, Sheikh Ahmed Zaki al-Yamani, announces on *Meet the Press* that his country will not lower production levels of oil until the price falls. He distances his government from the other members of the Organization of Petroleum Exporting Countries (OPEC) by saying that the current oil price

is too high. "It's not in the interests of the international community. And therefore we want it to come down a little bit lower."

Sheikh Yamani also makes a plea for sophisticated American arms. "We are surrounded by all types of countries who are focusing on the oil fields, on your own interests in this country, and we cannot be strong enough to defend ourselves, to defend our interests, which happen to be your own interests, without getting these arms."

August 9, 1981

President Anwar el-Sadat's Egypt is at peace with Israel since the Camp David agreement negotiated by President Carter. After meetings with President Reagan in Washington, Sadat speaks to *Meet the Press* live from Blair House.

BILL MONROE: Mr. President, you urged President Reagan to end the United States policy of not having contacts with the Palestine Liberation Organization. President Reagan reportedly repeated to you the pledge the U.S. has made to Israel six years ago, not to talk with the PLO.

SADAT: . . . I learned that Yasir Arafat came out in a press conference and said that they will respect the cease-fire. This is a great achievement. This moment I thought of the second step that should come after this and consolidate it, instead of leaving this cease-fire to dry, like everything that is fragile there in our area. So I proposed this dialogue, to talk between the States and the Palestinians, for the cause of peace.

Two months after his return to Cairo, President Sadat was assassinated.

From left to right: President Anwar el-Sadat of Egypt, Bill Monroe, Carl T. Rowan, Karen Elliott House, and Marvin Kalb.

August 23, 1981

Three weeks into a strike by air traffic controllers, Transportation Secretary Drew Lewis turns down the idea of negotiating with the strikers, saying that President Reagan considers this a matter of principle.

> LEWIS: I did discuss this with the president, and we feel very strongly that this is a breaking of an oath, the breaking of the law. It's not a union negotiation, not a union/management negotiation; it's a matter of the laws of this country. . . . These people forfeited their jobs. They left. They walked off.
>
> . . . As far as the long range goes, we do have over five thousand people that stuck with us, that stayed on the job; we have four thousand supervisors that are on the job. We plan to talk with those people, try to accommodate their needs, and then move on from there in terms of rebuilding the system. . . . We are going to have some temporary layoffs, but again we think the principle is important enough and the total economic impact on this country is not going to be that significant.

The Vietnam War continued to divide the country after it ended. Maya Lin's Vietnam Veterans Memorial in Washington, D.C., was destined to become the most visited monument in the United States and arguably the most moving, but it provoked hostility and anger before its completion in 1982.

When President Reagan fires the nation's striking air traffic controllers, it signals a radical change in industrial relations. The power of the unions is set to wane in the eighties, and the public will become familiar with "downsizing" and "restructuring," the *perestroika* of President Reagan's America.

November 1, 1981

Tax cutting is a cornerstone of the Reagan philosophy. But Bob Dole, Senate Finance Committee chairman, suggests on *Meet the Press* that broad tax rises may be needed to cut an increasingly alarming deficit.

> DOLE: If we are going to do something, we ought to find one or two big items and try to rally our troops to support one or two big increases, maybe an energy tax or some large item, rather than trying to pick off nineteen, twenty, twenty-five different areas, because you are going to have every special interest group in America descending on the Finance Committee in the Senate and the House Ways and Means Committee.

It is suggested to Senator Dole that the last stage of the Kemp-Roth personal tax cut may not be implemented.

> DOLE: I would hope we didn't do that. It would seem to me we'd be Carterizing Reagan policy. We'd be promising the people something on the one hand, and then taking it away or reducing it with the other. . . .
>
> I think there's a tendency of any new administration to look through rose-colored glasses and say, "Boy, just the fact that we were inaugurated is going to change the economy." The hard facts are that that doesn't work. It didn't work for President Carter; it hasn't worked for President Reagan.

November 29, 1981

Influence peddling by those with access to the White House is a story running through fifty years of *Meet the Press*. Richard V. Allen, assistant to the president for national security affairs, breaks major news on the program with his announcement that he is taking a leave of absence, with President Reagan's approval. Allen is having difficulty because of a thousand dollars given to him by a group of Japanese journalists for whom he tried to arrange an interview with first lady Nancy Reagan. "I did not know what I received was an envelope containing cash," he insists. Admitting the envelope was put in a safe in his office, he assures the panel that he has done "nothing wrong." The Justice Department supported his explanation.

March 21, 1982

Milton Friedman, Nobel Prize-winning economist, supports President Reagan's hostility to raising taxes to reduce the deficit.

> FRIEDMAN: I am strongly opposed to any retreat on the subject of taxes. I think raising taxes will not in fact reduce the deficit; it will simply increase spending. I too agree that the deficit is too large, but I think there is only one way that is appropriate to reduce it, and that is to cut spending. . . .
>
> My prediction is that the actual deficits over the coming years will be far smaller than is now forecast.

April 25, 1982

Israel's Prime Minister Menachem Begin is interviewed live in his Jerusalem office on the day the last part of the Sinai Peninsula is returned to Egypt under the terms of the Camp David agreement, negotiated by President Carter, Prime Minister Begin, and Egyptian President Sadat.

Moderator Bill Monroe joined NBC's Israel-based correspondent Art Kent for the interview in Jerusalem with Prime Minister Begin (April 25, 1982). Three correspondents in the Washington studio completed the panel. Monroe recalls the program's unique technical glitches. "Begin took his seat about two minutes before airtime. When the director, sitting in a big production truck outside the office, arranged for Begin to listen to one of the reporters in Washington to check out that area of communications, the panic began. Begin could not hear the Washington questioners. At thirty seconds to airtime, it was obvious we were about to go on the air with that link out."

A technician hurriedly retrieved a working earpiece from Art Kent—who did not have to hear the questions from Washington—and approached Begin from behind. "If you were a viewer of the program at that moment you were looking at a medium closeup of Menachem Begin," Monroe remembers. "All of a sudden, to his left and slightly behind him, appeared the midriff of a man whose upper body and head were out of the picture frame. It was something new for *Meet the Press* and undoubtedly for the prime minister of Israel. And now the viewer sees a pair of hands fiddling with the prime minister's left ear. Must be the hands, the alert viewer says to himself, that go with the belly. The hands extract an earpiece from the prime minister's ear. He goes on talking." Finally the hands inserted the replacement earpiece and withdrew.

Begin was answering a question as the end of the program approached, and Monroe heard the director's voice in his earpiece saying, "Say good-bye." "It was his customary terse guidance to me to thank the guest and wind up the program in no more than fifteen seconds. But neither the director nor I had planned for the final slapstick denouement of this unusual *Meet the Press*." They had forgotten that Begin's earpiece carried not only the voices of the Washington questioners but also the director's cues to Monroe. "So now, to my astonishment, Menachem Begin abruptly stopped talking in the middle of a sentence. He looked square into the camera, square at the television audience, and with a look of disbelief on his face he said, 'Say good-bye?'"

BEGIN: It is a great pity that he [Sadat] is not here with us to see the fruit of his efforts to bring about peace and reconciliation between the Egyptian people and the Israeli people. But his assassination took place, and he is not with us.

The prime minister summarizes Israel's attitude toward the agreement.

BEGIN: I do not agree with the cynics who say that the peace treaty is a piece of paper. It is not. It is the most serious commitment. And then I would like to add what our Egyptian friends know very well: If at any time they could commit a breach of their commitments under the peace treaty, then Israel's reaction will be swift.

Begin rejects the idea of negotiating a comparable land-for-peace agreement with Syria over the Golan Heights and reacts strongly to suggestions that Israel plans to annex the West Bank and the Gaza Strip.

BEGIN: You can annex foreign land. You can't annex your own country. Judea and Samaria are the parts of the land of Israel, or in foreign languages, Palestine, in which our nation was born.

June 13, 1982

Farouk Kaddoumi heads the political department of the PLO. He states his opinion succinctly: "I think Israel is a source of trouble, a source, and a threat to peace." He calls on international public opinion "to stop Israel doing any aggression against its neighbors, to withdraw from the West Bank and the Gaza Strip, to have the people of Palestine return to their homelands from where they have been uprooted. I am from Jaffa. My home was now occupied by a foreign immigrant. . . . We thank our brethren, the Lebanese, for our staying there, because we fight in order to go back to our homes."

. . .

MICHAEL J. BERLIN (*New York Post*): But, sir, how can you fight Israel if you can't get near it? . . .

KADDOUMI: We can fight inside the occupied territories. There are our people there, nothing difficult to a guerrilla warrior. . . . We are freedom fighters. . . .

BILL MONROE: Do you justify planting bombs in automobiles, for example, and marketplaces, killing civilians on the West Bank?

KADDOUMI: I don't think that the people of Palestine, when they resist—this is a self-defense. You see and read in the newspapers about the mass killing and the massacring. This invasion is a war of genocide against the Palestinians. You see that killing of one person is a crime, but killing a people is not a crime.

August 22, 1982

George Shultz makes an important statement on the Middle East in his first broadcast interview since becoming secretary of state on the resignation of Alexander M. Haig, Jr. Shultz calls for a long-term settlement of the Palestinian issue, say-

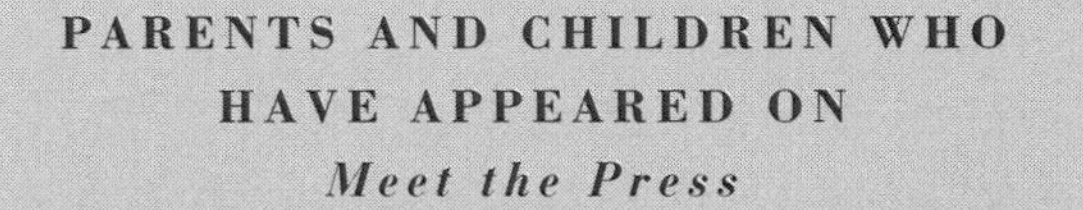

PARENTS AND CHILDREN WHO HAVE APPEARED ON *Meet the Press*

Edmund and Jerry BROWN

Tom and Ramsey CLARK

Tom and Chris DODD

Gerald and Jack FORD

Jawaharlal NEHRU and Indira GANDHI

Indira and Rajiv GANDHI

Albert Gore and Albert GORE, Jr.

Jesse Jackson and Jesse JACKSON, Jr.

Henry and Edgar KAISER

John F. Kennedy and John F. KENNEDY, Jr.

Henry Cabot and George Cabot LODGE

Eleanor, James, Elliott, and Franklin ROOSEVELT, Jr.

Adlai E. Stevenson II and Adlai E. STEVENSON III

Stuart and James SYMINGTON

Robert A. Taft, Sr., Mrs. Martha Taft, and Robert TAFT, Jr.

Eugene and Herman TALMADGE

Millard and Joseph TYDINGS

ing, "[T]he establishment of a situation where the Palestinian people can have some sense of dignity and control over their lives is very important and an essential part of any agreement." He considers the main point not to be an independent Palestinian state but "that the Palestinian people have a voice in determining the conditions under which they are governed." Asked if he means a Palestinian homeland on the West Bank and Gaza, he says, "Well, certainly that is a place that many of them call home, and a place that they'll live, and they should have a participation in determining the conditions under which they live." In this context the construction of Jewish settlements on the West Bank is "not constructive."

Shultz appeared on *Meet the Press* when the Israelis refused to allow the scheduled guest, West Bank Mayor Elias Freij, to travel to the United States for the *Meet the Press* interview. The following week *Meet the Press* sent Bill Monroe to Herzliya, Israel, to interview the mayor.

February 20, 1983

Americans are becoming increasingly aware of environmental problems at home. There are complaints about the Reagan administration's relaxation of clean air and water regulations, reflecting concern that environmental policy makers and enforcers have overstrong ties to industry. Sen. John H. Chafee (R-RI), chairman of the Senate subcommittee on environmental pollution, attacks President Reagan's appointments and policies.

> CHAFEE: He appointed these people who are enunciating his views. They are not my views, they aren't the views of many of the Republicans in the Senate and the House, and I don't think they are always the views of the American people.

Senator Chafee is joined on *Meet the Press* by House Interior Committee Chairman Morris K. Udall (D-AZ), a leading environmentalist.

> UDALL: Basically we are seeing the outcome of an administration which doesn't believe in the environment, which has made war on the environment, and which has people administering these key laws that don't believe in them.

February 20, 1983: Environmentalists are a growing political force in the 1980s. Some of their concerns are expressed on Meet the Press *by Rep. Morris Udall (left) and Sen. John H. Chafee (right).*

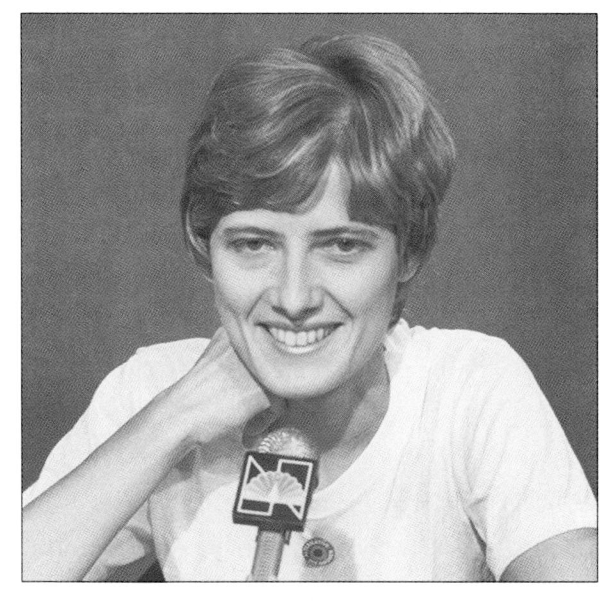

July 10, 1983: Petra Kelly, leader of West Germany's Green party, opposes the deployment of more nuclear missiles in Europe. "They cannot make us more deader than dead. You can only be dead once."

September 25, 1983: (left to right) Walter Mossberg, Rowland Evans, Mary Lord, John Dancy, Marvin Kalb, and Sen. Sam Nunn. Only Bob Dole has made more Meet the Press *appearances than Nunn.*

September 25, 1983

American troops have been transported to the Middle East, where they are acting as a peacekeeping force in Lebanon. Sen. Sam Nunn, chairman of the Armed Services Committee, warns that U.S. Marines in Lebanon need authority to defend themselves. "Right now," he says, "they are sitting ducks."

A month later a Muslim suicide attack kills 241 marines in their base. *Meet the Press,* alerted to the tragedy at 5:30 A.M. Sunday, scraps its scheduled political program and calls on Senator Nunn again, together with a new panel of foreign affairs specialists for the panel.

October 23, 1983

MARVIN KALB (NBC News): In the wake of the explosion in Beirut, Lebanon, this morning that killed perhaps as many as one hundred and twenty U.S. Marines and wounded many others, our [guest] today on *Meet the Press* [is] Sen. Sam Nunn of Georgia, considered the most influential Democrat on the Armed Services Committee. . . .

BILL MONROE (NBC News): You originally opposed our putting these marines into Lebanon. What is your reaction to this news?

NUNN: My first reaction is one of great sympathy to the families of the brave men that were killed.

My second reaction is that we need to do everything possible now to protect those marines who are still in Lebanon, because we have a unit that has been literally decimated. That unit has taken between fifteen and twenty percent casualties. In Vietnam or any other war we would consider that unit almost ineffective at this stage. So the second point I would like to make is, we've got to augment that unit, and we've got to do it very rapidly. . . .

The bottom line is, our marines have been in an untenable military position; they remain in an untenable military position. . . . I think the president owes the nation and the Marine Corps and our national security a quick but a very thoughtful analysis of our situation there, now. I don't think we've had that in the past.

December 4, 1983: After more than thirty-six years with Meet the Press, *Lawrence Spivak asks his last question. The guest is Jesse Jackson.*

October 30, 1983

The intervention of American forces to oust the government in Grenada was widely condemned in the United Nations Security Council, but U.S. ambassador to the UN Jeane Kirkpatrick defends the action.

KIRKPATRICK: I expect that most of the nations in the region will breathe a sigh of relief, as a matter of fact, at the success of the operation and at the removal of what a good number of them recognize was a clear and present danger to their own security. . . . I don't think it was an invasion. I think it was a rescue, and I think that we ought to stop calling it an invasion.

November 6, 1983

As chairman of the Joint Chiefs of Staff Gen. John Vessey was involved in planning the Grenada operation.

VESSEY: We planned the operation in a very short period of time, in about forty-eight hours. . . . As a result, we used more force than we probably needed to do the job, but the operation went reasonably well. . . . I think we have exposed what happens to countries that come under the Cuban and Soviet domination.

December 4, 1983

Lawrence Spivak makes his final appearance as a questioner on *Meet the Press*. The guest is Jesse Jackson.

December 18, 1983

Elizabeth Dole, secretary of transportation, is the wife of Sen. Bob Dole (R-KS).

MARIA RECIO (*Business Week*): Given your husband's own presidential ambitions, would you prefer to be the first lady president or the first lady?

DOLE: Well, let me just say that at this point I certainly have all the challenges that I need right where I am. I'm enjoying my responsibilities. I really have no plans to run myself. My husband of course has run for the presidency.

Recio asks her about the gender gap.

DOLE: There is a gender gap. My own view of it is . . . that any president sitting in the Oval Office today would be confronted with a number of problems that our changing society has produced. I have been a part of this change, in that I finished law school in 1965, when thirty percent of women were working. Today fifty-two percent are in the work force. We've seen a tremendous wave of women coming into the work force. We've seen, for example, women with children between the ages of seven and seventeen, sixty-three percent of them working. It's really revolutionary.

January 1, 1984

Two men who recently headed the Central Intelligence Agency, William Colby and Adm. Stansfield Turner, both state baldly that the U.S. Marines should be withdrawn from Lebanon.

COLBY: You should not send superpower forces to a peacekeeping mission. The marines are not a peacekeeping force.

TURNER: Marines are not appropriate to this task, particularly since the end of September, when we stopped being a peacekeeping force and entered into the conflict on the side of the government of President Gemayel. We are now seen as a protagonist, not a peacekeeper.

The White House has blamed the CIA for the Beirut massacre of the marines. Admiral Turner finds the charge outrageous.

TURNER: First, they have diverted so much of our human intelligence effort from collecting information, like on terrorism in Lebanon, to covert action, such as trying to destabilize the government of Nicaragua, that perhaps they are shorthanded. And secondly, Lebanon and Grenada are issues that this administration has made central focuses of U.S. attention. They could have, they should have, redoubled the effort on human intelligence in those countries.

. . .

BILL MONROE (NBC News): The United States now seems to be tilting toward Iraq in its war with Iran. Is that a good idea, Mr. Colby?

HUSBANDS AND WIVES ON *Meet the Press*

Howard BAKER and Nancy KASSEBAUM BAKER

Jimmy and Rosalynn CARTER

Bob and Elizabeth DOLE

Tom HAYDEN and Jane FONDA

Philip and Janey HART

William H. MASTERS and Virginia JOHNSON

Henry R. and Clare Boothe LUCE

George and Eleanor McGOVERN

James CARVILLE and Mary MATALIN

Ronald and Nancy REAGAN

William and Jill RUCKELSHAUS

Anatoly and Avital SHCHARANSKY

Robert and Martha TAFT

COLBY: I think we should pay attention when the Ayatollah Khomeini calls us the great Satan and sent Shiite terrorists in to blow up our people and our embassies.

Admiral Turner disagrees.

TURNER: Over the long run we have greater interests in Iran. . . . We don't want to open the door for [the Soviet Union] by becoming any more antagonistic to Iran than we have to despite the fact that they have a very, very odorous regime there today.

February 5, 1984

Vice President George Bush, himself a former director of Central Intelligence, admits that the political situation in Lebanon remains confused after the resignation of the Cabinet in Lebanon on the morning he comes to *Meet the Press*.

BUSH: Let's hope that out of these resignations you'll have a government formed that really more broadly represents the factions involved. . . . There's a lot of unpredictability.

Pressed about the large and growing deficit and alleged disarray in the administration on economic questions, the vice president replies.

BUSH: There's not disarray. Take your signals from the president. Work from the budget he sent up there. Give us another hundred billion dollars' worth of reductions over three years, have the tax reform that we're—that he's called for, go back and look at the cuts that he requested that he never got, and take your cues from those things, not by the who's up, who's down, inside the Beltway stuff.

March 18, 1984

Jim Wright, majority leader in the U.S. House of Representatives, is alarmed about the trend toward

In the mid-1980s there was little sign of weakness in the Communist façade, but some Western symbols were crossing the great divide and were sometimes altered in the process. In 1984 the Grill in Sarajevo was selling forty "Big Mek" hamburgers a day.

deregulation in many fields, begun in the Carter administration and developed by President Reagan.

WRIGHT: I would like very much to see some motion put into being to stop the momentum, the headlong drive to deregulating everything and creating the law of the jungle again, which existed a century ago.

. . . The causes of the deficits are the excessive tax cut of 1981, in which we gave ourselves the biggest tax cut in history, at the very same time we were launching the biggest military spending buildup in the peacetime history of this country. . . .

That's the reason why, while it took us one hundred and ninety-two years of constitutional government and thirty-nine presidential administrations, beginning with George Washington through Jimmy Carter, to amass a national debt of one trillion dollars, the policies upon which Ronald Reagan insisted and Congress lamentably assented, in 1981, if not radically altered, are going to double that and have us with a two-trillion-dollar deficit in five short years.

April 1, 1984

George Shultz rejects the idea of moving the U.S. Embassy from Tel Aviv to Jerusalem, saying it would offend religious sensibilities throughout the Muslim world.

September 30, 1984: Rep. Jack Kemp and Sen. Gary Hart (on the monitor).

When you run for public office in this country, especially for the presidency, you climb into a goldfish bowl.
—Rep. Richard A. Gephardt (D-MO), following the downfall of presidential candidate Gary Hart

October 14, 1984

Rep. Geraldine Ferraro of New York, the Democratic vice presidential candidate, faces questions about her ability to take over the presidency.

MARVIN KALB (NBC News): Ms. Ferraro, could you push the nuclear button?

FERRARO: I can do whatever is necessary in order to protect the security of this country.

KALB: Including that?

FERRARO: Yes.

. . .

KALB: And if you weren't a woman, do you think you would have been selected?

FERRARO: . . . I don't know if I were not a woman, if I would be judged in the same way on my candidacy. Whether or not I'd be asked questions like, Are you strong enough to push the button?

October 28, 1984

It is high season in the polling world as the presidential election nears. George Gallup assesses Ronald Reagan's hold on the American people.

GALLUP: The driving force in this election is clearly the economy. Going back fifty years of scientific polling, the two issues of peace and prosperity have controlled virtually all elections, and so the economy is certainly going in his [Reagan's] favor. Financial optimism is at a high point over the last five years. The mood in the country is brighter than it has been in seven years, largely because of economic factors.

As the pollsters predicted, Ronald Reagan is reelected President of the United States.

Roger Mudd of NBC News joined Marvin Kalb as a principal interviewer on *Meet the Press Decision '84*. These special editions of the program ran throughout the 1984 presidential campaign and featured on-the-scene reports and interviews.

Marvin Kalb, NBC News chief diplomatic correspondent, had been associated with the program since August 1980. Roger Mudd was NBC News chief political correspondent.

The experiment was judged a success—audiences were up 32 percent over the election period—and the two continued to share principal interviewer duties until June 2, 1985.

If we are going to attack the deficit, we can't set aside defense spending.
—Senate Majority Leader Bob Dole, December 2, 1984

June 23, 1985

The Lebanon hostage crisis plays out on *Meet the Press,* as Israeli Prime Minister Shimon Peres and Lebanese Shiite leader Nahbi Berri are interviewed about U.S. hostages held in Lebanon after

Shiite terrorists hijacked TWA Flight 847. The terrorists demand the release of Lebanese prisoners held in Israel. Peres says the Israelis "feel as strongly about American hostages as we would feel about our own," but "to surrender to terrorist blackmail" cannot be the solution.

PERES: It doesn't matter who surrenders—Israel or the United States. We shall break the united effort to bring an end to these terrible and unbelievable acts of cowardly people. . . . We support completely the position taken by the president of the United States and its administration not to surrender to blackmail.

Against a background of violent confrontations between black South Africans and the country's white government, Chief Buthulezi speaks to *Meet the Press* on August 4, 1985. He is often criticized by black militants for collaborating with the apartheid regime.

> BUTHULEZI: That is as much of bullshit as it would be to say that Andrew Young or Tom Bradley or Mayor Hatcher are collaborators merely because of their federal grants that are given to their cities.

Chief Buthulezi's passing reference to "bullshit" is the first obscenity on *Meet the Press* in almost forty years.

September 15, 1985

The South African ambassador to the United States, Herbert Boukes, gives the clearest indication to date that South Africa's white government may be flexible.

> BOUKES: The decision has been made, yes, to move away from apartheid, to dismantle apartheid.

November 3, 1985: King Hussein I of Jordan is interviewed by Tom Brokaw via satellite.

July 28, 1985: Dr. Edward Teller, senior research fellow at the Hoover Institution, is interviewed by Marvin Kalb. Teller first appeared on Meet the Press *in 1960.*

December 29, 1985

Terrorist incidents multiply. As *Meet the Press* moderator Marvin Kalb says, "Terrorism has emerged in 1985 as a new form of warfare." On December 27, 18 people are murdered and more than 120 wounded in terrorist attacks at airports in Rome and Vienna. Israel's Defense Minister Yitzhak Rabin and Ambassador Robert Oakley, the State Department's top official on counterterrorism, have extensive experience of terrorism in action.

> RABIN: We are in a war against terrorism, all the groups of terrorism, including—might be mainly—the Arafat group. We look at it not as one or two actions that took place in Europe. For us, it's a daily war against terrorism.

Oakley is asked if the danger could reach the United States.

> OAKLEY: I am certain that there are today a few acts of terrorism in the United States. Good work by the FBI and other law enforcement agencies, plus I think the general American attitude, abhorrence of organized violence—although there's plenty of spontaneous violence in this country—have kept terrorism down.

Terrorists deserve no quarter. Terrorists should have no place to hide.
—Secretary of State George P. Shultz, November 24, 1985, speaking after the hijacking of an EgyptAir passenger jet. Sixty people die when Egyptian commandos storm the plane in Malta.

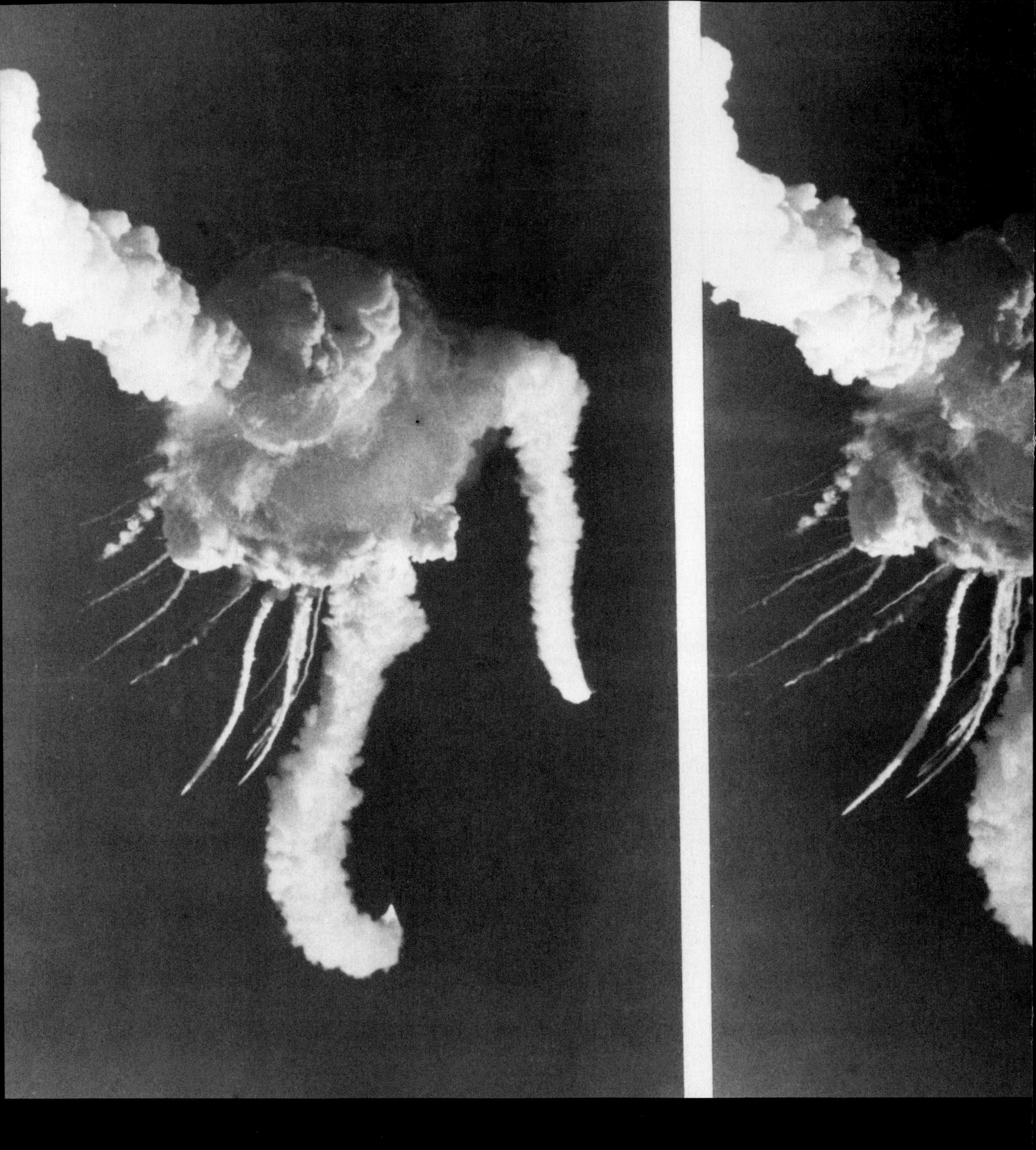

On January 28, 1986 the space shuttle Challenger *explodes soon after launch. Five days later Marvin Kalb's guests on* Meet the Press *are (opposite, left to right) acting administrator of NASA, Dr. William Graham, astronomer Dr. Carl Sagan, and Dr. Thomas Paine, chairman of the president's National Commission on Space.*

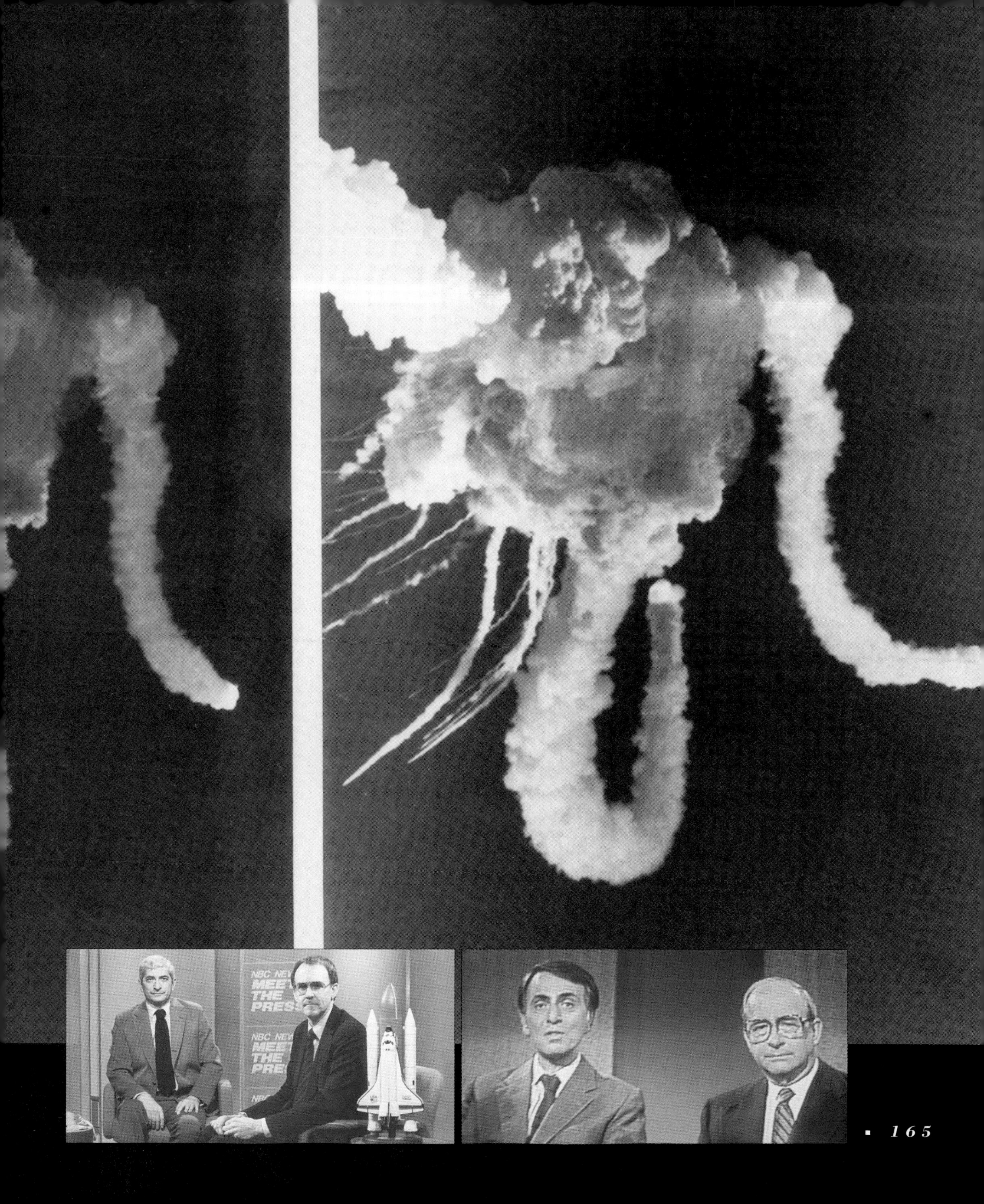

February 9, 1986

As accusations of ballot fraud mount, President Ferdinand Marcos of the Philippines talks about the election held two days before his *Meet the Press* appearance, in which both he and Corazon Aquino claim victory. Mrs. Aquino has promised daily demonstrations if she is not declared the winner. How will President Marcos respond?

> MARCOS: We'll let them demonstrate; probably we'll also counterdemonstrate, and we'll get our people to also shout in the streets.

Two weeks later, holed up in the presidential palace, President Marcos is interviewed by satellite again on *Meet the Press*.

February 23, 1986

In a historic edition of *Meet the Press* President Marcos speaks from the Presidential Palace, surrounded by unrest. Martial law has been declared, two of his top military men are leading a rebellion against him, and the streets of Manila are crowded with anti-Marcos demonstrators.

> MARVIN KALB (NBC News): If President Reagan and his administration were to ask you for the interests of the Philippine nation to step down and prepare an orderly transition to another government, would you listen to the president, sir?
>
> MARCOS: Look, I do not answer speculative questions. I do not believe that he will do so. I do not believe that he will derogate or degrade our constitution by pushing aside the proclamation, the canvass by our own parliament, and I do not believe in the answering of speculative questions.
>
> ROBERT NOVAK (*Chicago Sun-Times*): Mr. Pres—
>
> MARCOS: If that ever happens I—let me think about it. Let us talk about it.

This was considered the first time President Marcos had allowed the possibility of resignation.

Two days later President Marcos is forced from office, and Corazon Aquino, widow of an opposition leader murdered at Manila airport, becomes president.

March 9, 1986

The antigovernment contras in Nicaragua have been dubbed "freedom fighters" by President Reagan, who wants a reluctant Congress to grant them $100 million in new economic and military aid.

Rep. Michael Barnes (D-MD) urges the administration to accept a South American plan to pursue diplomatic channels with the Sandinista government rather than increase the military pressure. Barnes says, "It's hard to find anybody in the world who supports our policy."

But Assistant Secretary of State Elliott Abrams, who is passionately pro-contra, insists that "the president's not looking for compromise at this time."

May 11, 1986: (left to right) Marvin Kalb, Secretary of the Treasury James A. Baker III, and Senate Majority Leader Bob Dole.

Satellite transmissions featured prominently in Meet the Press's *1986 schedule. Some of the guests are shown above. Top row, left to right: President Ferdinand Marcos of the Philippines, Sen. Richard Lugar (R-IN), and Sen. Edward M. Kennedy (D-MA); middle row, left to right: Soviet dissidents Anatoly and Avital Shcharansky and Archbishop Desmond Tutu of South Africa; bottom row, left to right: National Education Association President Mary Futrell, American Federation of Teachers President Albert Shanker, and Ruth Daniloff, wife of imprisoned journalist Nick Daniloff.*

September 14, 1986

First lady Nancy Reagan has become an activist against drug use. Her "Just say no" campaign is a call to young people to resist peer pressure to try illegal drugs. She talks about the problem—and the solution—on *Meet the Press.*

REAGAN: It's not a Democratic problem. It's not a Republican problem. It's an American problem. It's up to the people to take a position now and stand up and be counted.

. . .

MARVIN KALB (NBC News): Do you feel that drug testing should be pursued throughout the U.S. government?

REAGAN: I think in—if somebody is in a sensitive position, yes, they should be tested, because then they're dealing with other people's lives, and yes, I think they should be tested.

. . .

KALB: Yes, but is there a point at which you would say, "Stop," and say this becomes an intrusion into someone's personal—

REAGAN: Well, it's awfully hard for me to look at it in those terms. I guess it's because of the five years talking to all these kids and all their parents and seeing so much and hearing so much. Because you're really talking about saving somebody's life or lots of people's lives.

January 11, 1987

President Reagan has admitted that mistakes were made in the affair that has come to be known as Iran-contra, a complicated secret deal in which the administration agreed to replace arms Israel sold to Iran in return for the release of the American hostages. Profit from the sale was used to finance the contras fighting the Nicaraguan government.

On *Meet the Press* Sen. William Cohen (R-ME), a member of the Senate intelligence panel that investigated the emerging scandal, says the president wanted to continue the policy even after a first delivery failed to obtain release of all the hostages. While praising the president's desire to pursue all avenues, he says President Reagan must assume responsibility for the policy.

COHEN: The fundamental mistake that was made was ever agreeing or allowing the sales of weapons. There the president has to accept full responsibility. . . . He in fact took foreign policy underground.

For all practical purposes, he eliminated the secretary of state, the secretary of defense, perhaps even the CIA, and certainly Congress.

February 8, 1987

Two former secretaries of state—Henry Kissinger and Cyrus Vance—discuss changes in the Soviet Union and the possibility of reaching an arms agreement with Soviet leader Mikhail Gorbachev.

VANCE: I think we are at a crossroads. Much is happening in the Soviet Union today that is very different from the past. There is an openness, there is a willingness on their part to discuss mistakes of the past, to talk about what has to be done in the future. I was there about a year ago, and the difference, even in that one year, from the kind of atmosphere that one feels when you go to Moscow today is very, very marked.

. . .

KISSINGER: Gorbachev is a totally new Soviet leader in my experience, capable of conducting a dialogue. It's the first time that I've met a group of Soviet leaders who would admit that on many of their reforms they didn't really know how to implement them, that there were many unanswered questions and a recognition of the domestic problems of the Soviet Union that I found unprecedented. So, from that point of view, it was interesting, even exciting.

April 5, 1987

Canadian Prime Minister Brian Mulroney makes news by proposing a treaty committing the United States and Canada to cutting acid rain emissions by 50 percent.

MULRONEY: Look, we are killing our common environment, and that to me is something that is completely unacceptable. The least we should be able to do for our children is to pass on a legacy of an unsullied environment. And we are in the process of corrupting that environment.

May 3, 1987

Daniel K. Inouye (D-HI), chairman of the Senate committee investigating the Iran-contra affair, says that President Reagan knew about money from the sale of arms to Iran being diverted to the Nicaraguan contras.

INOUYE: The president was aware that monies were being raised to support arms to the contras.

This is the first public statement from a committee member accusing the president of involvement. Later in the day, the president denies the accusation.

On May 3, 1987 Marvin Kalb takes his leave of *Meet the Press* and NBC.

KALB: This is my last program for *Meet the Press* and for NBC News. I have resigned to accept a professorship at Harvard University. . . . After thirty years as a network correspondent, I leave with a simple but very strong belief, and that is that our democracy is a very precious national asset that is most healthy, most admirable when there is an open and vigorous exchange between the press on the one side and the politician and policy maker on the other. That's what this program has been all about.

May 17, 1987

White House Chief of Staff Howard Baker says President Reagan broke no laws on Iran-contra.

BAKER: The president has done nothing illegal, . . . never tried to conceal the fact that he wanted the contras to survive, and there's nothing new about that.

Baker also supports the president on the question of attempts to buy the hostages' release with payments of one million dollars for each one.

BAKER: There really is a fundamental, fabulous difference between paying ransom to your captors in order to gain their release, and thus rewarding their crime, on the one hand, versus paying money to get past checkpoints in Iran, to bribe guards and to gain the release of your hostages.

MODERATORS OF *Meet the Press*

MARTHA ROUNTREE:
November 6, 1947 to November 1, 1953

NED BROOKS:
November 22, 1953 to December 26, 1965

LAWRENCE SPIVAK:
January 1, 1966 to November 9, 1975

During this period, several other moderators made irregular appearances:

Edwin Newman
Bryson Rash
Deena Clark
Neil Boggs
Bill Monroe
and others

BILL MONROE:
November 16, 1975 to September 9, 1984

MARVIN KALB AND ROGER MUDD:
September 16, 1984 to June 2, 1985

MARVIN KALB:
June 19, 1985 to May 3, 1987

CHRIS WALLACE:
May 10, 1987 to December 4, 1988

GARRICK UTLEY:
January 29, 1989 to December 1, 1991

TIM RUSSERT:
December 8, 1991 to present

May 24, 1987

After an Iraqi Exocet missile attack on the U.S. frigate *Stark* kills thirty-seven American sailors, Defense Secretary Caspar Weinberger warns that any Iranian attack on U.S. ships escorting Kuwaiti oil tankers through the Persian Gulf would be "a hostile act which would be responded to immediately or even prior thereto."

WEINBERGER: We believe the objective of keeping the shipping open, keeping the access to the oil fields open, not only for ourselves but for our allies, is a vital objective.

June 14, 1987

Former Secretary of State Henry Kissinger and Senate Armed Services Committee Chairman Sam Nunn (D-GA) express reservations about policy in the Persian Gulf.

KISSINGER: It isn't obvious to me that there is a new threat to shipping in the gulf. The level of attacks on shipping in the gulf this year seems to be about the same as it was last year.

NUNN: Even insurance rates [for gulf shipping] haven't gone up. And if there's anything that reflects reality, it's insurance rates.

KISSINGER: By our getting involved, in effect, on the Iraqi side, we are taking on a belligerent commitment in a war in which it isn't clear to me how it is going to end.

October 4, 1987

President Reagan's conservative appointments have changed the balance of the U.S. Supreme Court. Now there is vocal opposition to his nomination of Robert Bork. Former Rep. Barbara Jordan spoke against Bork in the Senate hearings on his appointment while Sen. Orrin Hatch (R-UT) is one of his leading supporters.

JORDAN: What the liberals—if you want to characterize the people who are opposing Judge Bork that way—what will be gained is the absence of a voice on the Supreme Court which would threaten to reverse centuries-long publicly held policy positions which this country is comfortable with. Judge Bork is the kind of voice that would see threatened those rights which everyone has become so familiar and so comfortable with and which are so important to the individual.

HATCH: Professor Jordan, could I make a comment there? I am a very good friend of Barbara Jordan's. We served together, we have worked together, we have worked opposite each other, but that is pure poppycock.

November 22, 1987

House Speaker Jim Wright (D-TX) has provoked outrage among conservatives by announcing plans to invite Soviet leader Mikhail Gorbachev to address the combined houses of Congress during his December visit to Washington. On *Meet the Press* Wright backs off.

> WRIGHT: Given the vehemence of their objection, it probably will be wise and will be decided by the White House that . . . let's have a less formal meeting.

But Wright insists the idea for the address came from the White House.

> WRIGHT: A week ago Friday I talked by telephone with Howard Baker, and he was precise enough to say the hour at which they expected to invite Gorbachev to speak—ten o'clock A.M. on the ninth of December.

December 6, 1987

The third summit meeting between President Reagan and Soviet leader Mikhail Gorbachev is about to begin. Speaking from Moscow, top Kremlin official Georgi Arbatov calls the occasion "a historic chance . . . for both our countries and the world" and announces that the talks can proceed without an agreement on "Star Wars," the Strategic Defense Initiative (SDI).

Arbatov also hints at a Soviet withdrawal in the long war in Afghanistan.

> ARBATOV: If the Americans stop supplying the—these bands who fight the government with armaments, we are ready to withdraw our troops.

White House Chief of Staff Howard Baker praises President Reagan's role in the negotiations.

> BAKER: Ronald Reagan had the courage to pick up his books and go home rather than give up on SDI.

December 13, 1987

President Reagan surprises the world by declaring after the successful Washington Summit that the Soviet Union no longer wants to conquer the world. Vice President George Bush begs to differ.

> BUSH: The jury's still out on the question. They haven't changed their fundamental belief about their system. . . . To suggest that we have some euphoric agreement now on where we go in the world is not true.

Nice smile but tough teeth.
—George Bush on Mikhail Gorbachev, December 13, 1987

December 20, 1987

Vice President George Bush and Senate Minority Leader Bob Dole (R-KS) are rivals for the presidential nomination.

CHRIS WALLACE (NBC News): Senator, you're running an ad now, comparing your background and George Bush's, and you end by saying Bob Dole is, quote, one of us.

DOLE: That's a pretty good ad.

WALLACE: What is George Bush? Is he some kind of alien creature?

DOLE: We don't say anything about George Bush. We're going to try and keep our campaign on a positive plane. . . . I've survived a few hard knocks in my lifetime. I didn't start at the top and stay at the top. I started at the bottom. With a lot of help from my friends, I'm somewhere up the ladder. . . .

He has a lot of advantages in his campaign. . . . One plane transports his limousine, another plane transports him—government planes.

February 21, 1988

Sen. Albert Gore, Jr. (D-TN), is a candidate for the 1988 Democratic presidential nomination. Chris Wallace asks him if he isn't just a Harvard-educated liberal passing himself off as a southern conservative.

GORE: Well, you know, the people of Tennessee have had an opportunity to hear those charges in five elections, and they've given a pretty resound-

GEORGE BUSH'S
Meet the Press
INTERVIEWS AND JOB TITLES

MARCH 21, 1971: permanent representative of the United States to the United Nations

JUNE 10, 1973: chairman, Republican National Committee

FEBRUARY 22, 1976: director, Central Intelligence

MAY 6, 1979: contender for the Republican presidential nomination

APRIL 20, 1980: contender for the Republican presidential nomination

SEPTEMBER 7, 1980: Republican vice presidential nominee

FEBRUARY 5, 1984: vice president of the United States

SEPTEMBER 16, 1984: vice president of the United States

APRIL 13, 1986: vice president of the United States

DECEMBER 13, 1987: vice president of the United States

George Bush served two terms in Congress but never appeared on *Meet the Press* during that time. He also served as head of the U.S. Liaison Mission to China.

ing verdict. . . . You know, the Republican party chairs all across the South are the ones that are pushing that line. They had a big strategy meeting a few weeks ago and decided that their top priority in 1988 had to be to stop Al Gore. What they are really saying is that they have decided who would be the strongest Democratic nominee.

March 6, 1988

Pat Robertson, Republican presidential candidate and television evangelist, beat George Bush in the Iowa primary. Robertson is shocked at what he sees as anti-Christian bias in the media.

ROBERTSON: I mentioned throwing down the gauntlet. What happened was I had to run the gauntlet. . . . Fun has been poked at me. My religious views have been ridiculed, I have been parodied.

Elizabeth Drew (*New Yorker*) asks him about school prayer.

ROBERTSON: What we are seeing in the schools of America is a total secularization of the process. Not only are we not praying, we are leaving every vestige of our religion out of our education. So we're training not only functional illiterates but cultural and moral illiterates as well. What I want is a return to moral values—right and wrong.

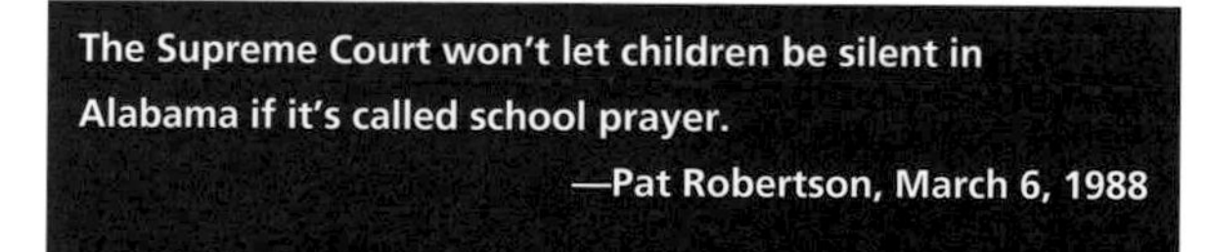

The Supreme Court won't let children be silent in Alabama if it's called school prayer.
—Pat Robertson, March 6, 1988

March 27, 1988

There is a cease-fire in the long battle between Nicaragua's Sandinista government and the contras. With Congress poised to give the contras humanitarian aid but no weapons, House Speaker Jim Wright (D-TX) reflects on the reasons for the cease-fire:

WRIGHT: I think it's war weariness. It's an exhaustion on both sides, with—what Joaquin Miller said: "War and its panoply, the lie that hides its ghastly mockery, that makes its glories out of women's tears, the toil of peasants through the burdened years." They are weary with that. The country is in a shambles. Both sides have suffered enough. They are the ones that bleed and die. It doesn't take much courage for people to sit up here in the air-conditioned comfort of Washington and decree that other people in another country will die. That isn't courage.

I've often said too that the best politics is poetry rather than prose. Jesse Jackson is a poet, Cuomo is a poet, and Dukakis is a word processor—that's what it gets down to.
—Richard Nixon, April 10, 1988

April 10, 1988

Former President Richard Nixon makes his first appearance on a Sunday interview program in twenty years. The interview begins with a current scandal—Iran-contra—and the possibility of a presidential pardon for White House aides Oliver North and John Poindexter if they are convicted in the affair.

NIXON: The answer to that, of course, is one that only the president should and can give. And the question he has to ask himself then is: Did these two men do what they did, believing, whether mistakenly or not, that they had the approval of the president, or were acting in order to serve his interests and would get that approval? If the president, after considering that, believes that that was the

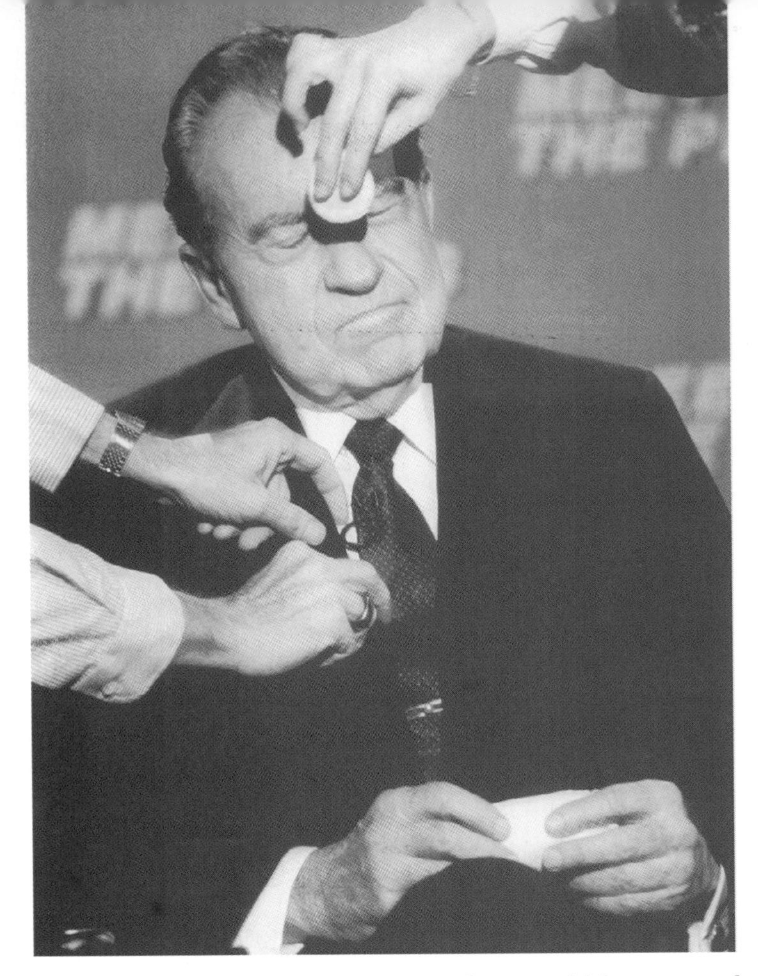

case, then he, the president, would have a good case for pardoning, because then the so-called crime would lack in intent.

JOHN CHANCELLOR (NBC News): Did those thoughts go through your mind when Haldeman was going to jail, and Ehrlichman? They worked for you.

NIXON: They certainly did, and it was a very, very difficult decision for me. Looking back, I probably should have pardoned them. I'm not sure that the country would have taken it at that time—it was a little stirred up, as you might imagine.

TOM BROKAW (NBC News): Some people have called this decade the decade of greed. Is that an apt description?

NIXON: There's nothing wrong at all with greed, provided that greed is one that contributes to the wealth of the country, so that the wealth of the country can then handle some of the problems that people have. Let me tell you, if some people weren't greedy, we wouldn't have the tax money that we could even be talking about more for education, more for health and the rest.

The interview turns to Watergate.

NIXON: Watergate was a breach of trust. I think, to keep it in perspective somewhat. . . . Nineteen seventy-two, as you know, was a very big year. A lot of things were going on. Winston Churchill once wrote that strong leaders usually do the big things well, but they foul up on small things, and then the small things become big. I should have read that before Watergate happened. In 1972 we went to China. We went to Russia. We ended the Vietnam War effectively by the end of the year. Those were the big things. And here was a small thing, and we fouled it up beyond belief. It was a great mistake. It was wrong, as I've pointed out over and over again. But under the circumstances now, people as they judge that period have to see what we accomplished and what we did wrong. And for the future I would advise all those that follow me in the position of president: Do the big things as well as you can, but when a small thing is there, deal with it, and deal with it fast; get it out of the way. Because if you don't, it's going to become big, and then it may destroy you.

May 22, 1988

A week before the fourth Reagan-Gorbachev summit, conservatives are worried about President Reagan's friendship with the Soviet leader. Sen. Gordon Humphrey (R-NH) articulates the problem.

> HUMPHREY: I suppose the president is bowing to what he sees as practical necessity. But I do think it's a mistake for the president—and, for that matter, Mrs. Thatcher and other Western leaders—to cast Mr. Gorbachev and the Soviet system as the equivalent of, say, President Reagan or a Western leader and the Western democracies. There is nothing that even begins to compare. So I really think it's a mistake for the president to be as fawning and as mushy-gushy, frankly, as he has been in recent months.

May 29, 1988

The Reagan-Gorbachev summit is about to begin in Moscow, and the Soviet Union has astonished the world with a sudden pullout from the long war in Afghanistan. President Reagan has annoyed the Russians by planning to meet with dissidents in Moscow. Soviet official Georgi Arbatov expresses Soviet displeasure.

> ARBATOV: You know, Gorbachev could come to the summit in Washington and bring a field kitchen and invite all the homeless of Washington to have free soup there. It would be a sincere gesture of sympathy to these poor people, but I don't think it will be a perfect manifestation of political tact.

Henry is difficult, some people think he's obnoxious—but he's a terrific negotiator.
—Richard Nixon on Henry Kissinger, April 10, 1988

May 15, 1988: Sen. John Kerry (D-MA) returns to Meet the Press. *He first appeared in 1971 as spokesman for Vietnam Veterans Against the War.*

June 12, 1988

Jesse Jackson is spoken of as a possible running mate for Democratic presidential candidate Michael Dukakis, but there are questions about Jackson's willingness to subordinate his ego for the benefit of the party:

> JACKSON: There's nothing wrong with having a big ego. So, I'm right to have a Rolls-Royce ego so long as [I] don't have a bicycle brain.

August 14, 1988

At the Republican National Convention the pro-life plank in the platform is contentious. Sen. Lowell Weicker (R-CT) and Sen. Gordon Humphrey (R-NH) disagree on the matter.

> WEICKER: I'm saying that even when the life of the mother is in danger or even if the woman is pregnant by virtue of rape or incest that she can't have an abortion funded by Medicaid, that just goes to show you that we're out of the area of common sense and into the area of extremism.
>
> HUMPHREY: I'm sure that George Bush would disagree with that. And he has supported the right to life plank in the Republican platform, and it's a good plank. It's a winning plank. . . .

WEICKER: We're tied in knots by this pro-life group. And we're not a pro-life party; we're a Republican party. And quite frankly the concerns of the people across the country go far beyond our position on abortion. And yet that seems to dominate every discussion that is ever raised by the far right within the party. . . .

Presidential nominee George Bush's problem is to convince America that he is more than a loyal vice president. His choice of a running mate is a crucial test.

HUMPHREY: We want a good solid Reagan conservative. Otherwise I think we are in big, big trouble. . . .

JOHN CHANCELLOR (NBC News): Dan Quayle, the senator from Indiana?

HUMPHREY: Very good, yes. Dan is very good.

August 21, 1988

Sen. Bob Dole was widely favored for the Republican vice presidential nomination, but George Bush picks Dan Quayle, and the spotlight is turned on the senator from Indiana. There are accusations that as a young man he used family influence to avoid combat in Vietnam, and Dole sees the furor hurting the Republicans.

February 14, 1988: Presidential candidate Rep. Jack Kemp (R-NY).

DOLE: Right now I'd guess there are a number of Reagan Democrats who are going to remain undecided or maybe go the other way.

I mean, they are out there in my little hometown. And I must tell you, in my generation, you knew who was in the Guard and who was in uniform and fighting for their country. So they are very sensitive about it. They didn't have anybody they could call, they couldn't influence anyone, say, "I asked my parent." Well, my father wore overalls. Who's he going to influence?

September 4, 1988

William Bennett, secretary of education, attacks Michael Dukakis's liberal "Brookline-Cambridge" background on *Meet the Press* and criticizes him for having vetoed a bill requiring the daily recitation of the Pledge of Allegiance in Massachusetts schools. George Bush is delighted with the attack and telephones Bennett to say so. This performance led to Bennett's appointment as drug czar in the new Bush administration.

February 7, 1988: Presidential hopefuls Bob Dole and Michael Dukakis explain their policies on Meet the Press.

January 31, 1988: Gen. Colin Powell (right) with House Majority Leader Thomas S. Foley (D-WA).

December 18, 1988

President Ronald Reagan blamed the biggest shortcoming of his tenure—the budget deficit—on what he called the "iron triangle" of Congress, the media, and special interest groups. Gen. Colin Powell, assistant to the president for national security affairs, defends the spending priorities of the Reagan years.

POWELL: I speak from experience. And somebody who was in a hollow army and has also seen an army in 1986 that is the finest fielded army we've ever had in peacetime—so the money was well spent.

April 2, 1989

Minority Whip Newt Gingrich (R-GA) is gaining a reputation for confrontational behavior. He is leading the campaign against Speaker Jim Wright, whose ethics violation case goes before the House Ethics Committee. Majority Leader Thomas Foley (D-WA) regrets the Gingrich tone.

FOLEY: The two of us are compelled, if we don't wish to—compelled to work together, if there is going to be any successful conclusion to the agenda of either the administration or the Congress. And this kind of raw and nasty partisanship, which Newt, with respect, is the master of and the spokesman for, can only distract us from getting the job done.

Elections are for the purpose of deciding who governs. Governance is what we're supposed to do now—not some running political warfare.

Gingrich is determined to stand firm on one issue: President Bush's "No new taxes" campaign pledge.

GINGRICH: I cannot imagine George Bush breaking the pledge he made for the entire '88 campaign and accepting any kind of significant tax change. And I think all of his loyal troops would far rather . . . reform the Pentagon than accept any significant tax increase.

I'm a hawk, but a cheap hawk.
—Newt Gingrich, April 2, 1989, on defense cuts

May 21, 1989

Tiananmen Square—Chinese government forces crush a student protest in Beijing, massacring more than one thousand. In moderator Garrick Utley's words, Tiananmen Square is "seven days that shook China and stunned the rest of the world, and it isn't over yet."

Winston Lord, former U.S. ambassador to China, insists that the importance of this event—as well as its horror—is incalculable.

LORD: What is clear already is that we are witnessing one of the most important historical

events since World War One; that China will never be the same; that if there is violence and bloodshed, it is the government's fault. They have made some grave, potentially tragic mistakes in recent weeks. . . .

For thousands of years there's been this fear of chaos, and that is why the leaders have been worried about how fast they can go with political reform as well as economic reform. . . . I think the Chinese people are coming together. I think the future is set in terms of a more open society. I think it'll take time, and there may be some tragic moments from here to there. But I think we're seeing a remarkable movement.

May 28, 1989

Israel's relations with the Bush administration begin uneasily. Israel is upset with Secretary of State Baker's call for Israel to give up notions of annexing the occupied territories of the West Bank and Gaza. Speaking by satellite from Rome, Secretary Baker is conciliatory, supporting Prime Minister Yitzhak Shamir's proposal for elections involving the Palestinians.

August 6, 1989: Benjamin Netanyahu.

BAKER: We are pressing the Palestinians in every way that we know how. Through our dialogue in Tunis, through our ambassador there with the PLO, we have suggested to the PLO that they permit Palestinians in the occupied territories to engage with Israel on this question of elections.

Secretary Baker is equally conciliatory toward Moscow, hinting at an end to sanctions following the withdrawal from Afghanistan.

June 4, 1989: Pro-democracy demonstrations (opposite) are crushed by Chinese government forces in Tiananmen Square, Beijing.

BAKER: The changes that we see there are dramatic, they are real, they are indeed revolutionary. We don't know yet whether [Gorbachev] individually will succeed. We want him to. There is no one in this administration that doesn't want the general secretary to succeed, because what he is doing is embracing the political and economic agenda of the West. The West has won. We've won the struggle of the past forty years; we've kept the peace for forty years. The Soviet Union is moving in our direction, and we ought to continue to encourage their moving in our direction.

July 23, 1989

Forty-one years after Whittaker Chambers named Alger Hiss on *Meet the Press* as a Communist in the State Department, there are echoes of the case. Top U.S. diplomat Felix Bloch is accused of spying, the first State Department official to be involved in an espionage case for decades. Sam Nunn, chairman of the Senate Armed Services Committee, assesses the damage.

NUNN: There's no doubt about the fact that the top people in the State Department, the top people in our embassy, have . . . knowledge about certain CIA operations. And so it could be very damaging.

November 12, 1989

Throughout Eastern Europe communism has been collapsing. The 1980s end with the fall of the Berlin Wall, symbol of a world divided by the cold war. At this truly historic moment *Meet the Press* talks to Helmut Schmidt, former chancellor of Germany, at the Brandenburg Gate in Berlin.

SCHMIDT: It is the first time that Germans established their freedom by a revolution, even by a very peaceful revolution. It has to be mentioned, though, that Hungary and Poland were coming ear-

November 12, 1989: The Berlin Wall is breached, and Secretary of Defense Dick Cheney (far left) says, "Mr. Gorbachev is going to be in for a very rough winter." The others (left to right) are Robert Novak, Elizabeth Drew, and John Cochran.

lier, and even earlier came Gorbachev's *perestroika* and *glasnost.* All this has to be seen in one context. And it's probable that also the East German Republic and the Czechoslovakian Republic will join the reformist course of Hungary and Poland.

Asked about possible reunification of the two Germanys, he says: "I think that unification is going to happen someday in the future, maybe even in the next century."

November 19, 1989

President Bush has been criticized for his restrained response to the breaching of the Berlin Wall. Former National Security Adviser Zbigniew Brzezinski thinks caution is correct.

BRZEZINSKI: Should he be doing an Indian war dance in front of the White House? I think he shouldn't gloat. Because for the Soviets this is a massive defeat. And let's face it, it really is.

I think what we have to do is be affirmatively engaged in promoting the process of change. And the process of change is taking place, and I think I can say it as a private person because our ideals and our system have really proven to be effective, to be superior, to be more responsive to the human condition.

Zbigniew Brzezinski first appeared on Meet the Press *on November 10, 1963 as director of the Research Institute on Communist Affairs at Columbia University.*

December 3, 1989

The decade ends well for U.S.-Soviet relations at the Bush-Gorbachev summit in Malta. Both leaders have given their aides specific instructions to advance the negotiations to reduce nuclear weapons and conventional forces in Europe. National Security Adviser Brent Scowcroft is in Malta with President Bush.

SCOWCROFT: I think there's no question that we're in a new phase. The world in which we all grew up and know—so familiar—the kind of confrontational world between the United States and the Soviet Union is changing. The post–World War Two world is collapsing about us, and I think it's premature to say what will follow. It's a very exciting time but also a very perilous time because it could all blow up.

December 10, 1989

One place where the world might still blow up is the Middle East, where the Palestinian problem remains unresolved. But Israel and Egypt—Egypt acting on behalf of the PLO—have agreed to an American plan for talks on the future of the territo-

November 1989: Germans hold hands on the Berlin Wall.

ries occupied by Israel and, specifically, elections for Palestinian self-rule. PLO Chairman Yasir Arafat makes it clear that there is a long way to go.

> ARAFAT: If they want the PLO to participate in this negotiation, definitc, I—wc have the right. It is—it is logical. . . .
>
> GARRICK UTLEY (NBC News): But Israel says it does not want to talk with any PLO representatives, only non-PLO Palestinians. So who will these people be?
>
> ARAFAT: With whom they—whom, with whom they are going to make peace? With goats?

December 24, 1989

The collapse of communism was bloodless until Romanians attempting to overthrow the Ceauçescu regime were brutally suppressed. Secretary of State James Baker is prompted to make an extraordinary statement on *Meet the Press,* saying that the United States would back Soviet intervention in Romania. This was reported as the first time since World War II that the United States has encouraged Soviet military intervention in another country. It is a measure of the change in the relationship between the two superpowers and a measure of *Meet the Press*'s standing that the secretary of state should choose to make his announcement on the program.

IN THE NEWS

1990

- Violeta Barrios de Chamorro defeats Daniel Ortega in Nicaragua's presidential election.
- Lech Walesa is elected president of Poland.
- Communists lose in East Germany's first free elections since World War II. Helmut Kohl is elected chancellor of a reunited Germany.
- Saddam Hussein's armies invade Kuwait, meeting little resistance. Operation Desert Shield forces leave for Saudi Arabia.
- President Bush vetoes a civil rights bill.
- In the battle against the budget deficit, taxes rise.

1991

- In Operation Desert Storm the coalition drives Iraq out of Kuwait.
- In the Iran-contra affair, charges against Lt. Col. Oliver North are dropped.
- After dramatic televised hearings, the Senate approves the nomination of Clarence Thomas to the Supreme Court.
- Charles Keating is convicted in the S&L debacle.

1992

- A jury acquits four police officers whose beating of Rodney King was caught on videotape. Rioting in South-Central Los Angeles leaves more than fifty dead, a neighborhood destroyed.
- The House Ethics Committee names the worst abusers in the House bank check-kiting affair.
- The Twenty-seventh Amendment to the U.S. Constitution, concerning congressional pay, becomes law. It was sent to the states for ratification in 1789.
- Unemployment reaches its highest level since 1984.
- Democrat Bill Clinton defeats George Bush and third-party candidate Ross Perot to become president of the United States. The Democrats control both houses of Congress.
- American troops land in Somalia to help in food distribution.

1993

- President Clinton appoints first lady Hillary Rodham Clinton to head a task force on health care reform.
- A terrorist car bomb explodes in the basement of the World Trade Center in New York. Six die, more than one thousand are injured.
- Four ATF agents are killed in a raid on the Branch Davidian compound in Waco, Texas.
- Janet Reno is sworn in as the nation's first woman attorney general.
- A federal jury finds two police officers guilty of violating Rodney King's civil rights.
- After a seven-week standoff at Waco, eighty Branch Davidians die when fire rages through the compound following a tear gas attack by government agents.
- President Clinton announces policy of "Don't ask, don't tell" on gays in the military.
- Deputy White House Counsel Vincent Foster is found shot dead.
- Islamic fundamentalist cleric Sheikh Abdel Rahman is indicted on World Trade Center bombing charges.
- House approves—and Senate ratifies—the North American Free Trade Agreement (NAFTA) with Canada and Mexico.
- President Clinton signs the Brady Bill, mandating a waiting period for gun buyers.
- Investigation of the Clintons' involvement in Whitewater begins.

1994

- An earthquake measuring 6.8 on the Richter scale devastates Los Angeles, claims over fifty lives.

THE 1990s

- Attorney General Janet Reno appoints Robert Fiske to investigate the Whitewater affair.
- President Clinton ends the trade embargo against Vietnam.
- CIA agent Aldrich Ames is charged with spying for Russia and pleads guilty.
- Four are found guilty of New York World Trade Center bombing.
- Paula Jones files suit against President Clinton for sexual harassment.
- Oliver North wins the Virginia Republican nomination for the U.S. Senate but loses the election.
- O. J. Simpson is charged with the murder of his ex-wife Nicole Brown Simpson and her friend Ronald Goldman.
- The Republican party wins control of both houses of Congress for the first time since 1952.

1995

- Rep. Newt Gingrich (R-GA) is elected Speaker of the House; implementation of the Republicans' Contract with America begins.
- President Clinton loans Mexico twenty billion dollars to prevent financial disaster.
- The Senate votes against a balanced budget amendment, and the House rejects a constitutional amendment on term limits for members of Congress.
- In America's worst-ever act of domestic terrorism, a massive truck bomb explodes outside the federal building in Oklahoma City, killing 168, injuring hundreds more. Timothy McVeigh is charged.
- U.S. space shuttle *Atlantis* docks with Russian space station *Mir.*
- A heat wave causes hundreds of deaths in Chicago.
- A jury finds O. J. Simpson not guilty of murdering Nicole Brown Simpson and Ronald Goldman.
- The Million Man March, organized by Nation of Islam leader Louis Farrakhan, draws hundreds of thousands of African American men to Washington, D.C.
- Israeli Prime Minister Yitzhak Rabin is assassinated in Tel Aviv by an Israeli opponent of the peace agreement with the PLO. Shimon Peres becomes prime minister. Israeli withdrawal from occupied territory continues. The killer receives a life sentence.
- A peace treaty is signed by the combatants in Bosnia and Herzegovina. The United States sends twenty thousand peacekeepers to Bosnia. Russia also commits forces.
- Stalled budget talks between Congress and the White House lead to extensive government closedown.
- The Dow Jones Industrial Average shows a year-on-year gain of one-third.

1996

- Cuban jets shoot down two planes flown by Miami-based Cuban exiles. The economic embargo is reinforced.
- Sen. Bob Dole wins the Republican presidential nomination and resigns from the Senate to campaign.
- Commerce Secretary Ron Brown is among the thirty-five killed when a USAF jet crashes in Croatia.
- Israeli shells hit a UN refugee camp in southern Lebanon, killing more than a hundred civilians.
- The Palestine National Council votes to end demands for the destruction of Israel.
- South Africa approves a postapartheid constitution.
- It is revealed the White House obtained FBI files on leading Republicans.
- TWA Flight 800 explodes in midair soon after takeoff from New York City.
- A pipe bomb explodes at the Atlanta Olympic Games.
- Bill Clinton and Al Gore defeat Republicans Bob Dole and Jack Kemp and the Reform party's Ross Perot in presidential election.

As America adjusts to the end of the long military confrontation with Moscow, a new villain appears in the Middle East: Saddam Hussein. Thoughts of a "peace dividend" fade when Saddam's armies invade Kuwait and refuse to leave. President Bush organizes a world coalition against the Iraqi leader, who boastfully promises the world the "mother of all battles." His forces are rapidly overwhelmed by Operation Desert Storm, which drives the Iraqis out of Kuwait. Before they retreat, they set fire to Kuwait's oil wells, turning the desert air black. Saddam himself retains life and power in Baghdad and remains a threat to regional peace.

In spite of leading the coalition to victory in the Gulf War, President Bush loses the 1992 presidential election to Gov. Bill Clinton of Arkansas. Ross Perot receives 19 percent of the vote, a strong third-party showing.

Rallying after the 1992 elections under Georgia Rep. Newt Gingrich, the Republicans offer the electorate a Contract with America, a conservative plan of action continuing and developing the Reagan philosophy. Inspired by the contract, the Republicans take control of Congress in 1994 for the first time in forty-two years. Although most elements of the contract pass the House of Representatives, a considerable part of it is rejected or modified by the Senate.

President Clinton faces calls for armed intervention in the former Yugoslavia when the collapse of communism sets ancient hatreds free in Bosnia and Herzegovina. Neighbors torture and slaughter neighbors in the name of Serbian nationalism. The European Union proves itself helpless to prevent the genocidal "ethnic cleansing," with its chilling Hitlerian echoes. President Clinton resists demands to bomb the Serbs and arm their Muslim victims.

In June 1994 a white Bronco driving slowly along a Los Angeles freeway is watched by the world on television. The nation becomes obsessed by the man inside the car: football hero O. J. Simpson, suspected of killing his ex-wife and her friend. Other news takes second place as the O. J. Simpson trial plays out on television.

Before the Simpson extravaganza the nation is briefly riveted and divided by the televised confirmation hearings into President Bush's Supreme Court nominee Clarence Thomas. Race and sex, rather than legal acumen, are the themes, as Anita Hill accuses Thomas of sexual harassment sometime ago. Thomas is confirmed, but sexual harassment has become a public issue. Accusations multiply, embroiling even the president, and workplace policy changes as a result.

Racial and sexual sensitivities are at the heart of a running argument concerning political correctness, a determination to include all and offend none. Many find its contortions absurd; others support it as simply civil. Opponents and proponents of political correctness express their views on confrontational radio talk shows, which thrive throughout the nation.

Campaign finance and influence peddling—issues as old as *Meet the Press*—are debated once again. Negative campaign commercials and allegations of misconduct in high places feed a worrying nationwide disaffection with professional politicians. "Washington insider" is used increasingly as a term of abuse rather than a recognition of public service, and the electorate demands term limits to unseat entrenched insiders. Many candidates express enthusiasm for the idea, but incumbents are less keen.

The nation unites in outrage when a Ryder truck loaded with explosives destroys the federal building in Oklahoma City. One hundred sixty-eight die and seven hundred are injured in the worst-ever act of domestic terrorism. The dead include many children in a day-care center.

America goes on-line in the 1990s. "Dot com" and "www" enter everyday speech, and Americans enter cyberspace, to talk to like-minded subgroups around the world. And all for the cost of a local phone call, if the line isn't busy.

Tim Russert became moderator of *Meet the Press* in December 1991. Under his energetic leadership, the program has reasserted its position as a significant force in the American democratic process. As the *National Journal* wrote, "Russert is known for doing his homework and concentrating on substance, thus making *Meet the Press* the newsiest and most influential of the Sunday morning shows." His weekly sign-off rings true: In the world of politics, "If it's Sunday, it's *Meet the Press*."

Tim's direct and forceful questioning is a method that makes news. Viewers have seen Tim pressing Bill Clinton, Newt Gingrich, Al Gore, Ross Perot, Louis Farrakhan, and Jack Kemp, and they have read all about it in the Monday-morning headlines.

Prior to joining NBC News, Tim Russert prepared for his career in journalism by developing a keen understanding of government and politics. Trained as a lawyer, he observed firsthand the inner workings of the executive and legislative branches as counselor in the governor's office in Albany, New York, in 1983 and 1984 and as a special counsel in the U.S. Senate from 1977 to 1982.

He joined NBC News in 1984 and was soon overseeing the *Today* show. He traveled with the program to China, Australia, and South America and in 1985 supervised the *Today* show's live broadcasts from Rome, negotiating and arranging the historic televised meeting with Pope John Paul II (another TV first for the NBC News Division).

He made his debut as a *Meet the Press* panelist on September 16, 1990, when the guests were House Speaker Thomas Foley and Senate Minority Leader Bob Dole. He took over the moderator's chair from Garrick Utley on December 8, 1991. Under his guidance, audience figures have risen, and the program has expanded to a full hour. He introduced the roundtable segment and the *Meet the Press* minute, footage chosen from the program's five decades that illuminates current events.

Tim Russert credits the source of his own strength to family and his South Buffalo Irish Catholic roots. He even produced a feature segment on the *NBC Nightly News* about his father, Big Russ, a retired truck driver and sanitation man. Tim wrote that "all of this was possible because of men like my dad. With strong family values, and a work ethic, they shaped our destiny . . . we stand on their shoulders."

He is married to Maureen Orth, an acclaimed writer for *Vanity Fair* magazine, and they have a son, Luke, who is twelve.

February 25, 1990

Gov. Bill Clinton of Arkansas answers questions about a problem reemerging as a major issue in the 1990s: health and insurance.

GARRICK UTLEY (NBC News): Are we headed towards a national health insurance system?

CLINTON: Yes, because we're getting the worst of all worlds today. You have thirty-seven million people uncovered. We're already spending twelve percent of GNP on health care, which is as high as anybody in the world. And we have inflation going up in medical costs at roughly three times the general rate of inflation. . . . I think there has to be a national solution to this problem. I think all of us would agree on that.

Health care reform was to dominate Bill Clinton's 1992 presidential campaign and the early years of his presidency.

April 22, 1990

On Earth Day, 1990, *Meet the Press* interviews Sen. Al Gore (D-TN), a prominent voice in environmental affairs. He is critical of President Bush's attitude toward a recent White House conference on global warming.

GORE: [T]he delegates from other countries expected a serious discussion, and instead they were confronted with administration participants who were formally advised—the memo was leaked to the press—they were advised to emphasize the uncertainties, don't get into the specifics. . . . The only remaining uncertainties are how rapidly the warming will occur, how much it will eventually be. . . . The fact is, President Bush is ducking Earth Day. Why doesn't he have anything to say on this occasion, when millions of Americans are calling for stronger action to protect the environment? Why is it that he would not allow himself to even say the words "global warming" at this major conference, which he called because he had pledged during his campaign to do it?

On Easter morning 1990 Senate Republican leader Robert J. Dole makes his twenty-sixth appearance on *Meet the Press*, breaking the record of twenty-five, held by Sen. Hubert H. Humphrey of Minnesota. Senator Dole is interviewed via satellite from Jerusalem, where he is completing a weeklong tour of Middle Eastern countries. He first faced the panel on July 16, 1972, as chairman of the Republican National Committee.

May 13, 1990

Campaign pledges are haunting President Bush. With a soaring budget deficit, the president's "Read my lips. No new taxes" promise looks shaky. White House Chief of Staff John Sununu discusses upcoming budget negotiations.

DAVID BRODER (*Washington Post*): Can you say this morning that the campaign pledge will be kept?

SUNUNU: The president is going into these discussions with no preconditions. And those lack of preconditions include no conditioning of the outcome in any respect at all.

BRODER: So you cannot say that the campaign pledge will be kept?

SUNUNU: We are saying that the president will go to that table consistent with the agreement he made with the leadership—no preconditions.

June 17, 1990

The American flag has become an election issue, pitting patriotism against freedom of expression.

Republicans propose a constitutional amendment to outlaw desecration of the flag, the so-called flag-burning amendment. Sen. Daniel P. Moynihan (D-NY) warns that anger against flag burners should not "provoke us into diminishing our rights. . . . You hate what the son of a bitch is saying, but he has the right to say it."

Rep. Newt Gingrich (R-GA) supports the amendment and attacks a Supreme Court ruling that a federal law banning desecration is unconstitutional.

June 17, 1990: Sen. Daniel P. Moynihan (left) and Rep. Newt Gingrich.

> GINGRICH: Why doesn't the country at large have the right to very narrowly amend the Constitution to rebuke these five lawyers?"

Gingrich's repeated dismissal of the Supreme Court as just "five lawyers" was criticized in a *Washington Post* editorial as an assault on America's democratic institutions.

July 22, 1990

Society remains profoundly divided over abortion. The issue comes into sharp focus as President Bush considers a nominee for the U.S. Supreme Court. Sen. Bob Dole (R-KS) is an abortion opponent but advises the president against a pro-life appointment. On *Meet the Press* Dole reveals he told the president that "I assumed the big 'A' word [abortion] would be the tough hurdle to climb."

> DOLE: If you have to vote someone who wants to overturn *Roe versus Wade,* it's going to be a bloodbath getting the nomination confirmed, and the same is true on the other side. . . .

July 29, 1990

As President Bush considers a conservative nominee to the Supreme Court, Rep. Newt Gingrich (R-GA), the Republican whip in the House of Representatives, continues to define a conservative agenda for the 1990s.

> GARRICK UTLEY (NBC News): Do you think that Mr. Bush is deserting the true conservatives, such as you and your colleagues?
>
> GINGRICH: No, and I don't think that in the long run the history of conservatism is a function of what President Bush decides or doesn't decide. I think the long-term trend towards new ideas, towards replacing the bureaucratic welfare state, towards smaller centralized government is going to continue, no matter what happens in Washington, D.C. . . . Washington is a city still dominated by a very liberal elite, and Capitol Hill is a capital dominated by a very Democratic liberal Congress.

August 5, 1990

While internal divisions split American opinion, the nation turns to an external threat. Three days after Saddam Hussein's troops invade Kuwait, and with U.S. oil supplies in jeopardy, former Secretary of State Henry Kissinger and Sen. William Cohen (R-ME) reflect on a menacing situation.

COHEN: We have a situation where we've had a wolf knocking at our door, and we persuaded ourselves that he's really a vegetarian. And I think this past week's incident indeed indicates that he likes red meat. I think we've made mistakes over the years with respect to Saddam Hussein. For years we've known he's been building chemical weapons capability, and the West has helped. For years we have supplied him with trade credits, purchased his oil. We have helped build this particular monster as such that is now swallowing up countries like Kuwait and threatens to—even if not invade Saudi Arabia, attack Saudi Arabia.

R. W. APPLE (*New York Times*): Do you think we have the stomach in any way to involve ourselves militarily in that part of the world?

KISSINGER: Well, it depends what kind of military action is contemplated. In the immediate future I don't believe that Iraq has any intention of invading Saudi Arabia. And I believe there is too much discussion of how we're going to protect Saudi Arabia and not enough discussion of how we're going to get them [the Iraqis] out of Kuwait.

August 12, 1990

There is no sign that Saddam Hussein is prepared to back off, even though he now faces the largest international military force assembled since World War II. An Arab coalition is united against Saddam, but how strong is it? John Cochran (NBC News) questions the Saudi Arabian ambassador, Prince Bandar bin Sultan.

COCHRAN: If Saddam should provoke Israel into military action—and that could happen—what happens to this Arab coalition that was so laboriously put together in Cairo? You can't fight as an ally of Israel against an Arab neighbor, can you?

PRINCE: [Saddam] has created a situation that's dangerous for everybody. He has changed the realities in the Middle East to a very negative way and in a very irresponsible way. . . . We must hold him responsible for what has happened—both the bringing of friendly forces to the area and that he must be responsible for all the repercussions.

August 12, 1990: Saudi Arabian Amb. Prince Bandar bin Sultan.

August 19, 1990

Saddam Hussein begins his "human shield" policy, moving U.S. nationals in Iraq to sensitive military sites. Rep. Les Aspin (D-WI), chairman of the Armed Services Committee, says the United States must not allow concern for the hostages to override military aims.

ASPIN: What it means is that there's got to be the right balance between concern for the hostages but not letting our policy be driven by the existence of hostages or be paralyzed by it. . . . In a sense this is an easier situation to deal with than, for example, the hostages that are somewhere lost in the morass of Lebanon. We at least know the address of the person responsible. So if we need to send a message, we know where to send it.

I question the response that says that we're going to go there and have our young people die so that we can have cheap oil here at home.

—Vietnam veteran Sen. Bob Kerrey (D-NB), August 26, 1990

September 16, 1990

As the nation prepares for war, budget discussions continue, with the focus on tax increases. Newt Gingrich has called Democrats "sick, pathetic, liberal, incompetent, tax-spending traitors." Sen. Bob Dole thinks this is going too far.

> DOLE: I think you have to limit personal attacks and personal insults. But I don't know, a new generation is coming along all the time, and may after they've been here awhile, they'll change their views.

September 30, 1990

In a highly significant development, Eduard Shevardnadze, foreign minister of the Soviet Union, makes the first public commitment of Soviet troops to military action against Iraq.

> SHEVARDNADZE (through an interpreter): I think that in principle we should seek to rule out the military option. I feel that Saddam Hussein and other Iraqi leaders have to understand—will understand—that there is simply no other way, that they have to decide to withdraw the troops. . . .We are a permanent member of the Security Council, and we will comply with any decision, with any resolution of the Security Council.

December 2, 1990

On *Meet the Press,* Secretary of State James Baker commits the United States not to attack if the Iraqis withdraw from Kuwait.

December 2, 1990: Guests Sen. Edward Kennedy (left) and James Baker.

> BAKER: There's never been any suggestion that force would be used if the United Nations resolutions were fully complied with.

The secretary of state repeats U.S. demands for "complete withdrawal from Kuwait, restoration of the legitimate government of Kuwait, freedom for the hostages." He utterly rejects Saddam's attempt to link the Palestinian issue to his withdrawal from Kuwait.

> BAKER: What we're going to say when he asks about the Palestinians is, "We don't think you invaded Kuwait to help the Palestinians. And if you did, all you have done is hurt the Palestinians."

Iraq releases the foreign hostages days later, and Sen. Sam Nunn (D-GA) is reported as saying Baker's statements on *Meet the Press* were an important factor in obtaining the hostages' freedom.

December 23, 1990

Throughout *Meet the Press*'s first fifty years there have been disagreements about a president's right to wage war without the approval of Congress. Senate Majority Leader George Mitchell (D-ME) objects to President Bush's belief that he can order an attack on Saddam Hussein without congressional approval.

> MITCHELL: The administration has said what they would like to see is a UN-type resolution, a blank-check authorization to say that the president, at some indefinite future time, under unspec-

ified circumstances, can make war. That would be a negation of the role of Congress in our system of government.

January 6, 1991

Saddam has been given a deadline to leave Kuwait. It expires on January 15. Secretary of State James Baker is about to meet the Iraqi foreign minister in Europe. The Iraqi ambassador to the United States, Mohammed al-Mashat, faces the press.

ANDREA MITCHELL (NBC News): Are you prepared, is your country prepared to withdraw from Kuwait before such talks can take place?

AL-MASHAT: Well, I pose this question to you—

GARRICK UTLEY (NBC News): Well, no. Answer the question. She asked a question, Ambassador.

AL-MASHAT: No, no, no.

UTLEY: She asked a question.

AL-MASHAT: Because this is an unfair question.

UTLEY: No, it's not an unfair question.

AL-MASHAT: Because the Israelis, they haven't even started to talk with the Palestinians with all the Security Council resolutions—

January 20, 1991

Saddam Hussein does not withdraw from Kuwait, and Operation Desert Storm therefore begins. With overwhelming air power, American forces under Gen. Norman Schwarzkopf attack Iraqi war installations in Baghdad. Reeling under assault, the Iraqis respond by attacking Israel with Scud missiles, trying to draw Israel into the war. Three days into the campaign General Schwarzkopf is interviewed from Saudi Arabia, amid fears that Saddam will deploy his chemical arsenal.

SCHWARZKOPF: I think the jury is still out on whether or not they have a chemical capability for their Scuds, but I would certainly say we're encouraged by the fact that they haven't used them so far.

January 20, 1991: Gen. H. Norman Schwarzkopf, U.S. commander in the Persian Gulf, expresses high confidence that Iraq's nuclear reactors "have been thoroughly damaged" by four days of bombing.

FRED FRANCIS (NBC News): General, what happened to the Iraqi Air Force? We were told yesterday the United States and its allies have killed ten Iraqi planes. They have better than five hundred combat aircraft. Can you tell the American people what's happened there?

SCHWARZKOPF: Yes. We've actually killed fifteen in air-to-air combat to date, but what's happening is they're just simply not flying. I think that's a fact. It's attributed to the fact that we have almost completely taken out their ground control radars. . . .

Saddam Hussein's defeated troops turned the desert black and deadly.

March 3, 1991

The war is over, the Iraqis are beaten, but Saddam Hussein still lurks in Baghdad. Is he still in control? Garrick Utley asks Secretary of State James Baker.

BAKER: As far as we know—we have no reason to believe that [he] isn't. . . .

THOMAS FRIEDMAN (*New York Times*): Can you state categorically now that we have destroyed Iraq's potential to develop nuclear weapons? . . .

BAKER: I think that we have seriously, seriously degraded their capability, if not destroyed it. I'm not in a position to go beyond what the military briefers have already said.

. . .

UTLEY: There hasn't been any terrorism, although Saddam called for a terrorist uprising. And some reports are saying today that this is because Syria, which needless to say over the years has been sponsoring terrorism, put the lid on it. . . .

BAKER: We made it very clear that if there is to be any kind of improvement in the relationship between the United States and Syria, they had to address this issue of terrorism.

. . .

JOHN DANCY (NBC News): Mr. Secretary, the United States pursued only limited aims during this war. You did not go after—at least overtly—Saddam Hussein. You did not attempt to occupy Iraq. One could argue that we are now going to be forced to live with the result of those limited aims. Was that a mistake: to pursue such a limited aim?

BAKER: No. I think it was absolutely the appropriate and correct policy to follow. We have not had any interest from the beginning of this—the president has been very clear on this—in occupying Iraq, moving up to Baghdad, street-to-street fighting in Basra or in Baghdad, or becoming an occupation force in Iraq.

April 28, 1991

The Brady Bill is named after James Brady, who was wounded and permanently handicapped in the assassination attempt against President Reagan. The bill requires a seven-day waiting period for police checks between buying a handgun and taking possession of it. Opponents—led by the influential National Rifle Association (NRA)—argue that it violates the constitutional right to bear arms.

Wayne LaPierre of the NRA prefers an instant computer check to what he sees as an intolerable wait. Rep. Charles Schumer (D-NY), chairman of the House Subcommittee on Crime and Criminal Justice, supports the bill.

SCHUMER: Okay, let me first say that not only have Richard Nixon and Ronald Reagan endorsed the bill, but I have just received letters from Jimmy Carter and Gerald Ford. So every past president, every living past president, has endorsed the Brady Bill, and we're asking George Bush.

Tim Russert (NBC News) pursues LaPierre on whether the NRA would revoke George Bush's membership if he signs the Brady Bill. Mr. LaPierre sidesteps the question.

LAPIERRE: President Bush is not supporting the Brady Bill, so that's not the issue. In fact the Justice Department has called the Brady Bill useless and a distraction from the real problem of taking violent criminals out of our streets and out of neighborhoods. . . .

GARRICK UTLEY (NBC News): Congressman, you feel the pressure of this. Are congressmen scared of the NRA?

SCHUMER: Yes, they are. The number of congressmen that have come over to me and said, "I know that Brady is right, I know that it will do a lot of good, but I'm afraid of the power of the NRA" is —you could count—I didn't have enough fingers and toes to count them.

May 5, 1991

The NRA is not alone in pressing its case in Washington. Special interest groups abound, and the Democratic Leadership Conference, headed by Bill Clinton, has been critical of party leaders on the issue. Elizabeth Drew (*New Yorker*) asks Governor Clinton if the congressional leadership is too subservient to the interest groups.

CLINTON: What we have said is that all the polls show and the presidential elections keep reminding us that a lot of voters who used to vote for us think that. And the reason I joined the Democratic Leadership Council was to try to unify Democrats who do get elected. . . .

May 5, 1991: Gov. Bill Clinton (D-AR).

GARRICK UTLEY (NBC News): Deep inside, do you think there is a good chance that a Democratic candidate could win the White House—not a chance, but a good chance?

CLINTON: Today? No. A year and a half from now? Maybe.

. . . If somebody would stand up and just be honest and say, listen, we . . . require both liberal and conservative elements and completely different approaches, and here's what I think, and if you want to vote for me, fine, and if you don't, stay with what you've got, but it's going to hurt our country, I think we'd have a chance to win.

September 8, 1991

Thoughts of bringing liberals and conservatives together seem farfetched as hearings on Clarence Thomas's nomination to the Supreme Court begin. George Bush's chief of staff, John Sununu, assesses the candidate's prospects.

SUNUNU: Things can come out in the hearing. . . . But we are comfortable going into this hearing that the confirmation process will go forward smoothly and that Clarence will be confirmed.

October 13, 1991

The televised hearings were anything but smooth. Anita Hill's accusations of sexual impropriety against Clarence Thomas added a prurient and controversial element. Members of the Senate Judiciary Committee were reluctant to discuss the ongoing proceedings on television, but two—Alan Simpson (R-WY) and Paul Simon (D-IL)—were persuaded late on Saturday evening to discuss developments on the following morning's *Meet the Press*. Senator Simpson, who claims he is receiving information damaging to Anita Hill's reputation, is angry about the personal attacks on Judge Thomas.

SIMPSON: I do gall and get strident about hypocrisy and things like that. . . . For one hundred and five days they have used anti-Semitism, the books he reads that are stacked in his garage, sexism, racism in reverse, the whole works.

Unlike Senator Simpson, Senator Simon finds Anita Hill credible, partly because "I find generally people who are lying don't volunteer to take lie detector tests." And he believes some good may come of the unseemly scenes.

SIMON: I think one of the—a public service has been performed by Anita Hill, whether you agree with her testimony or not, or believe it or not, in elevating this issue. We are as a nation today much more sensitive than we were a week ago.

Nancy Kassebaum (R-KS), one of only two women in the U.S. Senate, is watching the hearings on television in Kansas, and she questions Anita Hill's behavior.

KASSEBAUM: The charges don't quite match the actions. I would have thought she would have just left the employment. So I think that is something that in my mind hasn't really been fully answered. . . . I think it is very wrong to attack the credibility of Professor Hill, let me say, because I think that she speaks with great conviction, just as does Judge Thomas.

Judge Thomas is confirmed, but few reputations are enhanced by the process.

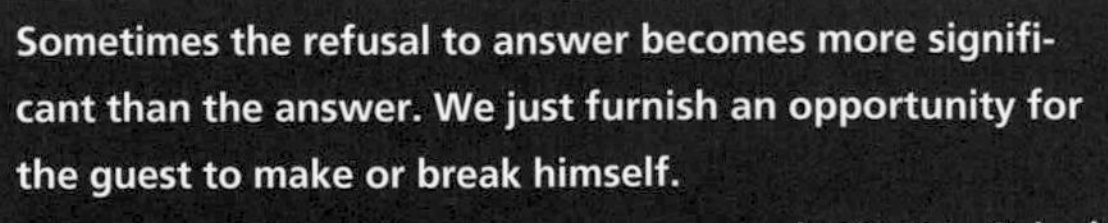

Sometimes the refusal to answer becomes more significant than the answer. We just furnish an opportunity for the guest to make or break himself.

—Lawrence Spivak

November 10, 1991

The colorful election for governor in Louisiana pits former Democratic Gov. Edwin Edwards—twice tried on federal racketeering charges—against youthful Nazi sympathizer and former Ku Klux Klan grand wizard David Duke. Duke has been

disowned by President Bush and the national Republican party, but he is running as a Republican. Utley's first comment to Edwards sums up the situation.

GARRICK UTLEY (NBC News): Voters can well ask why they should vote for either of you. Mr. Edwards first.

EDWARDS: They should vote for either of us because, unfortunately or fortunately, depending upon your views, we are on the ballot.

Duke claims he has turned over a new leaf.

DUKE: I have been too intolerant, and I am a Christian person, and I believe that we have a chance to find redemption in Christ and we have a chance to move forward in our lives. . . .

TIM RUSSERT (NBC News): What did you find so offensive and so objectionable about the United States of America that you found Nazi Germany to be preferable?

DUKE: All right, first off, I was never a member of a Nazi party or anything like that. My—what

THIRTEEN PEOPLE WHO HAVE APPEARED AS BOTH GUESTS AND REPORTERS ON *Meet the Press*

Pat Buchanan	David Gergen
William Buckley, Jr.	Richard Holbrooke
Richard Burt	Bill Moyers
Randolph Churchill	Kevin Phillips
Clifton Daniel	Strobe Talbott
Clayton Fritchey	James Wechsler
Bob Woodward	

happened to me is I was— . . . I became frustrated. I was a young man. I saw our United States government not allowing our soldiers, sailors, and marines to win in the Vietnam War. I felt frustrated. I looked for answers. I saw our schools declining with forced integration and forced busing, which hurt them. I was looking for answers, like many young people did in that period.

But Duke looks in vain for answers to Tim Russert's next questions.

RUSSERT: Sir, who are—what manufacturers are the three biggest employers in the state of Louisiana?

DUKE: Well, we have a number of employers in our state.

RUSSERT: But who are the three biggest manufacturers who are the biggest employers in the state of Louisiana?

DUKE: I couldn't give you the name right off, sir.

Mr. Duke is equally stumped by questions on poverty levels in his state. He loses the election.

January 5, 1992

Six weeks before the New Hampshire primary Gov. Bill Clinton (D-AR) is emerging as the front-runner in the race to become the Democratic candidate for president. He is making health care reform a key issue in his campaign, and he is critical of President Bush's plan to raise the Medicare contributions of the rich.

CLINTON: It's all a bonanza for the big health insurance companies and the health care bureaucracies. It'll be a disaster. It won't do anything to control costs. . . . Why charge people more for the same health care when you don't have the guts to go after the wasteful health insurance companies we've got, the wasteful health care cost system we've got? I don't think that's right.

Mass suspicion of career politicians is making term limits an election issue, and any candidate improves chances of election by claiming he or she is not a Washington insider.

CLINTON: I think anybody who knows anything about my career would say we've always had real competition in elections, and the only reason I've survived is that I've always run as an outsider, as the grass roots representative, as the agent of change—you've got to be for change.

January 12, 1992

Conservative columnist Patrick Buchanan is challenging George Bush for the 1992 Republican presidential nomination. He judges the president's recent trade talks in Japan "a fiasco" and says "he's got to start taking care of his own country first."

BUCHANAN: It is Mr. Bush's mistaken vision of the world. He looks at it as a globalist when all over the world economic nationalists are trying to seek advantage for their own country. . . .

April 5, 1992: Mario Cuomo, Democratic governor of New York, is interviewed on Meet the Press *for the third time.*

The Japanese are mercantilists. They are tough, energetic, competitive, hardworking—they've done a tremendous job. They want to make Japan first. I understand that. I don't have any problem with it.

In order to make us first, you . . . have got to create the climate in the United States we used to have, which was the best climate for investment in the world.

March 22, 1992

Gov. Bill Clinton (D-AR) is now the favorite for the 1992 Democratic presidential nomination. But there are questions about his past.

TIM RUSSERT: Can you assure the Democrats across the country this morning that there is nothing in your background that might emerge which would doom your candidacy and the Democratic party?

CLINTON: Well, I can assure you that there is nothing in my background which is inconsistent with what I have told you already. And I have done everything I could to be up front with the press and the American people. . . . I have the honesty and integrity and character to lead this country. . . .

RUSSERT: What role would Hillary Clinton play in your administration? . . . Would she in effect be a full partner, a copresident?

CLINTON: No, she wouldn't be a copresident. We have our differences of opinion, and in the end I have to decide. But we've always worked together, we care about the same things. She's one of the most caring and intelligent people I know, and I would rely on her heavily for advice and for input. . . .

RUSSERT: Her comment last week that she could have stayed home and baked cookies was taken by some as an insult to people who have chosen to be homemakers. Was that a mistake for her to have said that?

CLINTON: Well, I think it was certainly mistakenly interpreted, and I know that she regrets it very much. . . . But she never meant what she said to be interpreted as a slap at women who are homemakers and who raise children, because she believes, and I believe, that that is the most important work of our country.

April 19, 1992

Sen. George Mitchell (D-ME) believes personal attacks on political opponents are undermining America's confidence in the honesty of its politicians.

MITCHELL: Members of Congress spend hundreds of millions of dollars saying that they [Democrats] are dishonest, can't be trusted, and don't do what they say. It's not surprising that Americans come to believe they are dishonest, can't be trusted, and don't do what they say. . . . I don't think it will change until the American people register their disgust with it by defeating people who conduct negative campaigns.

May 3, 1992

Mass discontent with career politicians leads to the emergence of a strong third-party candidate, Ross Perot. In a week when a not guilty verdict in the case stemming from the police beating of Rodney

King leads to murderous riots and looting in Los Angeles, Perot appears on *Meet the Press,* where Tim Russert asks how he would handle the riots.

> PEROT: I'll sound-bite it for you. This is a place where the risk is high, the reward is low, and if you want people to put capital into those areas, you've got to give them an incentive. You've got a great man, Peter Ueberroth, that's moving in there. But if you look at his first words, he basically said it's going to take money, you folks are all going to have to climb into the ring. Now, real world: People with money, institutions with money, are very cautious to put it in high-risk areas.

Lisa Myers (NBC News) asks Perot about affirmative action.

> PEROT: God created heaven and earth in six days, but nobody else had done anything quite that fast. This is a complex undertaking. Real world: We're going to have to hunker down and stay on it. You know, and I know, the minute it goes off the front pages, most of the politicians will forget it. If I get stuck up here—this is the core of our melting pot. If it is a pot, let's assume it's made of china—we just broke it, right? We've got to put it back together again. It is precious, it is fragile. As a country we will lose if we let the melting pot break again and again and again.

Tim Russert presses Perot on his budget reduction figures, and the candidate is forced to admit, "I got bad information from a man whose name is a household word." Tim Russert pursues, pointing out that the Perot proposals could mean eliminating funding for mass transit, research into AIDS, breast cancer, and Alzheimer's disease.

> PEROT: Now the—this is an interesting game we're playing today. It would've been nice if you'd told me you wanted to talk about this and I'd had all my facts with me, but you didn't, right? Now—
>
> RUSSERT: Mr. Perot, you have said—
>
> PEROT: Wait just a second, wait just a second.
>
> RUSSERT: You have said that part of your four-hundred-billion-dollar deficit reduction plan—
>
> PEROT: Now, what I have also told your—
>
> RUSSERT: —is one hundred and eighty billion dollars—
>
> PEROT: Yes. May I finish?
>
> RUSSERT: May I finish? It was a simple question.
>
> PEROT: Well, you've already finished. Go ahead, finish again. It's your program. You can do anything you want with it. Go ahead.
>
> RUSSERT: Well, I'm trying to get a specific answer to a proposal you've made. That's fair.
>
> PEROT: Well, I am trying to answer it.
>
> RUSSERT: Please do, sir.
>
> PEROT: Are you sure you're finished?
>
> RUSSERT: Absolutely.
>
> PEROT: Okay, may I talk?
>
> RUSSERT: I wish you would.
>
> PEROT: Thank you.
>
> RUSSERT: Thank you.

After this exhilarating exchange, Tim Russert asks Ross Perot if he plans to run in the presidential election.

> PEROT: It's up to the American people. It's all in their hands. They have got to put me on the ballot in fifty states.
>
> RUSSERT: And if they do, it's a definite go?
>
> PEROT: If they do, I have told them that I will run. I will not belong to anybody but them, and I will be their servant. My word's good. It's that simple.

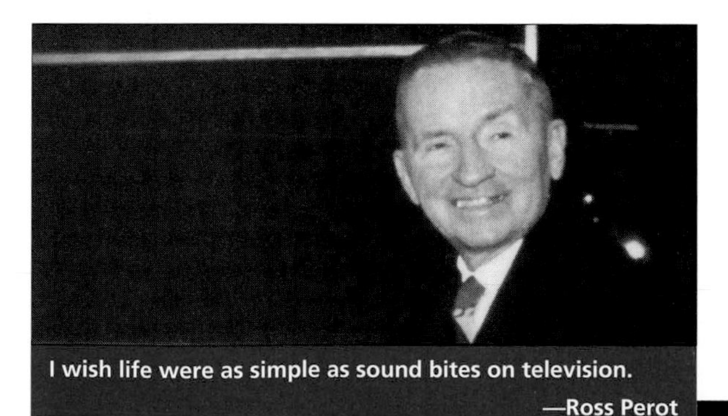

I wish life were as simple as sound bites on television.
—Ross Perot

From the start *Meet the Press* was a thirty-minute show, except for expanded special editions, but on September 20, 1992, it becomes one hour long, with the addition of a roundtable segment, in which members of the media discuss issues of the day. That month Larry King, host of CNN's *Larry King Live*, joins Tim Russert, David Broder, and Elizabeth Drew on the roundtable before traveling to Dallas to interview Ross Perot. There are rumors that Perot will use his appearance to declare he is back in the presidential race, prompting Tim Russert to ask Larry King about candidates' extensive use of talk shows in the campaign.

King points out that "talk shows were always a staple in America. In 1968 in Miami I interviewed Hubert Humphrey and Richard Nixon and George Wallace. They all were running for president. They came on, they took phone calls. Jimmy Carter ran in Iowa. He won by going on talk shows through Iowa. No one knew him. He went on talk shows."

September 27, 1992: (left to right) Tim Russert, David Broder, Elizabeth Drew, and roundtable guest Larry King.

April 18, 1993: Bob Dole (left) and talk show host Rush Limbaugh.

King thinks George Bush could use talk shows to boost his flagging campaign. "I think he's in big trouble, and I think he's got to come on more programs, I think he's got to get in touch with more people."

Bush lost the election to Clinton, and in April 1993 conservative radio host Rush Limbaugh is asked on the roundtable if there is a difference between Bill Clinton and George Bush.

LIMBAUGH: I don't think there is. You know, this administration loves to talk about the twelve years of Reagan-Bush, and I think when we are a little farther out, I think it's going to be the eight years of Bush-Clinton that the people are talking about, because there are a lot of economic similarities.

Making a second roundtable appearance on November 12, 1995, Rush Limbaugh talks about another possible president: Colin Powell.

LIMBAUGH: I have the same respect for his character that we've heard expressed everywhere. But I'm not really aware of the two or three things that General Powell has done that had sixty-six percent of the people saying, "Be our president. Be our president." What is that? And the press did not treat him as a suspect, which is unusual.

Political humorist Mark Russell addresses the issue of independent candidates running for president on the September 3, 1995, roundtable.

RUSSELL: Well, [Bill] Bradley, the reason he may run, the reason he's leaving the Senate—he has never been investigated by the Ethics Committee, so he's just not getting the media exposure that he should. And Colin Powell—I just—I don't know. People say, "Well, I'm for Colin Powell. He's great." I say, "Well, why? His issues? His opinions?" "Yeah." "Explain them." "No, he's great. He's just great." "Well, what—tell me a little more about him." "He's great. He's wonderful." And today that'll carry him.

May 10, 1992: Sen. Bill Bradley (D-NJ).

On the May 15, 1994, roundtable *Tonight Show* host Jay Leno suggests that Bob Dole may have been born in the wrong place to satisfy his presidential ambitions.

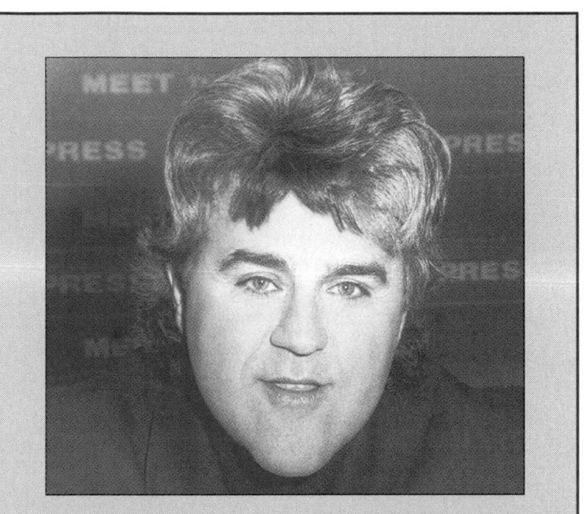

May 15, 1994: Jay Leno is the roundtable guest.

LENO: He's got a good sense of humor. . . . Americans don't like a sort of cranky sense of humor. I think he would be—if he was in England, he would be prime minister right now, because he has that sort of, that bent that I find very funny.

And what political stories do his audiences find funny?

LENO: Well, anytime—sex and money are always the best, and the Paula Jones thing seems to be the most fun for the audience, because there's something—everybody knows somebody who's done that, you know? And they are the kind of jokes people understand. . . . Most people don't have nuclear weapons in the backyard, but they have, well, the guy next door.

And what, wonders David Broder, would be Jay Leno's line about Tim Russert?

LENO: Well, I used to admire him as a kid, of course. I mean, he was Howdy Doody.

September 20, 1992

Vice President Dan Quayle is the guest on *Meet the Press*'s first regular one-hour program. Tim Russert questions him on the abortion issue, following the Republican party's adoption of the principle that all abortions should be banned, even in cases of rape or incest.

QUAYLE: If you want to talk about extreme positions, you can go look at the Democratic platform, where now they have taken out from the Democratic platform that a parent has a right to be informed when their daughter gets an abortion. You get informed if the schools give them an aspirin . . . but you are not informed if your daughter is going to receive an abortion. We think that is wrong. . . .

I mean, this is the issue. In *Roe versus Wade*, I have always said I thought it was an erroneous decision. Overturning *Roe versus Wade* would put it back to the states, and statutes like Pennsylvania will be created.

RUSSERT: So you are for overturning *Roe v. Wade*?

QUAYLE: Yes.

Vice President Quayle has been in the forefront of attacks on Bill Clinton about his draft history. But there are also question marks surrounding the vice president's own service record. Did he use family influence to join the Indiana National Guard during the Vietnam War?

QUAYLE: I never asked for any special treatment. Obviously if you join the National Guard, you have less of a chance to go to Vietnam. . . . But that's not the issue. See, the issue is not my military service in the National Guard or Bill Clinton's avoiding military service. The issue is the veracity of Bill Clinton. He will not tell the truth on this issue.

September 27, 1992

Pat Robertson is the president of the Christian Coalition, and he is a conservative. He is held partly responsible for the harsh tone of the Republican National Convention. Tim Russert asks Robertson about his convention reference to Bill Clinton's desire to appoint homosexuals to his administration.

RUSSERT: Aren't there homosexuals in George Bush's administration?

ROBERTSON: Well, I don't think he's going out actually asking for them. Bill Clinton indicated he would go about and solicit such people and ask for their point of view, and if they were active homosexuals, he would seek to put them on. And they've

said he is the most pro-homosexual candidate that has come on the national scene in history.

. . .

ELIZABETH DREW (*New Yorker*): Do you agree with Patrick Buchanan that there's a religious war going on?

ROBERTSON: . . . I do think that there is a cultural war, a war of values that's definitely going on, and this campaign in a sense is highlighting it. . . . I would like to see this nation return to some of the bedrock of loving husbands and loving wives, of stable families, of smaller government, of less intrusion into the business life of our nation, of values.

At the convention Pat Robertson said conservative activist Phyllis Schlafly had saved the Constitution from including homosexuality. On *Meet the Press,* following her son's revelation that he is gay, she is asked if homosexuality is a matter of choice or biology.

SCHLAFLY: I don't consider myself an expert on that. I don't know. That may be automatic. But your behavior is something you decide. And I think that people are to be held accountable for their behavior.

She holds strong views on sex education in schools.

SCHLAFLY: I think it's wrong to bring homosexual books into the elementary grades, which is now being done and promoted by the National Association for the Education of Young Children, and you've seen it in the New York schools.

I think the sex education courses that teach children that premarital sex is okay [are] wrong, and you know, that's what we've had for twenty years in this country, a nonjudgmental description of all kinds of sex acts with demonstrations of how to do it and with an attempt to break down the natural modesty of the girls.

December 6, 1992

President-elect Clinton's promise to end the military ban on homosexuals has stirred up much hostility. On *Meet the Press,* Secretary of Defense Dick Cheney explains why the Bush administration favors the ban.

CHENEY: People's private lives are their own business. The way I run the civilian side of the Pentagon is in accordance with that principle. But the military's different, because you have forced association. . . .

It's the judgment of our senior military commanders, which I concur in, that to force gays leading an overt, openly gay lifestyle into our military units would have a detrimental impact upon the cohesiveness of the units and our combat capabilities.

January 31, 1993: Quarterbacks Jack Kemp (left) and Roger Staubach assess the Buffalo Bills' chances against the Dallas Cowboys in Super Bowl XXVII.

January 10, 1993

Another Clinton campaign pledge is more universally welcomed: giving a tax cut to the hard-pressed middle class. Now it looks doubtful, as House Speaker Thomas Foley (D-WA) admits.

> FOLEY: I'm not sure, in the light of present circumstances, that [the tax cut] shouldn't be rethought. . . . It's a mistake for any president to say, "I'm going to keep my campaign promise no matter whether it hurts the country."

January 24, 1993

Two weeks after Speaker Foley's warning, Lloyd Bentsen—giving his first national television interview as treasury secretary—confirms on *Meet the Press* that the middle class should not expect a tax cut too soon. On the contrary, he raises the prospect of new taxes on energy, even on gasoline.

> BENTSEN: What you are going to see in this situation is some consumption tax is going to take place. . . . We have to do things to cut back on consumption and encourage investment for the creation of jobs in our country.

February 28, 1993

Two more broken Clinton campaign pledges are put to Secretary of State Warren Christopher. The first is to reverse President Bush's policy of returning Haitian refugees, the so-called boat people. And the secretary of state's answer echoes Speaker Foley's.

> CHRISTOPHER: I don't suppose you'd want anybody to keep a campaign promise if it was a very unsound policy.

During the campaign Bill Clinton also proposed to end the United Nations embargo on arms supplies to the Bosnian Muslims, involved in a bloody struggle with the Serbs.

Tim Russert (center) questions Secretary of State Warren Christopher (left).

> CHRISTOPHER: We found, when we consulted with our [European] allies, that if we would try to lift the arms embargo, they would probably abandon their humanitarian efforts. . . . I think we have to look at the reality of March 1993 rather than trying to look at the situation last September. Things that might have seemed feasible and possible then are probably not wise or prudent now.

The Serbian nationalists' aggression has made sizable inroads in Bosnia and Herzegovina, and Secretary Christopher admits for the first time in public that it may not be possible to force their withdrawal from the occupied territory.

> CHRISTOPHER: I suppose that it will never be able to be rolled back to the situation where it was a year and a half ago.

April 18, 1993

Health care reform was the cornerstone of the Clinton election campaign, and Hillary Rodham Clinton is leading a task force looking into health care provision and funding. But the reform plan is already running into opposition even within the

Democratic party. Senate Majority Leader George Mitchell warns against attempts to fund health care with new taxes.

> MITCHELL: I think it's a mistake to begin the discussion by talking about what type of tax, how much money, until you know what it is you are paying for.

When communism collapses, ancient hatreds break out bloodily in Bosnia, and the world has no easy solution.

May 2, 1993

The vice president, Al Gore, is asked about the need for new taxes to finance the health care reforms.

> GORE: [T]he health care task force is not talking about a value-added tax, as some of the indications earlier led some people to believe. . . . I think that the case for financing part of our health care reform by looking at the impact that tobacco has on medical costs is pretty strong.

The vice president also broaches the question of American military involvement in Bosnia.

TIM RUSSERT: What is our goal? What is our objective in Bosnia?

GORE: Well, to end the ethnic cleansing that has so horrified the conscience of the world and to prevent the changing of international boundaries by military force, a principle that has been well established in the world community for a long time, especially since World War Two. It was one of the guiding principles that the world came out of World War Two with.

September 19, 1993

The long-awaited—and late—Clinton health reform plan is about to be unveiled, and Counselor to the President David Gergen is excited.

GERGEN: We are on the verge of an historic moment.

Sen. Daniel P. Moynihan (D-NY) dampens the enthusiasm, calling the finance proposals "fantasy," and declaring that "they mustn't last."

MOYNIHAN: We are not going to get two hundred thirty-eight billion dollars out of Medicare and Medicaid in the next five years, to which we'll add ninety-one billion dollars in deficit reduction. That's not going to happen, needn't happen to get a better system.

October 31, 1993

Five weeks after publication, the Clinton health care plan is under siege. Rep. Dick Armey (R-TX) thinks the president must be ready to compromise.

ARMEY: We believe universal coverage is just a euphemism for the welfarization of health care. . . . When he sees his plan won't fly, then he'll look for something that can.

November 7, 1993

In a major *Meet the Press* exclusive, President Bill Clinton becomes the first sitting president to agree to an interview on any talk show since Jimmy Carter's *Meet the Press* appearance in 1980. The interview is conducted in the Oval Office.

TIM RUSSERT: Mr. President, this is our forty-sixth birthday. You are forty-seven. You strike me as the kind of guy who maybe watched the first program from your cradle.

CLINTON: I wish I could. I didn't have a television then. I was one when you started, but I was nine, I think, when we got our first television in 1956, so I couldn't start, but I did watch it often after that.

The president addresses his major interest: health care reform.

CLINTON: We tolerate conditions in America that are intolerable in other countries. Now, the condition we tolerate by not having everybody insured is higher health care costs. . . . We assume

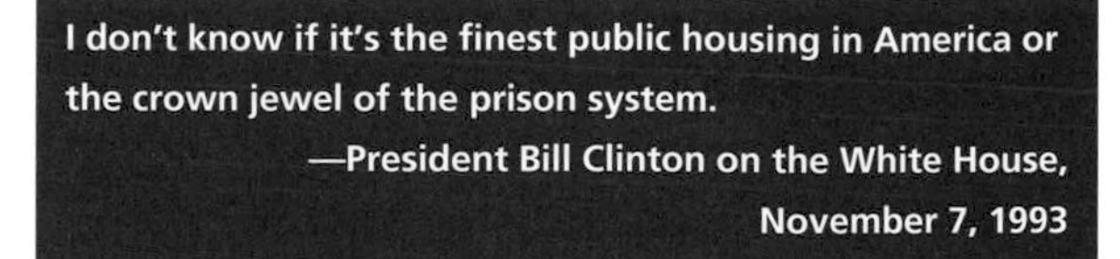
I don't know if it's the finest public housing in America or the crown jewel of the prison system.

—President Bill Clinton on the White House, November 7, 1993

that universal health coverage will cost more when every other country that has universal coverage is paying much less than we are and having less inflation.

President Clinton is also campaigning for NAFTA, the North American Free Trade Agreement, ending tariffs between the United States, Canada, and Mexico. Why are members of Congress so hard to convince of NAFTA's value?

CLINTON: I think frankly the vociferous, organized opposition of most of the unions telling these members in private they'll never give them any money again, they'll get them opponents in the primary, you know, the real roughshod, muscle-bound tactic, plus the fact that a lot of the business supporters of NAFTA have not gotten their employees and rank-and-file people to call and say they are for it. . . . But if all the presidents are for it, all the secretaries of state, all the Nobel Prize-winning economists—who never agreed on anything else in their lives, probably—and virtually all the governors are for it, it must be good for the American economy.

John F. Kennedy spoke passionately about trade union power on *Meet the Press* in the 1950s and 1960s. Another issue echoes the earliest days of *Meet the Press:* North Korea.

RUSSERT: Mr. President, a lot of growing concern about North Korea, a country that we fought some forty years ago. Will you allow North Korea to build the nuclear bomb?

CLINTON: North Korea cannot be allowed to develop a nuclear bomb. We have to be very firm about it. . . .

RUSSERT: There are eight hundred thousand North Korean troops amassed on the South Korean border. If the North Koreans invaded South Korea, would that in effect be an attack on the United States?

CLINTON: Absolutely. We have our soldiers there. They know that. We still have people stationed near the Bridge of No Return. I was up there on the bridge. I was in those bunkers with our young Americans. They know that any attack on South Korea is an attack on the United States.

Meet the Press has probably made more headlines than any other program in the history of television. When President Clinton was interviewed live in the Oval Office on November 7, 1993, the headlines were made before the program was over. In the early part of the program President Clinton was critical of the trade unions' tactics in the NAFTA debate. In the final minute of the program a note is passed to the president, who interrupts Tim Russert.

"Did you see what Gergen just did? He brought in this thing saying that the headline is now that Clinton accused labor of roughshod tactics and that's—[laughter] I mean, those guys are my friends. I just don't agree with them on NAFTA."

The House approved NAFTA on November 17, the Senate on November 20. _Meet the Press_ can claim to have influenced the fortunes of NAFTA. Press reports indicate that the August 1, 1993, _Meet the Press_ interview with Ross Perot—viewed by many commentators as a landmark in the decline of Perot as a political force—was a factor in the White House decision to approve a debate between Perot and Al Gore. The debate went ahead and was widely considered to have contributed to the vote of approval by Congress.

November 7, 1993: President Clinton refuses to rule out an invasion of Haiti.

Since the sensational 1946 Bilbo interview, racial issues have been covered on *Meet the Press*—desegregation and the civil rights movement, urban riots, the emergence of black power, and the continuing struggle for equal opportunity. Tom Brokaw (NBC News) asks the president if he thinks the racial climate in urban America is better or worse than a decade ago.

CLINTON: I think for middle-class people, it's much better. I think the level of comfort among people of different races is much higher. I think the appreciation for diversity is greater. I think for people who are outside the economic mainstream, it is much, much worse. . . .

And one thing I'd like to say to the rest of America is, you read these horrible stories about how many people get killed on the weekends. Most of the people that live in all those neighborhoods never break the law, work for a living, for modest wages, pay their taxes, trying to do right by their kids. I mean, this country is falling apart because we have allowed that—a whole group of us to drift away. It's not an underclass anymore, it's an outerclass.

The United States' concern with the Caribbean is another old and ongoing issue.

RUSSERT: Haiti. The military leaders have refused to meet. Your policy, United States policy, is to reinstate [the exiled president] Mr. Aristide. . . . Would you consider invading Haiti to reinstate Aristide?

CLINTON: . . . Last time the Americans went there, in 1915, we stayed nearly twenty years. So they [Aristide and Prime Minister Malval] have not asked for that. But I don't think we should rule anything in or out.

January 9, 1994

Daniel Patrick Moynihan (D-NY), powerful chairman of the Senate Finance Committee, deals the president's health care reform plans a mortal blow by declaring on *Meet the Press* that there is no health care crisis in America.

> MOYNIHAN: [T]here was a meeting in the Cabinet Room on Monday in response to Senator Dole's appearance on *Meet the Press* last Sunday, where he laid out some terms of health care. . . . [T]hey said, "And we won't have time for welfare until we get this health care bill." . . .
>
> We promised in that last presidential campaign that we would address the issue of welfare. In all truth, I don't want in any way to suggest that health is not a priority and that what the president makes a priority is a priority for me, but if you—we don't have a health care crisis in this country. We do have a welfare crisis.

April 3, 1994: Lt. Gen. Michael Rose, commander of the UN forces in Bosnia, speaks to Meet the Press *in Sarajevo.*

May 8, 1994

The Clinton administration is considering sending troops to Haiti. Randall Robinson, executive director of TransAfrica, has been on a hunger strike in Washington for twenty-seven days in an effort to change the administration's policy on repatriation.

The use of American troops overseas is a continuing subject of debate in the 1990s, whether in Bosnia, Somalia, or Haiti (below).

TIM RUSSERT: You say the end is within sight. Have you heard from the administration about a change in policy towards Haiti?

ROBINSON: About fifteen minutes ago I talked to National Security Adviser Anthony Lake, and he confirmed . . . that the administration has now committed itself to grant asylum hearings to fleeing Haitians, and that was the basis of my hunger strike in the first place. And with that commitment I will end my hunger strike today.

Later in the program deputy National Security Adviser Samuel Berger explains the policy change.

BERGER: [B]ecause of the increasing level of violence that has taken place in Haiti over the past several weeks, we have become increasingly concerned about that small percentage of Haitians who are fleeing not because of economic hardships but because of their political activities or political beliefs . . . that small group of people who are not necessarily fleeing to the American dream . . . , but they are fleeing the Haitian nightmare.

Asked about the astonishing longevity of *Meet the Press* in a medium where life expectancy is normally low, Lawrence Spivak said, "We found that the program generated enough excitement to compete in an entertainment medium because in addition to being informative, it had the following elements, which usually attract and hold an audience: big names, important in the news at the time; suspense—implicit in challenging questioning was the fact that the unexpected could happen at any moment—freshness, because the program was unrehearsed—the guest never knew the questions to be asked, the reporters never knew what the answer would be, both had to be on their toes ready for quick response—controversy—certain to result from any form of cross-examination—and, above all, fairness, both in the selection of the panel and in the questioning. The added dimension brought to the radio program by television came from the simple fact that most faces are revealing and great impact often resulted when facial expressions either matched or failed to match the words spoken."

July 31, 1994

The UN Security Council has approved an invasion of Haiti to overthrow the military dictatorship. UN Ambassador Madeleine Albright spells out the message to the Haitian government:

ALBRIGHT: You can leave soon and voluntarily, or you can leave soon and involuntarily.

August 7, 1994

The Whitewater investigation, although little understood by the public, continues to dog the White House. Kenneth Starr has been appointed special counsel, and he is a veteran of the Reagan-Bush administration. White House Chief of Staff Leon Panetta puts a brave face on the appointment.

PANETTA: The bottom line is: There are no criminal violations; there are no ethical violations; there were no violations of the law. There were, in fact, people who may have talked to each other too much. . . . I think we now know where the truth is, and I hope we can move on.

August 28, 1994

Thirty-five years after Fidel Castro's promise on *Meet the Press* to hold elections within four years, Cuba is still waiting to vote, and Castro is still in power. Large numbers of Cuban refugees are heading across the sea to Miami. Peter Tarnoff, undersecretary of state for political affairs, is asked to explain administration policy.

> TARNOFF: The United States is not interested in cutting a deal with Fidel Castro. . . . Our policy objective is to help achieve a democratic society in Cuba, with a free market economy, the liberation of political prisoners, and an open political system.
>
> . . .
>
> LISA MYERS (NBC News): Then the United States government is perfectly happy to see Fidel Castro reign over Cuba indefinitely as long as he makes economic and political reforms?
>
> TARNOFF: No. I think we are prepared to deal with whoever is the democratically elected leader of Cuba. It remains to be seen whether Fidel Castro would emerge as that person if there were free elections in Cuba.

Castro is not the Caribbean's only dictator, and Cuba is not America's only Caribbean problem. On the same program Robert Novak (*Chicago Sun-Times*) asks Sen. Richard Lugar (R-IN) and Rep. Lee Hamilton (D-IN) about the possibility of an invasion of Haiti.

> LUGAR: I would just say it's a terrible idea even to contemplate invading Haiti.
>
> HAMILTON: I hope we don't invade Haiti either.

November 4, 1994: As invasion approaches, Haitians in Port au Prince crowd onto a flatbed truck heading for the provinces.

September 11, 1994

There are differences of opinion between Congress and the White House over an invasion of Haiti. Congress demands a vote before any invasion, but Secretary of State Warren Christopher asserts, as administrations have asserted before him, that the president needs no congressional approval.

> CHRISTOPHER: We can't tie the hands of the president. The president may have to act in a situation very quickly and on his own constitutional authority.

And the secretary of state warns that the invasion date is fast approaching.

> CHRISTOPHER: I would say time is running out. I hope they [the government of General Cedras] leave very promptly, but their days are numbered, and they'll leave one way or the other, either soft or easy—soft or hard.

September 25, 1994

The mission to Haiti of former President Jimmy Carter, Gen. Colin Powell, and Sen. Sam Nunn averts a military invasion, but fifteen thousand U.S. troops are in Haiti, and U.S. Marines have been attacked by armed Haitians. Both houses of Congress have voted for "prompt" withdrawal. Secretary of Defense William Perry says on *Meet the Press* that the American forces should stay on the island until democratic elections are guaranteed. He is against fixing a withdrawal date.

PERRY: I would not like to have a date certain set. I think that complicates our operations.

Sen. Sam Nunn, chairman of the Armed Services Committee, expresses similar reservations.

NUNN: I'm reluctant to set dates certain for military missions which are inherently complicated and which can change very rapidly on the ground, but I think the majority of the Senate will insist on setting a date certain. . . . Someone asked me, you know, why do I think this agreement will be carried out when others have not? And my answer is four reasons: Army, Navy, Marines, and Air Force. We're in control.

Senator Nunn also pays tribute to Jimmy Carter's efforts.

NUNN: He is known around the world as a deeply religious man, a man of humanitarian convictions. In this instance, I think, it served this country well. . . . Jimmy Carter is an extraordinary American, . . . and without him this mission would have been an invasion; it would not have been a peaceful occupation. And there would have been, without any doubt, perhaps hundreds of Americans that were casualties, and certainly thousands and thousands of Haitians.

November 27, 1994

William Perry paints a grim picture of the situation in Bosnia and echoes an earlier statement on *Meet the Press* by Lord David Owen, European Community negotiator on Bosnia. Insisting that bombing is no solution, Lord Owen declared on May 30, 1993 that "you will not solve the problem at ten thousand feet." Perry concurs, saying that air strikes "cannot determine the outcome of the ground combat."

PERRY: The Serbs have occupied seventy percent of the country. There's no prospect as I see it of the Muslims' winning that back.

If you want a classic failure, this is a classic failure.
—Sen. Bob Dole on NATO's role in Bosnia, November 27, 1994

December 4, 1994

The Republicans become the majority party in Congress in the November 1994 midterm elections, and Rep. Newt Gingrich gives a classically confrontational *Meet the Press* performance.

LISA MYERS (NBC News): The first lady, Hillary Rodham Clinton, came after you last week, saying that your proposal to put the children of mothers who could not afford to support them in orphanages was both unbelievable and absurd. How do you respond to that?

GINGRICH: I'd ask her [to] go to Blockbuster and rent the Mickey Rooney movie about Boys Town. I mean, my answer to her, in part, is, you know, the little four-year-old who was thrown off the balcony in Chicago would have been a heck of a lot better off in Boys Town. . . . I don't understand liberals who live in enclaves of safety who say, "Oh, this would be a terrible thing. Look at the Norman Rockwell family that would break up." And the fact is we are allowing a brutalization and a degradation of children in this country, a destructiveness. We say to a thirteen-year-old drug addict who's pregnant, you know, "Put your baby in a Dumpster, that's okay, but we're not going to give you a boarding school, we're not going to give you a place for that child to grow up."

Hillary Rodham Clinton is a frequent subject of discussion on Meet the Press, *but she has never been interviewed on the program.*

Gingrich is also concerned that drug taking may be rife in the White House.

GINGRICH: My point is, you've got scattered throughout this administration counterculture people. I had a senior law enforcement official tell me that, in his judgment, up to a quarter of the White House staff, when they first came in, had used drugs in the last four or five years. Now that is a very serious private conversation.

Gingrich defends proposals to end antipoverty and food programs.

GINGRICH: The fact is we have established a principle which has created a culture of poverty that is devastating, and we have to reassert that to be a healthy, full American participant is to work. . . . I mean, can any serious American argue that the federalization of poverty has worked? That this is a system we're prepared to say is a success? And so let's get it back to the states. Let's have an experiment in Atlanta, an experiment in Los Angeles, an experiment in Chicago. The ones that work we ought to copy.

I think every American who's watching the show can think about twenty-five years back and ask yourself, what's the dumbest single thing you did, and be glad you are not running for president.

—Newt Gingrich, December 4, 1994

Gingrich's performance generated controversy and headlines. The Boys Town story attracted most press coverage, but the drug-taking accusations proved irresistible to many.

April 30, 1995

America is stunned by a horrific terrorist bombing in Oklahoma City, apparently the work of right-wing antigovernment extremists. Timothy McVeigh has been arrested in an investigation overseen by Attorney General Janet Reno. She is reluctant to discuss details of the investigation on *Meet the Press,* saying, "It wouldn't be wise for me to talk about what I know . . . for fear of disrupting the investigation."

TIM RUSSERT: Congresswoman Helen Chenoweth of Idaho is introducing legislation which says that a federal agent will have to register his firearm with a local sheriff and become deputized before he can carry out his duties. What would you think of that legislation?

RENO: . . . I think, clearly, there are principles

The ruined Murrah Federal Building in Oklahoma City, where 168 die in a terrorist bombing.

of federalism that apply here, and I think we should talk together about how we develop the partnership between federal and state law enforcement.

FBI Director Louis Freeh has drawn attention to legal restrictions on the agency's ability to investigate domestic groups that advocate violence before they turn to violent acts. The limits were set two decades ago when a Senate committee found the FBI to have been "consciously and repeatedly violating the laws and constitution by investigating the political activities of hundreds of thousands of American citizens." Is the attorney general concerned about history repeating itself?

RENO: I think what we need to do is to make sure that the guidelines are used not to investigate political action, but to investigate any lead that results in evidence that would lead us to violence and lead us to efforts to prevent violence. I think that can be done under the guidelines.

On the same program Wayne LaPierre, head of the National Rifle Association, is questioned about inflammatory language in an NRA fund-raising letter.

RUSSERT: You talked about "government thugs wearing black, armed to the teeth, wearing Nazi bucket helmets, black storm troopers." . . . Aren't you inciting people? Aren't you willing now to apologize for the tone of this letter?

LAPIERRE: That's like saying the weather report in Florida on the hurricane caused the damage rather than the hurricane.

RUSSERT: So you stand by this letter?

LAPIERRE: The fact is, if you talk to the victims of what's happening with these law enforcement abuses, they'll use very similar language. . . . Those words are not far—in fact, they're a pretty close description to what's happening in the real world.

May 7, 1995

House Speaker Newt Gingrich says the bombers reflect widespread disaffection with federal government.

GINGRICH: There is in rural America a genuine—and particularly in the West—a genuine fear of the federal government and of Washington, D.C., as a place that doesn't understand their way of life and doesn't understand their values.

Tim Russert asks the Speaker about his recent statements implying that the Democratic party is the enemy of normal Americans.

GINGRICH: What I was trying to say was a party which has consistently undervalued the family and which has consistently favored alternative lifestyles and said they are all normal, they are all equal, they are all valid, has to at some point say, "Gee, why do we have all these problems we didn't have in 1955?"

June 4, 1995

Sen. Bob Dole (R-KS) has been attacking Hollywood movies and rap music for encouraging dismal moral standards by exploiting violence and sex. In this context he is asked on *Meet the Press* about a steamy new novel from House Speaker Newt Gingrich.

DOLE: It's troubling to me. Maybe it's not troubling to Newt Gingrich.

Senator Dole has been particularly virulent about Time Warner productions, and he refuses on air to return money the corporation has contributed to his campaigns.

DOLE: I think it demonstrates that they didn't buy anything with Bob Dole . . . I'm not in their pocket or anyone else's pocket.

November 27,1994: Rebel Bosnian Muslim forces loyal to Fikret Abdic fire a mortar toward Bosnian government positions some three miles west of Bihac.

June 4, 1995: Madeleine Albright is interviewed as U.S. permanent representative to the UN. In January 1997 she granted Meet the Press *the first extended television interview following Senate confirmation of her appointment as secretary of state.*

Dole's comments were major news in Monday's newspapers. The headline DOLE RIPS NEWT'S SEXY NOVEL covered the front page of the *New York Post,* with the full story on pages four and five.

August 27, 1995

Goradze, Bosnia, is, in the words of Brian Williams (NBC News), "the situation that really won't go away." He asks Assistant Secretary of State Richard Holbrooke, who heads negotiations in the former Yugoslavia, why the new threat of NATO air strikes should be taken seriously.

> HOLBROOKE: [W]e have an agreement that if the Serbs attack the Goradze area, the NATO retaliatory strikes will go far beyond the previous pinpricks, these ineffectual, to my mind embarrassing NATO responses, which have only emphasized weakness rather than emphasized strength.

ROBERT NOVAK (*Chicago Sun-Times*): Mr. Secretary, you've spent the last week calling Dr. Karadzic, the leader of the Bosnian Serbs, a war criminal. . . . Do you really think, as a diplomat, it's helpful to call the person that you need the agreement from a war criminal?

HOLBROOKE: Bob, that's a very fair point. We've talked about it a lot. But the fact is an international tribunal in The Hague has indicted several people, including the man you just mentioned. . . . At Srebrenica a month ago, people were taken into a stadium, lined up, and massacred. It was a crime against humanity of the sort that we have rarely seen in Europe, and not since the days of Himmler and Stalin, and that's simply a fact and it has to be dealt with.

Bombing began days later, and in a live report from Belgrade on the following week's *Meet the Press,* NATO commander Adm. Leighton Smith tells the Serbs how to prevent another strike.

SMITH: Tim, it's very simple. No more attacks on Sarajevo or the other safe areas, get the weapons outside the twenty-kilometer exclusion zone, unimpeded movement of the humanitarian aid into Sarajevo and other places in Bosnia, and open the Sarajevo airport. . . .

TIM RUSSERT: It's fair to say the Bosnian Serbs have hours and not days to comply?

SMITH: That's a fair statement, Tim, yes.

Meet the Press periodically calls on NBC overseas correspondents to update breaking news stories. The September 3 program was unusual in that it contained three such reports, from Keith Miller in Belgrade, Tom Aspell in Sarajevo, and Diana Bishop in China, where tension with the Chinese government was growing as Hillary Rodham Clinton prepared to attend the UN Conference for Women in Beijing.

October 15, 1995

Hours before a scheduled appearance on *Meet the Press,* and the day before the Million Man March on Washington, Nation of Islam leader Louis Farrakhan cancels. The Rev. Jesse Jackson is joined in the studio by attorney Johnnie Cochran, in the headlines as attorney for O. J. Simpson. Tim Russert asks Cochran, "Will you be marching tomorrow?"

COCHRAN: No, I will not be marching. I'll be—because of business commitments, I'll be in New York tomorrow.

RUSSERT: Do you support the march?

COCHRAN: . . . . I think the sense of the march is positive, but there are some things that do concern me. So I will not be here personally. But I support black men everywhere who stand up. . . .

RUSSERT: Reverend Jackson, will you be marching tomorrow?

JACKSON: I'll be marching and speaking tomorrow. The compelling interests, the greater good is the disgraceful condition of the black community. Dr. King called it thirty-two years ago the shameful condition. The number one growth industry in urban America is jails. Half of all public housing built the last ten years has been jails. Today one-third of every black male age twenty to twenty-nine is trapped in the jail industrial complex at a cost of six billion dollars a year. . . . I feel that it is important that we have such a march to focus attention on the urban crisis. . . . If these men go back home with renewed commitment to direct action and voter registration, and we put on three million or four million more voters next year and focus on some economic development in our own communities and political alliances, it will change the course of our country.

October 16, 1995: The Million Man March in Washington, D.C.

October 22, 1995

There is talk of twenty thousand American troops heading for Bosnia as part of the peace agreement. Secretary of Defense William J. Perry points out that "we do not yet have a peace agreement," but discussions on troop deployment are taking place with Congress.

> PERRY: I believe that we have a compelling case for the president's decision to support this implementation force in Bosnia. I believe that we will make this case with the Congress and with the American people, and they will support it. . . .
>
> TIM RUSSERT: But if Congress did say no, you legally could send troops.
>
> PERRY: Indeed, the president has the constitutional authority to do that. . . . I cannot conceive of a major NATO operation without full American participation, indeed, without American leadership.

November 26, 1995

Tim Russert points out that it is hard to have the country focused on sending twenty thousand American troops to Bosnia when there's a budget debate going on. Sen. Daniel P. Moynihan (D-NY) agrees.

> MOYNIHAN: Get this out of the way so we can pursue the national interests and . . . see that those men and women we're sending overseas—they are overseas now—are in as secure a situation as they can be. Back them up by being united at home.

Assistant Secretary of State Richard Holbrooke, who brokered the Bosnian peace plan, explains why an American presence is essential to the peace process.

> HOLBROOKE: American leadership is essential to prevent a bloodbath and more human

tragedy. We spend a lot of money on refugees and reconstruction. Now, we want to spend less money—and it will be less money—to rebuild. . . . I think Americans will be able to take pride in this operation. It will be done safely. This is not a war.

December 17, 1995

The man who will command the American troops in Bosnia is Army Maj. Gen. Bill Nash. He talks live to Tim Russert from Germany.

> RUSSERT: How long before the twenty thousand American troops are on the ground in Bosnia?
>
> NASH: Well, we're starting to move, about three days ago, when the peace treaty was signed. . . . We are going to have a measured entry. It's going to be very deliberate in order to ensure that we take good care of our soldiers and have a safe deployment.

Sen. Bob Dole's support for the initially unpopular Bosnia mission was a critical factor in its success. Russert asks him if he has taken heat from some quarters in the Republican party for supporting the president.

> DOLE: I think sometimes you have to do the right thing. I mean, the easy vote was no, but . . . [w]e are there, and now the choice, in my view, is very clear: Support the troops. . . . The president made a commitment two years ago to send troops. We are the number one power in the world. We do have some responsibility, and our credibility is at stake.

Budget discussions have reached an impasse, and "nonessential" government services have been shut down.

> DOLE: The president has the Interior bill on his desk. He can sign it during this program, while he's watching the two of us, and all the parks will be open at noon today. . . . I'm very disappointed, I must say—having helped the president on NAFTA and helped the president on GATT, I think helping him to some extent in reference to Bosnia—that he would ignore us when it comes to the budget. . . .
>
> RUSSERT: And where can the president reach you if he wants to call you?
>
> DOLE: I've got a beeper.

I want to multiply Republicans, not divide Republicans.
—Sen. Bob Dole on the abortion issue, December 17, 1995

John DiJoseph, Meet the Press *photographer, retired in December 1995, at the age of eighty-nine. He had photographed every Washington origination of* Meet the Press *since its inception on radio in 1945, and many of the photographs in this book are his work.*

March 3, 1996

Sen. Bob Dole is ahead in the race for the Republican presidential nomination, but rival contender Pat Buchanan forecasts trouble ahead if Dole wins and chooses a supporter of abortion rights, such as

Colin Powell, as a running mate. Such a move by Dole "will split his party asunder, and many of my people will walk out no matter what I do," the candidate forecasts.

April 21, 1996

Bob Dole is the clear winner of the Republican primaries, and he will face Bill Clinton in the November presidential election. But will Ross Perot's Reform party be in the contest? Perot has said he will support a Democrat or a Republican if he is George Washington II.

PEROT: I used a terrible example when I said George Washington the Second. And this will tell your viewers all they want to know about American politics. If we were really considering George Washington the Second, we'd get all the image makers in, the sound bite experts, and they'd say, "You know, the guy has got wooden teeth. If he ever smiles, he's dead." So now I say, "Well, what about Abraham Lincoln?" They'd say, "Ross, the guy's got a beard. You know, he's not too pretty. You know, he's kind of awkward when he walks; never sell this guy." "Well, what about FDR, the guy who got us through the Depression and through World War Two?" "Sorry, Ross, never make it. Here's a guy in a wheelchair." "Okay, we've got Winston Churchill's identical twin, all of his great traits, but he's a U.S. citizen. What about him?" "Got to lose fifty pounds and quit smoking cigars and get a toupee."

What's my point, folks? Getting elected in America today has nothing to do with delivering results for you. It has everything to do with acting ability and theater. . . .

TIM RUSSERT: If your candidate is not Dole or Clinton, will the candidate of the Reform party insist on being part of the three nationally televised presidential debates?

February 4, 1996: Guests are Republican Governor Christine Todd Whitman of New Jersey (center), Colorado Democrat Gov. Roy Romer (on Whitman's left) and Republican Governors' Association chairman Gov. John Engler of Michigan (far right). On Whitman's right are Tim Russert and David Broder.

PEROT: Well, even in Haiti, I think they would let him, don't you? . . .

RUSSERT: Do you believe that if people in 1996 voted their conscience, you or the Reform party candidate could win?

PEROT: No ifs, ands, and buts. If people will vote their consciences—and folks, please don't be manipulated by "Watch my lips, no new taxes," Willie Horton ads—that was racist, that was negative, that's everything that's rotten about our country. We should love one another, not hate one another. They're going to be preaching hate and divisiveness all through '96 because we've got some groups that that's all they know how to do is try and search, destroy, and separate people.

July 21, 1996

After the opening ceremony for the 1996 Summer Olympic Games in Atlanta, *Meet the Press* interviews former President Jimmy Carter, who proposed the withdrawal of the U.S. team from the 1980 Moscow Olympics on *Meet the Press* (January 20, 1980). Carter believes America has an inspirational role to play in the world.

> CARTER: I think that's the one single thing about which I have learned more since I've been out of the White House, is how we can—potentially at least—help to elevate the life and the hope of people who pray for peace, who pray for freedom, who pray for human rights, who pray for the alleviation of their own suffering. And we now pay very little attention to them. That's the main thing I've learned.

An inspirational American was celebrated at the opening ceremony—Dr. Martin Luther King, Jr. Ambassador Andrew Young—who first appeared on *Meet the Press* as a young congressman in 1976 and later as the U.S. ambassador to the United Nations—worked alongside Dr. King and spearheaded the international campaign that helped bring the games to Atlanta.

> YOUNG: I think what we were saying was—to the world—this is how we got here. We got to this point because of Martin Luther King's emphasis on nonviolence, on the emphasis on human rights growing out of Martin Luther King with Jimmy Carter, and these are messages we want to share with the world. But we didn't want to say that we've got the problem solved.

Days later a bomb exploded at the Olympics, killing one person, injuring many more.

July 28, 1996

The mayor of Atlanta, Bill Campbell, speaks on *Meet the Press*.

> CAMPBELL: I visited several hospitals. I visited the families and several victims. It was a very touching scene, obviously, where the mother was killed. The young girl—her name is Fallon—is still in the hospital. But they all had the same resolve. They wanted the games to go on.

Rep. Newt Gingrich (R-GA) warns against fears of terrorism leading to an excess of domestic surveillance.

> GINGRICH: The worst thing we could do is decide to become a police state, both because in the long run it would increase terror as more and more people are alienated, but also because it is the ultimate defeat. The great joy of America is that we are a remarkably free country.

October 6, 1996

In his first Sunday-morning interview since being nominated the Republican candidate for vice president, Jack Kemp speaks on *Meet the Press* on the day of the first televised presidential debate of the 1996 campaign. He is committed to "total reform of the U.S. tax code to repeal the eighty-three-year-old system that's seven and a half million words long and is totally confusing, contradictory, and breeding corruption in America."

Kemp was the architect of Ronald Reagan's tax rate cuts.

> KEMP: We had to lower the rates. It was the right thing to do, but Congress overspent and, clearly, with a Republican Congress and Bob Dole as president, we could both cut the rates on capital and labor and the American family, hold down the growth of spending, bring budget equilibrium to this country and then reform the tax code and end the regulatory reign of terror on the American entrepreneur.
>
> . . .
>
> TIM RUSSERT: Let's talk about the fifteen percent tax cut, the centerpiece of your campaign. The American people—and you have seen the same data I have—just don't plain believe that you can cut taxes five hundred and fifty billion dollars and still balance the budget.

Betty Cole Dukert first joined *Meet the Press* as associate producer in 1956. Her tenure spans five

decades and some two thousand shows. She became the show's producer on Lawrence Spivak's retirement in 1975, senior producer in 1992, and is now executive producer of the program. Unflappable and gracious, she is universally respected by presidents and colleagues.

She still recalls her 1956 interview for a job with Lawrence Spivak. (At that time she was a production assistant at the NBC television station in Washington, D.C.) She reviewed her qualifications with Spivak: a degree in journalism; experience organizing the new Springfield, Missouri, radio station KICK (pay: $22.50 a week); a move to Washington to work briefly as a secretary at the USIA; a similar position with NBC, leading to her current position at WRC-TV. At WRC she worked as production assistant on a women's program, and on weekends she acted as production assistant for the network news operation.

Spivak appeared impressed by Betty's experience and offered her the job. "But," he warned, "before you accept, you should ask the person you will be replacing about my idiosyncrasies." Definitely interested, she did, and the conversation was a long one, for his idiosyncrasies were many. He was passionately hostile to smoking and just as passionately dedicated to his work. His hours were long, and, once she had the job, Betty's telephone would often ring late in the evening. But his devotion to a strong work ethic proved invaluable training to her and others who experienced the Spivak discipline for excellence.

Lawrence Spivak also disliked flying, and Betty has therefore traveled around the world for *Meet the Press*—to Vietnam, India, Lebanon, Israel, the Philippines, South Africa, and capital cities in Europe and South America. Her Rolodex is understandably extensive, a crucial tool. Old contacts and friends are major assets. If somebody is making news, she is likely to know his or her number. Forty years of guest lists prove her success.

The guests she likes to see are "the front-page figures in the news stories that seem likely to have lasting impact or importance." In a routine week guests should be lined up by Thursday, with Friday devoted to digging out background material. Saturday is a regular working day for Betty, and Sunday is showtime.

With such a demanding year-round schedule, it is not surprising that Betty met her husband, Joe Dukert, through *Meet the Press* at a Republican governors' conference in Palm Beach in 1968.

She says, "I think of *Meet the Press* as the meat-and-potatoes style of interview program. Some of these other programs today are like salad fads, in my estimation. The 'soft' talk shows serve a purpose, and I know there's a push by some to soften the hard-edged approach of traditional news programs to reflect what people are talking about over lunch or whatever. But we don't believe that's what people have tuned into *Meet the Press* all these years to see."

Betty Cole Dukert has truly witnessed history in the making at *Meet the Press*, and she has subtly helped that history be accurately reported to the millions of *Meet the Press* viewers since 1956.

April 1993: Betty Cole Dukert with Lawrence Spivak (center) and husband Joe Dukert.

KEMP: . . . It can be done. Bob and Jack Kemp can do it, and we can do it while balancing the budget, because it's designed to expand the size of our economy. . . . A new ad has President Clinton saying that "my job is to take care of the American people." And Bob Dole believes that his job is to find out where the American people want to go and help lead them there. We don't need the president of the United States to take care of us. We need him to create the climate in which we can work out our own happiness.

October 13, 1996

Allegations of dubious contributions to Democratic campaign coffers are mounting, along with assorted accusations of scandal involving the White House. Vice President Al Gore defends the administration.

TIM RUSSERT: Are you concerned that if [you are] reelected, the second term will be just riddled or saddled with ethical problems and investigations?

GORE: Oh, absolutely not, because what you are seeing with this five-year politically motivated investigation by the D'Amato committee and Senator Dole and this whole cottage industry—you would see them lose their motivation to continue spending millions of dollars on this. The whole purpose of it has been their effort to try to defeat Bill Clinton for reelection.

The vice president insists the administration is eager to reform campaign finance.

GORE: I'm sure you couldn't find a single campaign where there wasn't a time when the treasurer says, "Wait a minute," you know, "this one has to be sent back," or whatever. There have been no violations of law, no violations of the regulations. We've strictly complied with every single one of them. Now there is a difference between a legal resident of the United States who complies with all the laws, lives here, works here, et cetera. Under the law, as it exists, this is perfectly legal.

Tim Russert asks the vice president how he feels about minister Louis Farrakhan visiting Iraq, Iran, Libya, and Cuba.

GORE: Well, personally, I believe that what he has done and said is just completely outrageous. He has promoted anti-Semitism. He has promoted division between people of different racial and ethnic groups. That's un-American.

October 27, 1996

Reform party candidate Ross Perot thinks the character issue is an important consideration in the approaching presidential election.

PEROT: You should never let anybody be president of the United States . . . who does not have a strong moral-ethical base.

This leads him to prefer Bob Dole to President Clinton. Asked what he would do if forced to choose between the two, he says, "I think every American would pick [Bob Dole]."

November 24, 1996

This program was destined to influence the future of the Central Intelligence Agency, and it is a story as old as the cold war, deeply enmeshed in the history of *Meet the Press*. In 1948 ex-Communist Whittaker Chambers caused a sensation by publicly accusing Alger Hiss on *Meet the Press* of being a Communist. Almost fifty years later Hiss died, proclaiming his innocence to the last. That week President Clinton's national security adviser, Anthony Lake, is interviewed by Tim Russert.

RUSSERT: In our *Meet the Press* minute, we have Whittaker Chambers on this program talking about Alger Hiss. You are a student of history. Do you believe Alger Hiss was a spy?

LAKE: I've read a couple of books that certainly offered a lot of evidence that he may have been. I don't think it's conclusive.

These words come back to haunt Mr. Lake, when as director-designate of the CIA he faces the Senate Select Committee on Intelligence. Sen. Jon Kyl (R-AZ) forces Lake to admit his *Meet the Press* answer has been economical with the truth. The *Washington Post* reports Lake's claim to the committee that Tim Russert's question came "with twenty seconds to go in the program," when in fact it was halfway through the interview. Lake also changes his story, telling the committee, "I do believe Alger Hiss was guilty." Lake's hedging feeds Kyl's doubts about his "threshold of belief that someone is a spy" and his suitability for the CIA position. The incident plays a part in Lake's decision to withdraw his nomination during the nomination process.

> **Men in public office live by the voters they attract, and it is therefore hard for any politician to refuse to appear on a program that attracts an audience in the millions, and that makes important news across the country the next morning.**
>
> **—Lawrence Spivak**

December 22, 1996

The House Ethics Committee is reviewing admitted ethical wrongdoing by Speaker Newt Gingrich. Will he stay on as Speaker? House Majority Leader Dick Armey (R-TX) thinks so.

ARMEY: He has acknowledged that he's made these mistakes, that he is responsible, and he's accepted the ruling of the committee and, I think, with an enormous amount of grace and serious understanding of the importance of ethics to the American people.

Former New York Gov. Mario Cuomo thinks the Speaker's contrition lacks substance.

CUOMO: I think probably people are laughing at us all over America, all the politicians. The man lied. He got caught. He says, "I accept the responsibility, but I don't want to pay any price." All I have to do—if I get caught stealing a pair of sneakers, I go to Riker's Island. If I'm a welfare mother, you have to be personally responsible. . . . Put your actions where your words are. Step down. . . .

TIM RUSSERT: Let me move to another subject that's also in the news and bring you in, Reverend [Jesse] Jackson. That is the Board of Education in Oakland, California, has ruled that black English, Ebonics, should be taught as an official language. As a leader of African Americans in this country, what's your reaction to that?

JACKSON: That's an unacceptable surrender. It's teaching down to our children, and it must never happen. The second language, if they live in California, ought to be Spanish. . . . I understand their attempt to reach out to those children, but this is an unacceptable surrender, borderlining on disgrace. I hope that they will reverse that decision, accept the bigger challenge of teaching our youth, teaching them up and challenging them. They cannot get into the University of California. They cannot get a job at NBC or CBS or ABC unless they can master this language. I tell you, they can master it if they are challenged to do so.

As this pre-Christmas edition of *Meet the Press* ends, Tim Russert has a special announcement.

RUSSERT: In 1985, NBC News traveled to the Vatican and was greeted by Pope John Paul the Second. This month, we returned and were again greeted by the pope. We reminisced about his appearance on the *Today* program a decade ago. And when we told him *Meet the Press* will be celebrating its fiftieth anniversary, he noted that this was his fiftieth anniversary as a priest, and the Holy Father authorized the president of the Pontifical Council for Social Communications to offer these greetings: "I am happy to express special congratulations to NBC on the fiftieth anniversary of the program *Meet the Press,* which symbolizes the commitment of television news to bring information, understanding, and insight to those who seek to be responsible citizens in a dynamic democracy."

And to that I can only say amen.

January 12, 1997

The leader of the House Democrats, Richard Gephardt of Missouri, joins the debate on the Speaker's ethics problems, saying that "he should at least step down until the facts are out and until the House has made its judgment."

Tim Russert asks him about his apparently frosty relationship with Speaker Newt Gingrich.

> GEPHARDT: Well, Tim, it's obvious that over the two years we've had a relationship that hasn't been that close. And I really think, as I've said many times, it comes from the Speaker's belief that the Republicans don't really need to have much of a relationship with the Democrats.

Gephardt is a possible challenger for the Democratic nomination in the year 2000.

> GEPHARDT: The future will take care of itself. Nineteen ninety-eight is what I am looking at, and we are trying hard to win those ten seats back that we need to win a majority, so we can have a different outcome than we had on January the seventh, when I had to hand the gavel to Newt.

January 26, 1997

In her first extended television interview following Senate confirmation as secretary of state, Madeleine Albright—the first woman to hold the position—speaks about NATO expansion, which Russia sees as a threat.

> ALBRIGHT: We need to do for Central and Eastern Europe what was done for Western Europe after the Second World War. That is, try to provide some sense of stability, try to make sure that ethnic conflicts and border disputes don't overwhelm, and that is what NATO expansion is about. . . .
>
> NATO expansion will go forward, and the Russians need to understand that we want to have relations with them directly and also with NATO. . . . U.S.-Russian relations are very important to both countries.

This edition of *Meet the Press* was to have extraordinary—but not unprecedented—political repercussions. Finland's president, Martti Ahtisaari, who had become a *Meet the Press* viewer while working at the United Nations in New York in the 1980s, was watching the program. According to *USA Today* (March 17, 1997), when he heard Madeleine Albright say no venue had been fixed for the upcoming Clinton-Yeltsin summit,

HEADS OF STATE, PRESIDENTS, PREMIERS, AND PRIME MINISTERS ON *Meet the Press*

Country	Name	Date(s)
ARGENTINA	President Arturo Frondizi	1/25/59
AUSTRALIA	Prime Minister Harold E. Holt	6/11/67
	Prime Minister E. Gough Whitlam	10/6/74
BOSNIA	Prime Minister Haris Silajdzic	4/3/94
BRITISH GUIANA	Premier Cheddi Jagan	10/15/61
CANADA	Prime Minister Pierre Elliott Trudeau	2/27/77
	Prime Minister Brian Mulroney	4/5/87
CHILE	President Salvador Allende	10/31/71
CHINA	Premier Zhao Ziyang	9/27/87
CUBA	Premier Fidel Castro	4/19/59
CYPRUS	President (Archbishop) Makarios	9/15/57
EGYPT	President Anwar el-Sadat	9/9/79, 8/9/81
EL SALVADOR	President-elect José Napoleon Duarte	5/20/84
ETHIOPIA	Emperor Haile Selassie	10/6/63
FRANCE	Premier Pierre Mendès-France	11/21/54
	Premier Guy Mollet	3/3/57
	President Valéry Giscard d'Estaing	5/23/76
	President François Mitterrand	3/25/84
	Premier Michel Rocard	7/16/89
GERMANY	Chancellor Konrad Adenauer	3/20/60, 4/16/61
	Chancellor Ludwig Erhard	12/1/63, 6/6/65
	Chancellor Kurt Georg Kiesinger	8/20/67
	Chancellor Willy Brandt *(Brandt was also interviewed three times before becoming chancellor and once afterward.)*	4/12/70
	Chancellor Helmut Schmidt *(Schmidt was also interviewed three times after becoming chancellor.)*	12/8/74
	Chancellor Helmut Kohl	3/4/84
GHANA	President Kwame Nkrumah	7/27/58
GREAT BRITAIN	Anthony Eden *(before becoming prime minister)*	9/2/51
	Prime Minister Harold Wilson	4/7/63, 9/19/65
	Prime Minister Edward Heath	2/4/73
	Former Prime Minister Alexander Douglas-Home	10/2/60
INDIA	Prime Minister Jawaharlal Nehru	11/5/61
	Indira Gandhi *(before becoming prime minister)*	4/26/64
	Prime Minister Indira Gandhi	4/3/66, 10/25/70, 11/7/71, 8/24/75
	Prime Minister Morarji Desai	6/11/78

HEADS OF STATE, PRESIDENTS, PREMIERS, AND PRIME MINISTERS ON *Meet the Press (continued)*

Country	Guest	Dates
INDIA (CONTINUED)	Prime Minister Rajiv Gandhi	6/16/85
IRAN	Shah Mohammad Reza Pahlavi	10/26/69, 7/29/73, 5/18/75
ISRAEL	Prime Minister Moshe Sharett	11/13/55
	Foreign Minister Golda Meir	12/2/56
	Prime Minister Golda Meir	9/8/69
	Prime Minister Menachem Begin *(First show was as former underground leader and fund raiser)*	12/12/48, 4/6/75, 7/24/77, 5/7/78, 11/16/80, 9/13/81, 4/25/82
	Prime Minister Yitzhak Rabin	9/15/74, 2/1/76
	Prime Minister Shimon Peres	12/2/79, 8/8/82,12/31/84, 6/23/85
	Former President David Ben-Gurion	3/5/67
	Benjamin Netanyahu *(as deputy foreign minister)*	8/6/89, 8/11/91
ITALY	Prime Minister Mario Scelba	4/3/55
JAPAN	Prime Minister Kakuei Tanaka	8/5/73
JORDAN	King Hussein I	4/19/64, 4/13/69, 4/2/72, 5/4/75,12/4/77, 6/22/80, 11/3/85
MOROCCO	King Hassan II	3/31/63
NICARAGUA	President Anastasio Somoza	3/19/67
PAKISTAN	Prime Minister Mohammad Ayub Khan	7/16/61
	Prime Minister Zulfikar Ali Bhutto	9/23/73
	Prime Minister Mohammad Zia-ul-Haq	12/12/82
PHILIPPINES	President Carlos García	6/22/58
	President Diosdado Macapagal	10/11/64
	President Ferdinand Marcos	9/18/66, 10/8/72, 9/19/82, 2/9/86, 2/23/86
RHODESIA/NYASALAND	Prime Minister Sir Roy Welensky	10/27/63
RHODESIA	Prime Minister Ian Smith	10/8/78
RUSSIA/SOVIET UNION	Former President of Russia Mikhail Gorbachev	3/28/93
SINGAPORE	Premier Lee Kuan Yew	10/22/67, 4/15/73
SOUTH AFRICA	President Pieter W. Botha	11/19/79
SWEDEN	Prime Minister Olof Palme	6/7/70
TOGO	President Sylvanus Olympio	3/25/62
TUNISIA	President Habib Bourguiba	5/7/61
UNITED STATES OF AMERICA		
as president	President Gerald Ford	11/9/75
	President Jimmy Carter	1/20/80
	President Bill Clinton	11/7/93
postpresident	Former President Gerald Ford	11/2/80
	Former President Jimmy Carter	3/29/87, 7/21/96, 4/27/97
	Former President Herbert Hoover	12/11/55, 8/9/59
	Former President Richard M. Nixon	4/10/88

HEADS OF STATE, PRESIDENTS, PREMIERS, AND PRIME MINISTERS ON *Meet the Press (continued)*

prepresident	John F. Kennedy	12/2/51, 11/9/52, 2/14/54, 10/28/56, 11/9/58, 1/3/60, 7/17/60, 10/16/60
	Lyndon B. Johnson	7/10/60, 10/9/60
	Richard M. Nixon	9/14/52, 9/11/60, 10/6/62, 10/7/62, 9/12/65, 10/23/66, 11/3/68
	Gerald Ford	1/16/66, 1/8/67, 7/28/68, 1/5/69, 1/18/70, 1/14/73, 1/6/74
	Jimmy Carter	6/2/74, 12/15/74, 1/11/76, 7/11/76
	Ronald Reagan	1/9/66, 9/11/66, 5/26/68, 9/12/71, 1/20/74, 3/7/76, 5/1/77
	George W. Bush	3/21/71, 6/10/73, 2/22/76, 5/6/79, 4/20/80, 9/7/80, 2/5/84, 9/16/84, 4/13/86, 12/13/87
	Bill Clinton	9/6/87, 2/25/90, 5/5/91, 1/5/92, 3/22/92
VIETNAM, SOUTH	President Nguyen Van Thieu	9/10/67
YUGOSLAVIA	Former King Peter	1/2/49
ZIMBABWE	President Robert Mugabe	8/24/80

"Ahtisaari ordered an aide to telephone U.S. Ambassador Derek Shearer and suggest Helsinki. Within two weeks, the United States and Russia had accepted the offer." *USA Today* quoted Ambassador Shearer as commenting, "You've got a Finnish president who watches *Meet the Press*. It just wouldn't have happened this way in the old days."

But *Meet the Press* did help set up the first peacetime summit conference after World War II. In March 1955 Sen. Walter George's call for a meeting of the heads of state was taken up by President Eisenhower and led directly to the 1955 Geneva Summit Conference with Nikita Khrushchev.

February 9, 1997

Like *Meet the Press,* the National Basketball Association celebrates its fiftieth anniversary in 1997. At the NBA All-Star Game in Cleveland, Tim Russert talks to Michael Jordan (Chicago Bulls), Charles Barkley (Houston Rockets), and Grant Hill (Detroit Pistons) about role models.

JORDAN: I think, you know, we have an obligation. It wasn't an obligation that we chose. It was bestowed upon us because of the success that we have gathered. But I think when your parents are there every day, they have much more influence on that kid than . . . we do. What we do is generalized. It's over a group of people. And we try to do that to

February 2, 1997: *Meet the Press* becomes the first network television program ever to broadcast live in digital high definition. Mike Sherlock, NBC's executive vice president for technology, recalled that "NBC was the first network to successfully broadcast in color, the first network to broadcast in stereo, and now we are the first network to broadcast a regularly scheduled network program in the new digital high definition standard."

The historic broadcast was from NBC's station WRC-TV in Washington, D.C., host station for the high-definition model station WHD-TV. Studio guests saw the high-definition images on a wide screen monitor, and the program was recorded for posterity.

The event added to *Meet the Press*'s technological firsts, including first live satellite interview (with British Prime Minister Harold Wilson, September 19, 1965), first news program to be broadcast in color (February 14, 1954), and first news program to be televised on a regular basis in color (September 25, 1960).

The *Meet the Press* set, inaugurated in 1996, was designed with the extra quality demands of high-definition television in mind. In the program's early days sets changed frequently and often resembled hotel rooms, taking their cue from the Washington hotel in whose bowels the studio was located. In 1954 a set was established that lasted five years, to be replaced by a version that was in use for eighteen years until it was donated to the Smithsonian Institution in 1977.

the best of our abilities. But the influence is going to come from a day-to-day basis.

BARKLEY: I think the athletes are secondary role models. Your parents are your primary role models. They—there's not many Grant Hills or Michael Jordans out there. Every kid wants to be, but they are not going to be. That's unrealistic. They have a better chance of being what their mother or father are. And that's reality. . . .

I'm from a single-parent family. And my mother and grandmother raised me and they were strong. They taught me great discipline and how to work hard. . . . White people do not owe us anything but an opportunity. We have to sooner or later step up, get educated ourselves, stop having kids out of wedlock, stop gang-banging and things like that. . . . There are a lot of strong black women out there, and there are a lot of strong black men out there raising their kids, seeing if they can handle it. But just not having one parent, that's a crutch.

April 13, 1997

The interview with Nation of Islam leader Louis Farrakhan on April 13 brought a new twist to the *Meet the Press* experience with security measures. In addition to inspections by advance teams and some thirty aides and security men accompanying him to the studio, the *Meet the Press* makeup artist was requested to surrender all applicators used to apply powder or other elements to the minister, including tissues used after the program to remove it. When questioned about the purpose, an aide said it was to ensure that no slow-acting poison was involved.

The experience of fifty years on the air has prepared *Meet the Press* to take such an original request in its stride. After all, a nervous Sen. Joseph McCarthy, fearful of an assassination attempt, faced the panel in 1951 with a loaded gun in his lap. Five years earlier, in *Meet the*

February 9, 1997: National Basketball Association stars Charles Barkley (left) and Michael Jordan (center) talk to Tim Russert (right). The NBA and Meet the Press *both celebrate their fiftieth anniversary in 1997.*

Press's radio days, Sen. Theodore Bilbo took out a gun license specifically in order to arm himself for his appearance on the program. In 1960, former Soviet intelligence agent Alexander Kaznacheev arrived at the studio heavily disguised in a red wig and matching mustache, suspecting that a Kremlin assassin was lurking on Nebraska Avenue.

Many of the program's guests have had good reason to fear the assassin. President John F. Kennedy, his brother Sen. Robert F. Kennedy, Dr. Martin Luther King, Jr., President Anwar el-Sadat, Prime Minister Indira Gandhi, Gov. George Wallace, President Ronald Reagan—the list is chillingly long.

Some of the issues discussed by these leaders and others remain unresolved. The country carries its racial problems into the twenty-first century, the corruption of politics by money is a major concern, just as it was when John F. Kennedy appeared on the program as a young congressman, and violence is a constant threat in the Middle East, almost fifty years after Menachem Begin made his first appearance on *Meet the Press*. But there is real cause for hope. *Meet the Press* has covered the rise and fall of communism from Senator McCarthy's witch-hunts through the cold war years to the arms agreements of the Gorbachev years and the collapse of the Soviet Union. A peaceful resolution of this global conflict would have seemed impossible to the program's guests as the superpowers confronted each other in Berlin.

The program's cofounder, Lawrence E. Spivak, believed that *Meet the Press* could make a real contribution to democracy by forcing those in power to account for their actions in public view. Fifty years of programs prove him right. As *Meet the Press* celebrates its golden anniversary, the future is as unpredictable as ever, but one thing can be counted on—if it's Sunday, it's *Meet the Press*.

(*Meet the Press* celebrates the fiftieth anniversary of its NBC television debut in November 1997. Book production schedules dictated an earlier cutoff date for this book.)

PRESS
FUJINON
JIMBORGMAN
TV LISTINGS
"WE CAN WATCH CLINTON ON MTV, BUSH ON 'LETTERMAN', PEROT ON 'ARSENIO'..... OR MADONNA ON 'MEET THE PRESS'...."

Index

As the oldest program in television and the main NBC network production originating in Washington, Meet the Press *has long been considered a prime assignment for technical personnel and has won special affection and devotion from them. A number of crew members have worked on the program each week for twenty-five years or more. A young cameraman getting his first assignment to* Meet the Press *once told the producers, "I want you to know, before I get blasé about it, how exciting it is to me to get to work on this program after seeing it at home for as long as I can remember."*

Jackson | Abraham Beame | Elmo R. Zumwalt Jr. | Paul McCracken | Charles Black | Martha Griffiths | Russell Roth | Wilbur Cohen | C. Jackson Grayson | Albert Shanker | Yitzhak Rabin | Alan Greenspan | E. Gough Whitlam | Lloyd Bentsen | Wayne Hays | Leon Jaworski John Hannah | Jean Mayer | Sterling Wortman | Lester R. Brown | Mary Louise Smith | John Glenn | William Saxbe Francoise Giroud | Terry Sanford | Yvonne Burke Helmut Schmidt | Henry Reuss | Mike McCormack | John Brademas | Ella Grasso | Al Ullman | Joseph Sisco | Frank Zarb | William Coleman, Jr. | Willy Brandt | Menachem Begin | Thomas A. Murphy | Reginald Jones | Irving Shapiro | Arthur Wood | Walter Wriston | Donald C. Cook | Robert McCloskey | Arthur Burns | Calvin Rampton | Christopher Bond | James Longley | Edwin Edwards | Fredrick von Hayek | Coleman Young | Richard Carver | Fred Hofheinz | Alexander Solzhenitsyn Alejandro Orfila | Fred Ikle | Patrick Murphy | Hubert Williams | Edward Davis | Robert DiGrazia | Joseph McNamara | James Parsons | Frank Church | Robert Georgine | John Ryor | Prince Saud Al-Faisal | Edmund G. Brown., Jr. | Henry Kissinger | Hugh Carey | L. William Seidman | Philip Hart | Janey Hart **1976-1980** John Marcum | Birch Bayh | Jimmy Carter | Fred Harris | Milton Shapp | Lloyd Bentsen | Henry M. Jackson | Terry Sanford Morris Udall | Rogers Morton | Yitzhak Rabin | Yasser Arafat | Meldrim Thomson | William Loeb | George Bush Thomas Kleppe | Ronald Reagan | Dick Clark | George C. Wallace | Walter Heller | Bob Woodward | Carl Bernstein Donald Rumsfeld | Barry Goldwater | John J. Rhodes Paul Laxalt | Valery Giscard d'Estaing | Barbara Jordan Mervyn Dymally | Vernon Jordan | Jesse Jackson | A. Jay Cooper | John Ehrlichman | John Connally | Hamilton Jordan | Robert Strauss | Michael Dukakis | Robert Ray Wendell Anderson | Mills Godwin | Andrew Young Eugene McCarthy | Richard Schweiker | Elliot Richardson | John Sears | Nelson Rockefeller | Charles Mathias | Eldridge Cleaver | Leonard Woodcock | Robert Dole | Carl Sagan | Gerald Soffen | Rosalynn Carter William Scranton | James Corman | Guy Vander Jagt Tom Anderson | Peter Camejo | Lyndon LaRouche | Roger MacBride | Milton Friedman | Jack Ford | Dixy Lee Ray Benjamin Hooks | James R. Thompson | Derek Bok Richard Bolling | Philip Burton | John J. McFall | Jim Wright | Mike Mansfield | William Simon | Edward Levi Jack Watson, Jr. | Charles Schultze | Howard Baker | Lloyd McBride | Ed Sadlowski | Brock Adams | Bert Lance Pierre Elliott Trudeau | Harold Brown | Michael Blumenthal | Joseph Califano | Alan Cranston | Bob Packwood | Russell Long | Ralph Nader | John Swearingen | Roy Chapin | W. Donham Crawford | Carl Bagge | Denis Hayes | Gary Hart | Robert Byrd | Douglas Fraser | Robert Giaimo | Kenneth Gibson | George Moscone | Harvey Sloane | Tom Moody | Lewis Murphy John Culver | Jake Garn | Millicent Fenwick | Donald Fraser | James Schlesinger | Ray Marshall | Menachem Begin | Peter Jay | John B. Anderson | Ellsworth Bunker Sol Linowitz | Strom Thurmond | Jesse Helms | Arthur Upton | Lane Kirkland | William Milliken | John D. Rockefeller IV | Pete du Pont | Jerry Apodaca | George Busbee | Parren Mitchell | Griffin Bell | Cyrus Vance Henry Ford II | Walter Mondale | Jacob Javits | Audrey Rowe-Colom | Phyllis Schlafly | Liz Carpenter | Margaret Mealey | Eleanor Smeal | Abba Eban | King Hussein | Thomas P. O'Neill | Daniel Moynihan | Theodore Hesburgh | Arthur Okun | Bill Brock | Leon Jaworski Moshe Dayan | Arnold R. Miller | Edmund G. Brown, Jr. Bob Bergland | Patricia Roberts Harris | Alan Greenspan Barry Bosworth | Alexander Haig | Dean Rusk | George W. Ball | Harrison Williams | Orrin Hatch | Zbigniew Brzezinski | Morarji Desai | Howard Jarvis | Irving Selikoff Paul Kotin | Sidney Wolfe | Donald Kennedy | Anthony Mazzocchi | Eleanor Holmes Norton | John K. Galbraith William Steiger | John C. White | James Abourezk | John Ryor | Jerry Wurf | Jack Kemp | Henry Kissinger | Ian Smith | Ndabaningi Sithole | George McGovern | Evelle Younger | Alfred Kahn | Pieter Botha | Leonel Castillo Patrick Steptoe | Patricia Derian | Edmund Muskie Juanita Kreps | David W. Belin | John Glenn | Walter Levy Richard Stone | Paul Findley | Ezer Weizman | Jerry McAfee | Shahriar Rouhani | William Masters | Virginia Johnson | Paul Nitze | John Dingell | John Brademas Frank Church | Helena Arocena | Robert Cox | Benjamin Civiletti | William Winpisinger | Anwar Sadat | Neil Goldschmidt | Tom Hayden | Jane Fonda | Thomas A. Murphy | Armand Hammer | Marshall Shulman | Edward M. Kennedy | Shimon Peres | Sadegh Ghotbzadeh | R.K. Ramazani | Billy Graham | Douglas Costle | Edwin Meese Michael Barnes | Robert Mugabe | Patrick Lucey | Sam Nunn | Jerry Falwell | Richard V. Allen | Gerald Ford John Sawhill | Joseph Biden | Charles Percy | Philip Crane Gar Alperovitz | Henry Bellmon | Ernest F. Hollings | Spiro Agnew | Athalie Range | George Shultz | Philip Caldwell **1981-1987** Martin Anderson | Howard Baker | Jack Watson, Jr. | Charles Percy | James R. Jones | Jack Kemp James McClure | Jim Wright | Donald Regan | Jesse Helms Walter Heller | T.H. Bell | Douglas Fraser | Alexander Haig Jean Kirkpatrick | John Glenn | Ahmed Z. Yamani William Webster | David Stockman | Thomas Foley Caspar Weinberger | Richard Schweiker | Paul Tsongas Edwin Meese | Saadoon Hammadi | Cyrus Vance Walter Wriston | Richard Hatcher | Richard Carver | Gary Hart | Dan Rostenkowski | Henry M. Jackson | William French Smith | Anwar Sadat | Griffin Bell | James Thompson | Robert Poli | Murray Weidenbaum Kenneth Blaylock | Menachem Begin | Thomas Sowell Paul Laxalt | John Tower | James Tobin | Walter Mondale Bob Dole | James Baker III | Richard V. Allen | Vernon Jordan | Alan Cranston | George Kennan | Alan Greenspan | Richard Snelling | Bruce Babbitt | Bill Bradley | Malcolm Baldrige | James Watt | Guillermo Ungo | Pete Domenici | Michael Barnes | Robert Dornan Milton Friedman | Richard Bolling | Robert McNamara Edward M. Kennedy | Henry Kaufman | Trent Lott Farouk Kaddoumi | Eugene Rostow | Orrin Hatch | John K. Galbraith | Indira Gandhi | Shimon Peres | George Shultz | Eilas Freij | Rashad Shawa | Bill Brock | Ferdinand Marcos | Nicholas Veliotes | Lester Thurow | John R. Block Reubin Askew | Tony Coelho | Guy Vander Jagt | William L. Armstrong | Martin Feldstein | Mark Hatfield Mohammad Zia-ul-Haq | Henry Reuss | Millicent Fenwick | Moshe Arens | John Chafee | Morris Udall | Paul Volcker | Richard Burt | Noel Gayler | Albert Gore, Jr. Harold Washington | Richard Perle | Ernest F. Hollings Sol Linowitz | Alan K. Simpson | Timothy Wirth | Richard Gephardt | Brent Scowcroft | Stansfield Turner | Nancy L. Kassebaum | Petra Kelly | Bob Michel | Toney Anaya Christopher J. Dodd | Philip Caldwell | Lane Kirkland Ernest Boyer | Sam Nunn | Marshall Shulman | Frank Borman | Eric Rouleau | John W. Vessey, Jr. | George McGovern | Kenneth Adelman | William Ruckelshaus Jesse Jackson | Elizabeth Dole | John Danforth | Bob Edgar | William Colby | Kenneth Dam | Robert S. Strauss George Bush | Helmut Kohl | Andrew Young | Francois Mitterrand | Joseph Biden | Robert McFarlane | Jose Napoleon Duarte | Charles Manatt | Dianne Feinstein Wilson Goode | Romano Mazzoli | Lloyd Bentsen Charles Robb | Albert Shanker | William Bolger | Moe Biller | James A. Johnson | Richard Wirthlin | Richard Leone | Geraldine Ferraro | David Aaron | George Gallup, Jr. | William Schneider | Michael Dukakis | Bob Graham Mark White | Richard Lugar | Daniel Moynihan | Donald Engen | Marvin Kalb | Roger Mudd | John Chancellor Tom Brokaw | Barry Goldwater | Paul Kirk, Jr. | William J. Bennett | William Friday | William Janklow | Les Aspin James Schlesinger | Harry Summers, Jr. | James Webb Max Cleland | Franz-Joseph Strauss | Dick Cheney Richard Darman | Rajiv Gandhi | Patrick Leahy | Samuel Lewis | Peter Ueberroth | Edward Teller | Gatsha Buthelezi | Stephen Solarz | John Chettle | Clayton Yeutter | Georgi Arbatov | Michael Armacost | Mario Cuomo | William Gray III | Herbert Beukes | Charles Grassley | David Pryor | Shafik El-Hout | Judith Kipper Vernon Walters | King Hussein | | Gerard C. Smith Michael Deaver | Helmut Schmidt | Roald Sagdeev Julyan Semyanov | Stephen Trott | Pat Robertson Thomas P. O'Neill | Robert Oakley | Yitzhak Rabin Richard Shadyac | David Newsom | James Miller III | Phil Gramm | Bob Packwood | Carl Sagan | Thomas O. Paine William Graham | Anatoly Shcharansky | Avital Shcharansky | David Durenberger | Juan Ponce Enrile Fidel Ramos | William J. Crowe, Jr. | Elliott Abrams Alfonso Robelo | James Sasser | John Herrington